UNCOUPLING

DIANE VAUGHAN

Vintage Books
A Division of Random House, Inc.
New York

UNCOUPLING

Turning Points in Intimate Relationships

VINTAGE BOOKS EDITION, JULY 1990

Copyright © 1986 by Oxford University Press, Inc.

All rights reserved under International and Pan-American Copyright
Conventions. Published in the United States by Vintage Books, a
division of Random House, Inc., New York. Originally published, in
hardcover, by Oxford University Press, Inc., in 1986 and, in softcover,
by Vintage Books, a division of Random House, Inc., in 1987.

Library of Congress Cataloging-in-Publication Data

Vaughan, Diane.
Uncoupling : turning points in intimate relationships / Diane
Vaughan.
p.   cm.
Includes bibliographical references.
ISBN 0-679-73002-8
1. Divorce.   2. Separation (Psychology)   I. Title.
HQ814.V38   1990
306.89—dc20   89-40709
CIP

Manufactured in the United States of America
79B8

For my friend,
BEV KLINGENSMITH,
who believed that relationships are worth the struggle

ACKNOWLEDGMENTS

When I was a graduate student, I heard a well-known professor remark, "Scholarly work is excruciatingly lonely sometimes." I since have found this to be true. Often, when overwhelmed by the tedium of transcribing tapes and creating card files or the difficulty of interpreting a seemingly uninterpretable event, I have recalled his comment. The word "sometimes" is an important qualifier, however, for pleasure, comfort, and excitement also accompany the often relentless isolation with ideas. Moreover, research is a social activity, and isolation is interrupted by engagement with others whose interest, encouragement, and criticism are as central to scholarly work as the parts of the creative process which, of necessity, must be done alone.

I acknowledge those who have contributed to this research. Without them, the research process would have been the lonely endeavor of which I was warned. In particular, I thank Laurel Richardson and the members of her Sociology of Gender seminar at The Ohio State University for providing the creative environment in which *Uncoupling* had its beginnings in 1976. And I am grateful to Peter L. Berger, not only because his work was the source of my initial inspiration, but for his valuable comments on my first explorations of this topic. The substantive support of the National Institute of Mental Health allowed me to continue the research at Yale University as a post-doctoral fellow. During this period, I completed most of the fieldwork, profiting from the comments of Albert J. Reiss, Jr. and the members of the post-doctoral seminar on the Sociology of Social Control, as well as from the insights of Kai T. Erikson and the graduate writing seminar members. My thanks also to Marlene Brask and Betty Dahill, who assisted in typing interview transcripts.

Uncoupling became a three-city project, as I moved to Boston. While a visiting scholar at the Wellesley College Center for Research on Women, I completed the interviewing and analyzed the data. During this time, both my work and my self benefited from association with Jane Traupman. I began writing while teaching at Boston College, where I continue to draw on the ideas and support of faculty and graduate students. The arduous task of translating my stapled, scotch-taped, diagram-laden prose into print fell to Kathleen Crowell, Martha Roth, Shirley Urban, and Sara White. Not only were they patient and efficient, but, as first readers of the manuscript, responsive and supportive. My thanks also for the help of Janet Wirth-Cauchon and Sara Schoonmaker, who assisted with administrative tasks and word-processing, respectively.

As the manuscript approached final form, I was fortunate to have the review comments of several colleagues who read parts or all of this work: Jack Ammerman, Nancy Ammerman, Lee J. Cuba, M. C. Devilbiss, Patricia Ewick, William A. Gamson, David A. Karp, Stephen J. Pfohl, and Albert J. Reiss, Jr. Meticulous scholars all, I am grateful for their insights. My thanks also to Susan Rabiner, my editor at Oxford University Press, and to the staff who helped produce this book, especially Joan Bossert, Laura Brown, Peg Munves, Helena Schwarz, Jeff Seroy, and Rosemary Wellner. I am indebted to still others who are not identified with particular stages of the research process, but who have contributed in informal ways throughout: Mildred Fox, Sandra Joshel, Margo MacLeod, David M. Petersen, John Tryneski, Eleanor Westney, and Stanton Wheeler. My special thanks to Tina Packer and Dennis Krausnick, who opened their home, their ice cream freezer, and Shakespeare and Company to me in a last idyllic summer of writing, and to Patricia Ewick and Lee J. Cuba who, both as colleagues and as friends, have nurtured my ideas over the years.

Three final debts: to my parents, who laid the foundation for this book by teaching me that life derives its richness from our relationships with others and that every individual life is fascinating if only we take the time to inquire; to my children, who continue to instruct me in these lessons by following the course that their grandparents set; and to the people who made this book possible by sharing their intimate relationships with me.

Boston   D.V.
April 1986

CONTENTS

UNCOUPLING

Introduction

I was married for twenty years. As I reflected on the relationship after our separation, the marriage seemed to have been coming slowly apart for the last ten. Certainly we had our good times, but I could retrospectively pick out turning points—moments when the relationship changed, times when the distance between us increased. These turning points did not hinge around arguments or the typical emotional catastrophes that beset any relationship. Instead, they appeared to be related to changes in each of our social worlds. For example, I started college because I realized I was never going to have the steady companionship of my partner and needed something of my own to do. This step, innocently taken, changed me—and us. As our marriage aged, we reacted to our difficulties by altering our relation to the world around us. Those changes, in turn, affected the relationship, changing us as individuals and our relationship to each other.

What's more, when I thought about our relationship in terms of our maneuverings in the social world, it seemed as if our marriage had eroded slowly and steadily over time in a regular, orderly way. Although we personally experienced the ending of the relationship as chaotic and disruptive, its demise took on a kind of social rhythm. That an experience could be orderly and disorderly at the same time was counterintuitive. Perhaps this orderliness was because ours was a long marriage and thus its ending extended over a long period, giving the appearance of an orderly dissolution. Perhaps it was a natural reflection of my occupation then: a graduate student in sociology, being trained to look for order.

During the same period, I came across an article describing marriage

3

as a process in which two individuals renegotiate who they are with respect to each other and the world around them.[1] They restructure their lives around each other. They create common friends, belongings, memories, and a common future. They redefine themselves as a couple, in their own eyes and in the eyes of others, who respond to the coupled identity they are creating. They are invited out as a twosome, mail comes addressed to both, the IRS taxes them jointly. Single friends may hesitate to call, while the two people are readily incorporated into the social world of those who also are coupled. The coupled identity they create is constantly reaffirmed, not only by the words and deeds of others, but also by the way others come to take the relationship for granted. This continual public confirmation gives them a stable location in the social world and validates their identity.

These ideas immediately captured my interest, for what appeared to have happened as my own relationship deteriorated was a reversal of this process: we slowly and over time began redefining ourselves as separate people. Rather than an abrupt ending, ours appeared to have been a gradual transition. Long before we physically separated, we had been separating socially—developing separate friends, experiences, and futures. We reacted to our changing relationship in ways that altered the definitions that we held of ourselves and that others held of us.

In order to answer the questions raised by my own experience and further stimulated by my reading, I began interviewing people about how their relationships ended. I wanted to learn about the relationships of people who had lived together as well as those who were married. Thus, my interest was not simply on divorce, but on "uncoupling"— how people make transitions out of intimate relationships. Having publicly lived with and been sexually intimate with another person were the primary criteria, not sexual preference or marital status. Collecting biographies of individual relationships seemed the obvious method of going about this, because I wanted to understand not only the unfolding of events over time, but also how people ordered those events. Consequently, I asked people to tell me about their relationships, beginning with the moment they first sensed something was wrong. I tape recorded their narratives, interjecting occasional questions.

My concern always has been with how—not why—people make transitions out of relationships. Many times the people I talked to did not understand why themselves. Even when they thought they knew, the reasons changed, so that what seemed to explain it at one time often did not seem important six months later. The interviews reinforced my interest, for no matter whether the relationship was of short or long duration, no matter whether the partners were rich or poor, gay or straight, young or old, living together or married, giving up the relationship was hard for both people.

One woman told me she had a premonition before she was married that the marriage was a mistake. The week before the wedding, she dreamed she was dressed all in white, but was wearing black shoes. On the second day of the honeymoon, she and her husband had a disagreement. In the heat of the argument that followed, he pulled the wedding ring from his finger, threw it across the room, and punched her in the nose. Before they left for the hospital, she searched the floor of the room until she found the ring and replaced it on his finger. This scenario recurred throughout their relationship. Six years later, they were in Japan, walking on a snowy night. An argument began, and in yet another episode of the all too familiar pattern, he threw his ring away and hit her. She said, "You know, it took me three hours of crawling around in the snow in the dark, but I finally found that ring."

This woman's search for the ring in the snow symbolizes the priority our relationships assume in our lives. So important are they that we hang on to them even though we may not be all that happy. And why do we stay in unhappy relationships? We do it because we believe in commitment. We do it because we feel bound by the law. We do it because we don't want to hurt the other person. We do it because we are afraid nothing better may be out there. We do it because we believe in our own goodness, in our own ability to fix things. We do it because we are not quitters. We do it because getting out costs money, time, energy, and other relationships and we simply can't afford to go. We do it for our children. We do it for our parents. We do it for God.

Given all the constraints, it's a wonder we ever end relationships. Nonetheless, we do. So universal is this experience that we all have expertise. Considering the many factors that compel us to stay in unhappy relationships and the frequency with which we end them, the question of how we manage to disentangle ourselves and go on seems an obvious one. Yet research on how people make transitions out of relationships is sparse. Although a voluminous literature exists on separation and divorce, it by and large ignores the negotiations between partners over time.[2] Research on couples who live together and then separate is anything but voluminous. It, too, fails to address the question of "how."[3]

As a result of my inquiry, I discovered that transitions out of relationships have certain common characteristics. Sociologically, uncoupling occurs in a uniform way—a describable pattern. In order to uncouple, two people must disentangle not only their belongings but their identities. In a reversal of coupling, the partners redefine themselves, both in their own eyes and in the eyes of others, as separate entities once again. Getting out of a relationship entails a redefinition of self at several levels: in the private thoughts of the individual, between partners, and in the larger social context in which the relationship exists. As these changing definitions become increasingly public—first between the two, then to family and friends, and finally to acquaintances and strangers—the response of others perpetuates the separate paths the partners have begun. Uncoupling is complete when the partners have defined themselves and are defined by others as separate and independent of each other—when being partners is no longer a major source of identity. Instead, identity comes from other sources.

Uncoupling is primarily a tale of two transitions: one that begins before the other. Most often, one person wants out while the other person wants the relationship to continue. Although both partners must go through all the same stages of the transition in order to uncouple, the transition begins and ends at different times for each. By the time the still-loving partner realizes the relationship is in serious trouble, the other person is already gone in a number of ways. The rejected partner then embarks on a transition that the other person began long before. Understanding uncoupling consequently hinges on examining the process in relation to whether one is the initiator or the partner being left behind. Admittedly, identifying who is the initiator and who is being left behind is not so easy in some cases. Over the course of a long relationship, these roles may be passed back and forth, with one person assuming the role of initiator at one time and the other acting to end the relationship at another. How these roles get passed back and forth is, in fact, one of the more intriguing aspects of the process.

I will describe these two transitions, from the initiator's first tinge of unhappiness to the conclusion of the uncoupling process. The text parallels the experience in many ways. In life, the partner who is being left behind enters the process late. Mirroring reality, that individual's actions and thoughts do not appear until Chapter 4. Chapter 6, "Trying," is long, but that is because often in life, trying is long. The book itself is an artifact of one of the patterns in the process. Readers will discover that occasionally people turn to writing when they are uncoupling. They work through their experience on paper, reinterpreting it until it makes sense to them. Obviously, this book began because of my need to understand and redefine my own marriage experience. Moreover, writing it has served me in this same way in the caring relationships I have known since then. Those who read this book may be similarly implicated, however, for frequently people in the midst of uncoupling search partner; a few had reconciled with the old. Considering the intimacy of the subject matter, the reader might wonder how I found these individuals who discussed their private lives with me. I sent letters to people whose divorces were listed in the newspaper; I advertised; I recruited from singles groups, counseling centers, and lesbian and gay organizations; I inquired of people I met. Always I asked for the names of others who might be willing to talk to me.

Beyond these formal efforts, I found people serendipitously. Everyone has data on this topic. When asked "What do you do?," I replied, "I do research on how people make transitions out of relationships" and invariably the other person would begin telling me about his or her own relationship or that of some friend or relative. Once I went to a local newspaper office to place an ad for interviewees. Two women behind the counter volunteered to be interviewed, plus three men who were waiting in the line behind me. This has happened in bus stations, in diners, at parties, on boat docks, at ballgames, at the dentist, in supermarkets, and in taxis.

In addition, I interviewed professional counselors: social workers, psychologists, psychiatrists, and clergy. I sat in on groups for the newly separated and the divorced. A particularly efficient method of learning about uncoupling was to give material I'd written on the topic to people who reacted to my developing ideas by comparison with their own lives. A more informal contribution came from personal experience and the experiences of friends. In addition, autobiographical accounts, films, newspapers, periodicals, and conversations have yielded a large number of illustrations of certain points. So numerous are the resources I've drawn from, so easy and constant is access to this information, that often the problem was not how to get information but how to get some distance from it.

Interviews, observations, and other sources notwithstanding, I make no pretense of having gotten to the bottom of things. I believe that relationships are dynamic and that change, rather than stability, is their normal condition.[4] They are, in fact, so complex that it may be impossible even for the participants to unravel all the intricacies of their experience with each other. I simply have tried to isolate one transition from the many that occur throughout a relationship, taking as the beginning the participants' reality: when it began for them. By dwelling on the patterns in uncoupling—the similarities across all experiences—I do not mean to reduce to sameness the experience of difference that, for example, gays feel from heterosexuals, women from men, the economically disadvantaged from the advantaged, or the old from the young. Differences do exist. Uncoupling is common in certain ways, uncomfor information to guide them as they contemplate and experience the major life event.

While *Uncoupling* is primarily about relationships, it addresses additional concerns that traditionally have been central to sociology. This book is also about power. It considers how cues and signals can be manipulated to foster desired impressions. It exposes the constraining characteristics of the social circles to which individuals belong. It shows how individuals define social situations. It demonstrates the discrepancies between the inner mental world and public performance. It explores identity and the way it is constructed, negotiated, maintained, and transformed. And it examines the connection between the individual act and the social world.

While my purpose here is to orient the reader to what is in this book, I must mention what is left out. In order to examine the sociological dynamics of uncoupling, I have isolated individual experience from the larger environment in which it occurs. The intimate relationships whose biographies yielded the substance of this book are located in a particular place at a particular moment in history. Their transition experiences cannot be assumed to be a universal form, applicable to other types of family units in other times and other places, or to social relations in general. Questions remain to be asked that are different from the ones I've asked, questions that explore the connection between particular social, economic, and cultural environments and the individual lives within them. These, too, are questions that traditionally have been central to sociology.

Neither is the emotional impact on the individual the central issue here. Not that the individual experience is unimportant. Uncoupling is a dramatic life event, whose importance is reflected in the eagerness of people to discuss their relationships even years later. Indeed, in attempting to put the story in chronological order, there was no one who was not visited again by sorrow and loss in the telling of it, regardless of the passage of time. Though the psychological dimensions of uncoupling are obviously important, a researcher has the luxury of selectivity. I have tapered and molded the psychological, necessarily a part of uncoupling, to be subservient to the sociological rhythms of the process.

I interviewed 103 people, most of whom had a high school education or better. Several individuals were interviewed more than once, which allowed me to monitor their transitions over time. Nearly all were separated or divorced, although a few were still in their relationships and were considering separation or divorce. For some, the separation was recent, while for others, it happened years ago. Some had found a new mon in others. While my purpose is to examine the similarities, I have pointed out differences in the text and in discursive notes. As is always the case, the research methods shape what is found. The direction and extent to which my methods have affected the contents of this book are discussed in the Postscript.

A Caveat

Sociology is possible only because human behavior is patterned. Students in a classroom tend to sit in the same part of the room each day—often in the same seat. Concertgoers tend to applaud simultaneously and at appropriate intervals. Elevator passengers almost invariably face the front. The potential gift of sociology is to uncover the patterns and regularities from among many incidents and observations so that perhaps people may recognize their own isolated experience within the context of the experiences of others. But the path of each individual life is unique and unpredictable. Bear in mind that the patterns I describe in uncoupling are derived from the retrospective accounts of many people who have uncoupled. By definition, they have gone through most, if not all, of the stages described in this book. But someone reading this book may experience many of these stages without uncoupling. The process can be reversed, halted, or delayed—or accelerated—by the actions of the two people involved. People do have the ability to change their individual circumstances. And, as will soon become clear, possessing information is a first step toward doing that.

ONE

Secrets

W_E ALL are secret-keepers in our intimate relationships. We keep secrets from our partners about daily encounters, former lovers, true feelings about sex, friends, in-laws, finances, personal hopes, and worries about work, health, love, and life.[1] It may be, in fact, that keeping these secrets makes all relationships possible. If our partners knew every thought, every nuance of our selves, our relationships would run the risk of succumbing from either constant turmoil or—perhaps worse—a tedious matter-of-factness devoid of surprises.[2] Whatever their contribution to the maintenance of our unions, secrets also contribute to their collapse.

Uncoupling begins with a secret. One of the partners starts to feel uncomfortable in the relationship. The world the two of them have built together no longer "fits." Often these feelings appear very early. Indeed, many report that they "felt it was a mistake" prior to combining households; prior to the wedding; on the wedding day; on the honeymoon.

> *I was never psychologically married. I always felt strained by attempts that coupled me into a marital unit. I was just never comfortable as "Mrs." I never got used to my last name. I never wanted it. The day after my marriage was probably the most depressed day of my life because I had lost my singularity. I became, in the eyes of the world, a man's wife. And I was never comfortable and happy with it. It didn't make any difference who the man was.* [GRADUATE STUDENT, AGE 26, DIVORCED AFTER 2 YEARS[3]]

After we decided to live together, Carl and I began to talk about what furniture we would use from each of our apartments to furnish the new one. When it came right down to getting rid of some of my things and sharing others, I wasn't willing to make that commitment and those compromises for him. I realized that I wasn't ready for a live-in lover. I never told him this. We'd already told our friends, and it just seemed too late to back out. [BARTENDER/WRITER, AGE 32, SEPARATED AFTER LIVING TOGETHER 13 MONTHS]

As a matter of fact, my first trauma with being married was about a half an hour after we left our wedding reception. I loved the party we had, but when I left with him to go off, I was miserable. I just felt like, "What have I done?" It wasn't just the leaving home, 'though that's how Bill explained it. He said, "Well, you're really going to miss your family." The implication was that I was upset because I was leaving my family, but I knew (it's very clear to me and it was clear to me at that moment) that that was not what was bothering me. Yes, I was going to miss them, but I knew they would always be there. What I didn't like was who I was leaving with. I had a feeling of, "What have I done? I've done something very wrong to myself." I made this life decision. It was irreversible. I was stuck. [SECRETARY, AGE 25, DIVORCED AFTER 4 YEARS]

These disquieting feelings often get dismissed as the cold feet the partners have heard so much about, or are laid aside with the thought that all relationships are difficult in the beginning. The discomfort is seen as ''just an emotional reaction that everybody goes through—people get married and it's traumatic and you calm down after that.'' But afterwards the uneasiness may not disappear. It lingers, grows stronger, or goes away for a while, then returns. Of course, dissatisfaction does not always appear so early. It may come after years of comfort in a relationship, and its cause and moment of origin may be unclear.

I don't think I can be very precise about when an awareness began of trouble in the marriage itself. I think I thought more about needing to be away from the relationship than feeling like I wanted it to be over. There was a two-year period when a lot of things in my life were changing. It was sometime during those two years that I had the first inklings of change in the relationship. It was very subtle. There was no confrontation during the two years. Just an increase in discomfort with a whole lot of things. One of them was the marriage. [PSYCHOLOGIST, AGE 44, DIVORCED AFTER 12 YEARS]

Probably all of us, at some point, feel dissatisfied with our relationships. The thought, however, remains an occasional one, an unexplored and unacted on notion, appearing (or called into service) at difficult moments. But dissatisfaction, whatever its source, does not signal a relationship's end. When relationships do end, the unhappiness is both explored and acted on. Disenchantment becomes more than fleeting anger, disappointment, or regret that comes and goes. The unhappy partner fastens on it, harboring and exploring it. This secret is different from the other secrets partners keep from each other. This secret is not about daily encounters, finances, or in-laws. This secret is about the relationship. The dissatisfied partner privately acknowledges that the relationship is a source of discomfort. Some complain of feeling dislocated; their identity as partner conflicts with their sense of self and their place in the world.[4] Others complain of losing identity. This discomfort resides internally, to be weighed and considered: a secret often difficult to accept and understand, and even more difficult to share.

Thus, uncoupling begins as a quiet, unilateral process. The assumption that relationships take place in each other's presence obscures the evaluative, reflective, assessing work that we do without the input of our partners.[5] We walk around harboring and mulling over the secrets of our unhappiness. Perhaps they are unarticulated in the beginning because our feelings are nebulous. Perhaps they remain unspoken because we are uncertain as to their cause, their depth, and their implications. Perhaps we are afraid to share them for fear of discovering or validating the other person's unhappiness. For whatever reason, we won't do it until we are absolutely sure. So the dissatisfied partner creates a private niche in which to weigh the fragile, disturbing new notions, to assess present actions and future possibilities, to make estimates, to consider, to reject, to act, to wait, and, perhaps ultimately, to choose.

By the simple and innocent act of solitary reflection, the dissatisfied partner unintentionally initiates a breach between the two. The breach is created by information: one who owns it, one who does not; one who can assess it, one who cannot. At its base, this breach may perhaps be thought of as moral—a breach of trust—yet not to be ignored are its social implications. The dissatisfied partner unwittingly creates a power imbalance. A secret gives its owner the ability to control the flow of information. The secret-keeper can hold back information, consider it privately, and shape it in ways that influence the present and future.[6]

Secrecy allows plans to be developed, changed, executed, or given up without open inspection, the intrusion of alternative viewpoints, feedback, or correction.[7] Although secrecy protects the unhappy partner's capacity to explore and assess, the other person, by being excluded, is at the same time prevented from adequately understanding the developing (and potentially threatening) situation. As a consequence, the other person is precluded from acting.[8] The advantage automatically lies with the dissatisfied partner. A precarious advantage at this point, true, but important to note because power differences play a critical role in uncoupling, and they appear here, in the earliest beginnings of the transition.

At some point, the dissatisfied partner tries to remedy the situation. To relieve personal discomfort, the unhappy person initiates actions which, if effective, would bring self-concept and the identity bestowed by the relationship into harmony.[9] The initiator begins to try to tell the partner that something is wrong. Getting this message across is important, for negotiation cannot begin until both partners agree that a problem exists. For the relationship to be reshaped to meet the initiator's needs more adequately, the initiator must first capture the other person's attention. This is no simple task. While the initiator has identified the relationship as a source of dissatisfaction, the reasons for this unhappiness may still be vague and undefined—incomprehensible to the initiator and consequently inexplicable to the other person. For the initiator who has not only acknowledged that the relationship is troubled, but has begun to come to some understanding of why this is so, the task is no easier. The partner (we will assume) is reasonably content and committed to the relationship. Whether out of fear of hurting the other person, out of uncertainty, or both, the initiator finds that the words are difficult to formulate and express.

Unable to articulate true feelings, thoughts, and moods easily, the initiator does not directly confront the partner in a way that allows the partner to address the basic issue ("I am unhappy in the relationship and this is why"). Instead, the initiator begins to display discontent through cues and hints, by deeds as often as by words. Discontent displayed by deeds—a disgruntled glance, a goodnight kiss omitted, an activity scheduled that permanently conflicts with a time understood to be "our time"—may be difficult to interpret or, if seized on by the partner, explained away. When discontent does surface in words, initiators tend to attach their complaints to the problems of everyday life with the other person. "You embarrass me when you laugh so loud." "I wish you would get home for dinner in time to eat with the children." The emphasis is on the other person's daily failings. The complaints are intermittent and mundane. Not surprisingly, the partner responds to them on the level at which they are raised—as small problems.

not serious trouble. Perhaps at this point the initiator does not even recognize the extent of the problem. Perhaps at this point, it is small.

NEGOTIATING FOR CHANGE

The initiator's complaints are more than an attempt to communicate unhappiness, however. They are also the initiator's first attempt to save the relationship. By lodging complaints, the initiator tries to change the partner to be more in keeping with the initiator's sense of self and place in the world. Thus, the focus on daily failings is an honest one, for, as George Eliot notes, "it is in these acts called trivialities that the seeds of joy are forever wasted." [10] The initiator tries to correct the partner's daily failings in the hope that the partner will become a more interesting, more attractive person—and, hence, a more suitable partner. Some try to change the partner both in appearance and behavior. They may suggest changes in weight, clothing, or hair. They may point out specific traits that annoy them, such as choice of friends, drinking habits, temperament, conversation style, sexual technique (or lack of it), leisure pursuits, or financial management.

Some initiators encourage their partners toward a new activity.

She had never shown much interest in what I did and I wanted her to be able to understand it—who I dealt with, why I liked it—and, also, I wanted to be able to share things with her that happened at the plant. So I said to her, "Listen. Have I got a deal for you. How would you like to come to my office one morning a week? See what it's like, meet the people, I'll explain things to you. Come on a regular basis, I'll pay you for your time, then we can go have a fancy lunch someplace, wherever you want." [DIVISION MANAGER, AGE 54, DIVORCED AFTER 19 YEARS OF MARRIAGE]

After her father died, she started going from one thing to another. Really, nothing seemed to hold her interest. Her vitality was down and she was really focused inward to the point that I felt more and more concerned. She was drinking more than usual, which made the time we had together not very good time. I thought exercise was the right answer—some formal program where there would be a routine and some other women, so I got us both a trial membership at Women's World for her birthday. [POTTER, AGE 32, SEPARATED AFTER LIVING TOGETHER 9 YEARS]

The initiator may encourage the partner to take that evening course, have a night out with friends, attend the convention, go hunting, visit the family for a week, join the basketball league, accept that business opportunity, although it means working on Saturday. (What makes the other person more attractive is often not the new activity but a consequence of it—the partner is around less.)

Sometimes initiators bend their energies toward more sweeping changes. Rather than eliminating a particular trait or adding a new one, they try to modify the partner's personal style or chosen direction in life.

Somehow I had misjudged her—who she was and what she was capable of. Maybe I thought she was someone she was not, or maybe she was that person but now she wasn't any more. I felt disappointed and also worried that I might have something to do with it. She needed something of her own, some friends of her own. I encouraged her to get out in the world and get involved. That if she got started trying things, she would find herself. [SECRETARY, AGE 26, SEPARATED AFTER LIVING TOGETHER 5 YEARS]

I think I thought at the time when we first married that there were things I didn't like. Maybe I should have said something then, but I just thought they'd change, you know, like other people have said. It would get better. Or that I'd be happier with her. Then I got so I— I, how can I put it—would dress her. I mean I would look at her and say this is what I want, this is how it should be, not the way you are. In a way, I suppose I tried to rebuild her, the way I thought she should be. [FINANCE OFFICER, AGE 33, DIVORCED AFTER 7 YEARS]

I think there was one half-hearted attempt by me to save our relationship. I was aware of his dependence on the marriage to provide all his happiness and it wasn't providing it. I wanted him to go to graduate school, but he postponed it, against my wishes. I wanted him to pursue his own life. I didn't want him to sacrifice for me. I wanted him to become more exciting to me in the process. I was aware that I was trying to persuade him to be a different person. [GRADUATE STUDENT, AGE 26, DIVORCED AFTER 2 YEARS]

Sometimes the initiator's attempts to reshape the partner "to be a different person" focus on some aspect of the partner's behavior which, because of its apparent deep-rooted, chronic nature, seems beyond the ability of the partner to change. Perhaps the partner is overweight, depressed, unable to keep a job, addicted to drugs or alcohol, given to abusing the spouse or children, or experiencing some other difficulty for which professional help appears to be the logical solution. The initiator urges the partner to get help: to find a social worker, a counselor, a clinic, a doctor, or some self-help group.[11]

Although the initiator tries to improve the relationship by eliminating the other person's perceived flaws, these efforts seldom result in immediate success. The initiator frequently finds that attempts to reach the other person fall short. While the initiator has a clear sense that all is not well, only bits and pieces of this news have reached the partner. The real issue—that the initiator doesn't like life with the partner—remains hidden beneath the camouflage of complaints about "small stuff"—the problems of everyday life. The secret remains a secret. Thus, the partner's awareness of the extent of the initiator's discomfort, if the partner is aware at all at this point, goes no further than these minor complaints: "She doesn't like my friends"; "I am too fat"; "We have a problem with money." While the initiator defines the relationship as troubled, the partner does not. Change cannot occur unless both define it similarly. Not ready to make a break or even to think of the relationship as over, the initiator continues to try to bring the other person to a common sense that all is not well.

Meanwhile, the initiator remains unhappy. Whatever the reason, the relationship is not meeting the initiator's needs. Consequently, in an attempt to make an uncomfortable situation more comfortable, initiators often channel their energies in a second direction. Concurrent with their efforts to change the partner, initiators try to change the relationship. Some initiators try to modify the structure of the relationship by adding a new member—a baby.[12]

> *I got very concerned about starting a family. He couldn't see it, wasn't ready for it, didn't want to be married, was totally happy with the way things were going. I began lobbying hard for it, desperately wanting a family and I found out he felt just as desperate about keeping things the same.* [BOOKKEEPER-CLERK, AGE 29, SEPARATED AFTER LIVING TOGETHER 4 YEARS]

Some initiators attempt to change the division of labor.

> *I was trying to push harder and harder for a nontraditional marriage to meet my needs. As he moved into the world, his occupation, he went in just about the totally opposite direction. All he knew was all of his friends had wives. Yes, their wives were working, but their wives were also into working for the marriage: working to get the home, working so that eventually they could stop working and have children. And they were still filling most of the duties that surrounded being a wife, in spite of the fact that they were teachers, or nurses, or anything. I had something different in mind.* [MUSIC TEACHER, AGE 28, SEPARATED AFTER 6 YEARS OF MARRIAGE]

Some try to alter the relationship by renegotiating the rules. The rules that initiators most often try to convert relate to the quality and quantity of their participation in the relationship—or in other relationships.

When we decided to live together, we agreed we'd be monogamous. For me this was easy because I had always been monogamous, but he hadn't been. I think one of the reasons he decided to try it was the AIDS scare. Lots of people were looking for a regular partner. But after a while, he got restless and started talking about opening up the relationship, as long as we didn't bring anybody home. [SALES CLERK, RETAIL CLOTHING, AGE 35, SEPARATED AFTER LIVING TOGETHER 2 YEARS]

Although the initiator may try to negotiate with the partner to change the relationship, the partner may not go along with the initiator's wishes. Sometimes, realizing the negotiations will be difficult (or, in fact, a lost cause), the initiator makes changes without the partner. While two people must negotiate in order to create a relationship, change can be effected by only one—without gaining the consent of the other.[13] Thus, the initiator can (and often does) change the relationship without the aid, consent, or sometimes even the knowledge of the other person.

This feat is possible because the capacity for secrets is built into our relationships from the start.[14] An intimate relationship is the smallest organization we create. In the creation of other, more formal organizations, the founders openly and formally negotiate with each other about the way their enterprise will be run. They discuss and decide on the structure of the organization and its rules, often putting many of these decisions in writing. And while other rules develop about how the work will get done and about members' rights and obligations that are never formalized or mutually acknowledged, at least the essential elements of operation are discussed and arrived at through formal negotiation.

When we decide to live with another person, however, these things are informally negotiated, and sometimes never negotiated at all. Even though we bring with us rules and assumptions that we have learned from our experiences in other intimate relationships, from parents and friends, from books, movies, and television, this accumulated insight and wisdom seldom gets articulated.[15] The early days of a relationship pass relatively untended. Each partner goes about daily activities happily assuming that common plans and expectations are being realized, when, in fact, the plans and expectations may not be common at all.[16] Two people can be in the same relationship for some time, operating on different sets of rules and not know it—until one of them violates a rule held dear by the other. Then that rule gets discussed.[17]

More often, however, the informality of our intimate arrangements, plus the fact that each partner frequently operates independently (and thus out of sight) of the other, allow hidden sets of rules to remain hidden. Not only can we go along day after day unaware of the assumptions our partner holds about the relationship, but it also is possible for us to be ignorant of our own rules. In a situation where hidden assumptions are commonplace and often go undiscovered (as one partner said after her marriage ended, "I never knew Joe even believed in divorce. I just assumed, because he was Catholic, that he didn't"), one partner readily may change the relationship without gaining the consent of the other.

> *Bob wanted us both to devote our time to the store. Around the middle of the second year, I got tired spending every waking hour running the register, stocking shelves, and trying to do the bookwork, and we also started getting on each other a lot. I started thinking, you know, more and more about doing something else, but he would hear none of it, and I just decided to forget about taking the pill.* [BOOKKEEPER-CLERK, AGE 29, SEPARATED AFTER LIVING TOGETHER 4 YEARS]

Some changes that are initiated by only one of the partners are more likely to attract the other person's attention than others; for example, having a baby, or changing the division of labor. Harder to detect and thus likely to remain secret are changes in the rules of the relationship. The rules that are changed without the partner's knowledge usually concern the quality or quantity of the initiator's participation in the relationship. Sometimes initiators impose limits on their participation, as in this case:

> *I finally came to the point where I realized I was never going to have the kind of relationship I had hoped for. I didn't want to end it, because of the children, but I wasn't going to let it hurt me anymore. The children and I were going to be the main unit, and if he occasionally wanted to participate, fine—and if not, we would go ahead without him. I was no longer willing to let being with him be the determining factor as to whether I was happy or not. I ceased planning our lives around his presence or absence and began looking out for myself.* [STUDENT, AGE 39, DIVORCED AFTER 20 YEARS]

For others, the rules that are altered may be related to the quality and quantity of their participation in *other* relationships.

> *I had reconceptualized what marriage was. I decided sexual fidelity was not essential for marriage. I never told her that. And I didn't even have anyone I was interested in having that intimate a relationship with—I just did a philosophical thing. I just decided it was OK*

for me to have whatever of what quality of other relationships I needed to have. Something like that—of that caliber—was something I could never talk to her about. So I did it all by myself. I read things and decided it. I was at peace with me. I knew that we could stay married, whatever that meant. OK, I can stay legally tied to you, and I can probably live in this house with you, and I can have my life and still be in this situation with you, but you need some resources, because I don't want to be all for you, and I did tell her that. But I couldn't tell her this total head trip I'd been through because she wouldn't understand. [GRADUATE STUDENT, AGE 26, DIVORCED AFTER 4 YEARS]

In the beginning, initiators deal with their troubled relationships in these ways. They focus on the problems in the relationship and try to change things to suit their needs. They try to alter the other person or to change the relationship in order to reduce their discomfort and increase the self-validation they receive from the union. And perhaps they succeed. As a result of their efforts, change occurs, and they stay with the other person. In other words, these responses may hold relationships together. (Or perhaps no change results, but they remain anyway. This we will discuss later.) But these strategies also appear in relationships that end, yet additional changes follow. The unhappiness remains, and the initiator tries a third course of action. The initiator begins to explore and invest energy in other directions. In the process, this dissatisfied partner begins to create an identity independent of that bestowed by the relationship.

SEARCHING FOR IDENTITY: REDEFINITION OF SELF

No longer finding the relationship compatible with sense of self, initiators turn to alternatives that supply the self-validation they seek.[18] They may invest additional energy in some ongoing activity or may search out some new interest.[19] Sometimes an alternative is discovered unexpectedly. The initiator may have accepted the problems in the relationship, assuming the disappointments as a fact of life. By stumbling into an experience that uncovers attractive and enticing opportunities, the initiator finds that home, if not boring, is at least routine. Outside recognition becomes more important and valuable than what is coming from the relationship. The discovery transforms the formerly complacent initiator into a seeker, looking elsewhere for recognition and rewards—or vigorously pursuing what so serendipitously has presented itself.[20]

But it is not simply a matter of finding something else to do. This process involves discovery of self-worth and affirmation from a source other than the relationship. Initiators may find it in education:

I decided to enroll in graduate school. It was as if all of my life until then I had been surrounded by mirrors that faced outward and covered me up. People who looked at me saw not me, but reflections of themselves in relation to me. I was Michael's mother, Bill's wife. When I was at school, it was as if all the mirrors were taken away and people saw me for the first time. Just me—Peggy. [TEACHER, AGE 51, SEPARATED AFTER 26 YEARS OF MARRIAGE]

Some initiators discover it in parenting, cultivating a special relationship with one or more of their children.[21]

Being around home was a drag. Alice was always after me about the house, or my mother or something and there was no peace. I never had any peace. I started doing things all the time with my son. We would take weekends and work on the car, or go fishing. During the week we would check out the ads for auto supplies and go around looking for parts. Usually we'd stop in at the bar. Alice hated this, because he wasn't really old enough to drink, but an occasional beer wasn't hurting him. We were just having some man-to-man talk and fun. [SALES ENGINEER, AGE 38, SEPARATED AFTER 19 YEARS OF MARRIAGE]

Perhaps the initiator begins to rely more on friends, either strengthening existing ties or forming new ones, finding companionship that is missing in the relationship.

He was going out with other people and I had to see some other people in my life also. It wasn't that type of thing that I would see one person one night and then a few nights later see another person and then in the middle of the night, see another person. I always managed to—I was making friends where Ned was having tricks, bringing over tricks. He wasn't making friends. I was making friends. I needed them desperately. I needed that love that I wasn't getting from any other direction. I wasn't getting it—fortunately I was able to find it elsewhere. [CALLIGRAPHER, AGE 29, SEPARATED AFTER 7 YEARS OF LIVING TOGETHER]

It may be that no single alternative is sufficient. Instead, the initiator draws on many people and many activities. Some seem to find stability and a sense of self by creating a lifestyle that onlookers might think frenetic: rushing from one thing to another, heavily overscheduled, always expected somewhere else. Some find self-realization in work: from a new job, from rewards intrinsic to doing the work itself, from praise bestowed by co-workers, or from the independence that comes with earning a wage.

I was often uncomfortable at home. Especially when her son was around, because there was no clear way in which I fit in with them. She was obviously concerned about the boy having a good upbringing, but didn't really try to incorporate me into the parenting, probably for lots of reasons. Instead of going along with them or hanging around on the edges, as I came to think of it, I signed up for the 3 to 11 shift, which was bad in some ways because by not being around them, I was also not being around her, but it was good because I started feeling good from 3 to 11 everyday instead of feeling stressed, and like I didn't belong. [NURSE, AGE 28, SEPARATED AFTER LIVING TOGETHER 3 YEARS]

The feeling that something is amiss may propel initiators to devote energy to some cause. They may volunteer at the fire department, hospital, or school. They may join a political campaign or work on some public issue. Many turn to self-improvement—an EST course, a book discussion group, therapy—some activity where the focus is personal maintenance or change. Initiators may become preoccupied with dieting, weight lifting, bowling, or jogging. They may enroll in adult education classes, learning new skills such as photography, bridge, word-processing, or auto repair. Latent or wished-for talents may be cultivated: dance classes, music lessons, art courses—all entailing long hours to master. Although "self-improvement" is common parlance for these undertakings, the term also accurately describes the deeper consequences of such activities. Initiators take on improvement *of the self* by turning elsewhere for the rewards and identity substantiation that the relationship is not providing.

Initiators may find self-realization in a return to some former lifestyle that was displaced by the relationship. People often resume ties with their family of origin. A young woman whose husband traveled a lot reported relying on her own family for the family life she had expected with her husband but which never materialized: extended phone conversations on a daily basis with brothers and sisters, dinners several times a week with parents, and a social life centered around family participation in religious celebrations, children's birthdays, and school activities. One man, who complained that his wife was so absorbed in the children that she paid no attention to him, began stopping by his widowed mother's house on the way home from work to take care of the lawn and keep her house in good repair. In exchange, she gave him dinner. He returned to his wife, having contributed elsewhere, having been fed and nurtured elsewhere.

Others report returning, not to their family of origin, but to elements of the single lifestyle they had enjoyed before they decided to live with their partner. Initiators may renew and strengthen ties with friends from their single days, resuming former pursuits: playing cards, doing the bar scene, playing pick-up basketball, shopping with girlfriends. Some turn not to others but to self. They discover—or rediscover—that they are their own best resource. In quiet times, they find self-validation in their capacity to be alone.

Obviously, many of these alternatives are also pursued in stable relationships where both partners are deeply committed to each other.[22] The individual interests of each become part and parcel of the relationship, adding depth and breadth to the life of each partner and simultaneously to the relationship. In many cases, the pursuit of other interests may be exactly the stuff that allows the initiator to remain in a troubled relationship. The initiator supplements the relationship by incorporating these activities into his or her ongoing lifestyle.[23] Mollified by having needs met elsewhere, the initiator drifts into a stable existence with the partner. Relieved of demands it could not meet, the relationship endures.

Despite this ability to shore up failing relationships and enhance healthy ones, the pursuit of other interests can and does contribute to their demise. When relationships end, the initiator eventually gives the new focus priority over the relationship. We make choices about how we spend our time and energy, choosing activities to the degree it is rewarding to do so or punishing not to.[24] But one choice often precludes the possibility of others. As the initiator draws identity from and gives energy to the alternative, what she or he draws from and gives to the relationship diminishes. The initiator continues (for the time being) to go home, but, like the man who routinely stopped by his mother's house every evening, does so having contributed elsewhere, having been fed and nurtured elsewhere.

Furthermore, in relationships that end, these alternatives are not shared with the partner. Unlike a healthy relationship in which the partners grow in new directions but maintain bonds of interdependence between their separate interests, uncoupling is characterized by the pursuit of alternatives in ways that sever ties instead of strengthen them. The initiator begins creating a social world from which the partner is excluded. Sometimes the activity itself prevents the participation of the partner.

Ricky got into female impersonation, mostly for the art of it. He got to be very good at it. He won prizes in competitions in bars. But the drag got to be too much for me. It took hours and months preparing—finding the right dress, sewing it to fit, then the make-up. Ricky

*got to spending so much more money and time on it, and he and Tom
would do it together. I was excluded because I wasn't good at it. I
wasn't pretty enough for the drag, and I really had no interest in
it.* [SERVICE COORDINATOR/STUDENT, AGE 28, SEPARATED AFTER LIVING TO-
GETHER 1 YEAR]

Then, rather than taking the partner along by bringing news of the
activity home or including the partner in the social life that accompanies
the separate ventures, the initiator may bracket that part of life, shutting
out the partner. Sometimes the initiator may try to get the partner to
participate, but the partner declines—or goes along with it for a while,
then drops out. The attempt to have the partner vicariously join in may
be stymied because the partner finds the initiator's alternative interest
boring or simply inpenetrable. Or the partner may view the initiator's
interest as objectionable. The initiator may be unwilling or unable to
bridge this gap and thus either not talk about the activity at all, or discuss it in a way that either maintains or constructs barriers to the partner's participation. Although silence creates distance, talk can have the
same effect. To minimize tensions, the initiator withholds information.

In many cases, the partner is aware of the initiator's commitment
elsewhere. But knowledge of the existence of some alternative is not
the same as participation in it, even vicariously. Though bits and pieces
of information may be passed on to the partner, they represent the trivialities of the initiator's experience. The important problems, the difficult moments, the sweet victories, the favorite anecdotes are shared only
superficially, if at all. Because the initiator controls the flow of information, the partner's understanding of and access to these experiences
of the initiator's are limited. Thus, secrets multiply, increasing the
asymmetry and widening the breach between the two.

The initiator may choose some socially disvalued alternative that calls
for even greater secrecy.[25] He or she may turn to others for sex, creating
multiple nonshareable secrets.

*I traveled quite frequently to the Midwest and fortunately I ran into
one of these girls that was corn-fed and healthy and that occupied my
time for some amount of time. After I found this new acquaintance, I
found others. I made it a point to travel as much as possible and I
think I reestablished some faith in myself.* [SALES REPRESENTATIVE, AGE
36, DIVORCED AFTER 11 YEARS]

Having many lovers can be a satisfying alternative, for from them initiators may derive self-validation without making a commitment, without developing an intimate connection with another person. Initiators
may remain in the relationship, more or less contented by the multiple

alternatives they have found. Often, however, the field narrows to one, as the initiator stumbles into a new intimate relationship that becomes singular and serious, precipitating a transition out of the old relationship.[26] Not all who become involved in a new intimate relationship do so by first casting a wide net, however. The result is nonetheless the same. The initiator discovers the possibility of an alternative intimate relationship, and responds by cultivating it.

I would see him all the time when we went out dancing. Then when I joined the poetry workshop, I saw him there. After a while I found that going to the poetry workshop and going dancing were the things I most looked forward to, and I realized it was not because of who I was with, but because of who I would see while I was there. After a while, we became lovers. His relationship was not working out well either, so we consoled each other. [ILLUSTRATOR, AGE 24, SEPARATED AFTER LIVING TOGETHER 18 MONTHS]

I had never had an affair. I had never thought about having an affair. I was still not saying, "I'm gonna get a divorce," but I was feeling like I didn't want him anymore—that feeling, but not associating that feeling with divorce. At that time I went to my best friend to seek some emotional support, but she was going through an upheaval and life crisis herself and was absolutely unavailable for me. So I turned to her husband. And we were both in the same situation—we just fell into each other's arms. Oh my God! We'd known each other for years and here we were. [LEARNING DISABILITIES TEACHER, AGE 49, DIVORCED AFTER 23 YEARS]

The new relationship can be a fantasy relationship, more imagined than real. The initiator's choice is someone who is distant in some way. The new love may live in another city, be coupled to someone else and thus unavailable much of the time, or be emotionally distant, not reciprocating the initiator's feelings of love. The unavailability of the other person, however, does not affect the degree to which the initiator derives self-validation from the relationship, nor does it diminish the initiator's involvement.[27] Despite the elusive quality of this new lover, the initiator maintains the relationship with little contribution or effort from the other person: collecting anecdotes to relate in future conversations, writing letters, going over past encounters, planning future ones. The initiator devotes energy to the fantasy as to an available lover; the difference is that the relationship finds its expression mostly in thoughts rather than in day-to-day encounters. Perhaps part of the attraction is the distance itself. The initiator can care about and derive identity from the other person without jeopardizing his or her present lifestyle.

When another person becomes a part of the memories of the initiator, neither the experiences of today nor the plans for tomorrow can be shared with the partner. To acknowledge to the partner that time, energy, and commitment are flowing into another intimate relationship would precipitate a crisis the initiator is not ready to confront.[28] Unlike other alternatives to the relationship, where bits and pieces of trivia about daily affairs can be exchanged with the partner, bits and pieces of trivia can seldom be exchanged when the daily affair *is* an affair. Hence, the initiator works hard at secret-keeping when the alternative is a lover.

The need for secrecy is compounded when the initiator has not only formed a new intimate relationship, but also has changed sexual preference.[29] The care and caution the initiator takes in concealing information about the relationship is extreme. The initiator potentially faces a dual transition: uncoupling from the partner and from a heterosexual lifestyle. She or he needs privacy to explore the implications of these major changes, so incompatible with what others have come to expect. In order to protect the opportunity to think things through, the initiator strives to present an image of self consistent with that of the past, carefully guarding against the introduction of discrepant information.[30]

Secrets create the possibility of a private niche that protects fledging thoughts and fledging identities.[31] By the effective monitoring of information, the initiator can create a separate world that the partner does not even know exists.[32] Consequently, the initiator begins the threads of a life apart from the other person. The creation of this separate world is reinforced when information not shared with the partner is disclosed elsewhere, creating or strengthening ties elsewhere while weakening the bond between the partners.[33]

I shared important things with the children that I didn't share with him. It's almost as if I purposefully punished him by not telling him. Some good thing would happen and I'd come home and tell them and wouldn't tell him. [ASSISTANT PROFESSOR, AGE 37, DIVORCED AFTER 19 YEARS]

I found my friendship with her became more and more important. We shared so much. Yet all those years we were never sexually intimate. I think intellectual infidelity has a much more serious effect on a relationship than sexual infidelity. I can give my body to anybody and still stay in my relationship. But if I give my mind, I'm gone. [OFFICE MANAGER, AGE 52, DIVORCED AFTER 26 YEARS]

The initiator has begun to create a social location apart from that shared with the partner. This is not an activity engaged in with malice aforethought. Rather, it occurs as the initiator attempts to ease his or her life situation. The social consequences, however, are serious, for the initiator's response has a divisive effect on the couple. One secret leads to others and, as secrets multiply, the partner is increasingly excluded from the initiator's world. In beginning a life independent of the partner, the initiator has taken the first tentative steps toward a transition out of the relationship. In search of self-validation, the initiator finds it. Inadvertently, the initiator has begun to create an identity independent of the partner and partnership. How ironic that our intimate relationships, so often viewed as providing the stable, solid core of our existence in a fluctuating and unpredictable world,[34] are themselves so fragile that they can be undermined by a series of responses to a personal problem—responses intended only to relieve the immediate discomfort of one of the partners.

TWO

The Display of Discontent

UNCOUPLING is thus simple and unintentional in its beginnings. In the process of seeking self-validation outside the relationship, the dissatisfied partner creates a small territory that confirms an identity independent of the coupled identity created with the other person. As time passes, the initiator reacts in additional ways that further divide the couple. The initiator (who for some undetermined amount of time and with varying degrees of diligence has been trying unsuccessfully to change the partner and the relationship in certain hoped-for directions) tires of the effort. Now doubting that the situation can be readily salvaged by pushing for change, the initiator begins to view the relationship as unsaveable. Disillusioned by the inability to resolve unhappiness at home, the initiator becomes increasingly preoccupied with the ways partner and relationship fail. The dissatisfied initiator focuses more and more on the flaws, minimizing the positive aspects.[1]

The initiator's accentuation of the negative is a reversal of the somewhat mystical process that draws us to another in the first place. When we fall in love, we abstract the good from our beginning knowledge about the other person. We focus on positive traits. We see similarities and compatibilities with our partners—or if we notice differences, we view them as complementary. As the relationship matures, our sense of the other adjusts to the reality: along with the characteristics we admire, our beloved (alas) has some flaws. We are forced to acknowledge that there are no angels—only fallen angels. As relationships become troubled, our focus shifts again, this time to negative qualities. We redefine our partners and relate to them in terms of their objectionable traits. We see more the differences than the similarities—or regard the differences now as troublesome and unattractive. Out of our increasing unhappiness, we start to dwell on and even exaggerate our partner's flaws.[2]

I was unhappy with her, it didn't really matter what she did, nothing was right. Our last year, she was pregnant a good part of the time and when I look back now there were times I really feel I was downright mean, and she had a rough time. It was bad enough she was carrying a child I found was mine, but I mean I used to like to think when a women is pregnant it's the most beautiful part of her life or she's the most beautiful. Yes, to an extent it's a miracle, I think it is, but on the other hand you can't tell me she's beautiful, she just isn't. I mean, you know, you just get fatter and fatter. [FINANCE OFFICER, AGE 33, DIVORCED AFTER 7 YEARS]

Not only do initiators redefine their partners in negative terms, but they also reconstruct the history of the relationship, reordering their reminiscences into a negative chronology of events.[3] The good times are forgotten or explained away. An enjoyable vacation together, for example, may be interpreted as "enjoyable because we went with friends," or "but I always loved getting out in the woods, it wouldn't matter who I was with," or accepted as pleasant because it was an idiosyncratic event. "Sure, we had a good time, but that's because we were on vacation. On a day-to-day basis, we were miserable." The bad times form the salient memories. In explaining how they came to create this union in the first place, initiators seldom mention love. Obviously, people form intimate relationships for complex reasons, not all of which they recognize at the time—or later. When they uncouple, they reinterpret the coupling process. They sift through those reasons, eliminating or downplaying the ones that justify the union on the basis of anything but accident, necessity, or even outright mistake.

We got together because we were both on the rebound. In all honesty, probably anybody would have looked good to me. I was so needy I stunk. [ILLUSTRATOR, AGE 24, SEPARATED AFTER LIVING TOGETHER 18 MONTHS]

I finished my degree, it seemed like there was this natural break in my life, and it was time to get married. And Nancy just happened to be the one standing there at the time. [ENGINEER, AGE 54, SEPARATED AFTER 28 YEARS OF MARRIAGE]

I had my own room at home and it certainly was big enough for two, but as an adult you can't get away with having a girlfriend overnight—the same friend—on a regular basis without causing a hassle.

I was ready for my own place and she had been looking, too, so we found an apartment and moved in together. It was simply a matter of convenience. [MODEL/SALESCLERK, AGE 26, SEPARATED AFTER LIVING TO-GETHER 2 YEARS]

Everything was wrong. And I really was caught up in a lot of things. But it was also real clear—the evidence was fairly unmistakable—that we had gotten married much more for other peoples' reasons than our own and that we really hadn't had much of an opportunity to rationally choose someone who we'd made sure we wanted to spend the rest of our lives with and that we really hadn't even thought about whether we were even committed to that idea. It had all been done in a thoughtless, clearly naive and immature way. I didn't date any-one other than her after I was 17 years old. [PSYCHOLOGIST, AGE 44, DI-VORCED AFTER 12 YEARS]

In reordering the history of the relationship, the initiator also reassesses its personal significance.[4] The initiator may conclude that the relation-ship has all along been wrong—but now its true meaning is correctly understood.

Somewhere along in the last couple of years I started thinking of my feelings toward her as ones I might have toward a sister. That meta-phor, of the sister, helped me understand and deal better with the situation. It meant that the intensity of the relationship was not im-proper. It was just misconceived and improperly expressed. And there wasn't anything wrong with having strong feelings. What was wrong was trying to behave as a couple. And I didn't have sexual feelings for her and I didn't have interest in trying to be sexual. [LAWYER, AGE 35, SEPARATED AFTER LIVING TOGETHER 10 YEARS]

The initiator may allow that the relationship was meaningful once, but no longer is. Or the initiator may come to believe that the relationship is destructive for one partner or the other, for both, or for the kids.

From the start I needed to believe that the relationship was bad for Paul, too. Maybe that's a part of it, for to believe that this was good for Paul would cause me too much personal pain, and I couldn't handle it. I can't honestly say except from my perspective, that the relationship was bad for him. I think he could have gone the rest of his life with me, because that was all he needed or wanted out of his life. [LEATHER CRAFTSMAN, AGE 42, SEPARATED AFTER LIVING TOGETHER 12 YEARS]

Our ability to do this—to alter our past history and our sense of who our partner is—derives from the fact that the events constituting our lives are subject to alternate interpretations, not just by outsiders, but by ourselves.[5] As our lives change directions, we attempt to maintain consistency by assigning major importance to some facts or events that formerly seemed minor. Some are given new meaning. Some are preserved and highlighted, while others are ignored, downplayed, or discarded.[6] We busy ourselves with interpretation and reinterpretation, constantly working to bring our past into consistency with our present.[7] When we become unhappy, we seek to explain failure in the present by reinterpreting the past. Of the myriad things that could be noticed, we notice only those that are important for our immediate situation and proceed, as Berger puts it, to "correct fortune by remaking history."[8]

Home provides a fertile arena for exercising our natural talents at reordering incidents and identities. There we create an intimate environment with another person whom we love and trust. We feel safe with that other person. Yet that intimate environment, intended as a safe haven, can become the place where we are not safe at all, but the most vulnerable. For in the loving and trusting and being ourselves, we let the other person see all our failures, all our flaws. That person knows us in a total way that the rest of the world does not.[9] This knowledge of the other that accompanies intimacy can at any moment convert that safe haven into a dangerous place, for we each possess information that can be used to do the other in.[10]

Our propensity to redefine partner and relationship negatively is further enhanced should we glimpse a potential alternative lifestyle, against which the relationship is compared and found wanting.[11]

I went to the school for six weeks. I loved being on my own, loved not thinking about my problems, met two really exciting wonderful women, and one of them I had an affair with. What that suggested to me was that one of the things that I've always felt itchy about in my marriage was that I never was on my own. I went literally from the Boy Scouts to fatherhood. I was never a bachelor, I never dated anybody, I never lived on my own, I never learned to cook my own food. The first delight I had up there was being on my own. I really liked it. I had a certain schedule I had to keep, in fact an intense one, but the relief of being alone and of being only myself, not coming as somebody's partner, was really wonderfully exhilarating. [ADMINISTRATOR, AGE 44, SEPARATED AFTER 23 YEARS OF MARRIAGE]

I went out to dinner with one of the women from my women's group. And we went to a Chinese restaurant, and we sat there and talked for three hours! Between dinner and talking, I thought to myself, I've never done that with Dick. If I'd gone out to dinner with him, we would have eaten in silence or relative silence while we talked about some trivia. And I thought, how sad—what, am I going to spend my life with a man that I really don't have a whole lot to say to? But where am I going to find one that's different? [HOUSEWIFE, AGE 36, SEPARATED AFTER 12 YEARS OF MARRIAGE]

What Melanie's presence in my life made vivid was the weakness in my marriage, being that loss of a real love. That loss of real sharing, and involvement with something else that can contribute to love. I was very torn up by the implications for my own life of loving a woman, of sexually loving a woman, but the deepness of my love for Melanie during that period made me realize that a marriage that didn't have close to that deepness was absurd. It was farcical. [AMATEUR PHOTOGRAPHER, AGE 28, DIVORCED AFTER 6 YEARS]

I went to work for an individual who was a very bright person in terms of his job. Over a period of 5 or 6 years working for that man, my salary went up from like $14,000 to $42,000 a year and prestige-wise I probably was more highly thought of than he was. So my character development, my confidence in my own ability multiplied at the same time as my check did. The thought that I couldn't control my own personal destiny but that I could control everyone else's that I worked with just got to be something I couldn't stand. It's very difficult to go from being king at the office, to being a slave at home when you do it at 5:30 every day, it's very difficult. [DIRECTOR OF DISTRIBUTION, AGE 36, DIVORCED AFTER 11 YEARS]

The experience expands the range of possible choices,[12] throwing the relationship's failings into broad relief. The alternative precipitates an awakening—awakening to competencies undiscovered, needs unmet, possibilities unrecognized. As a result, the negative aspects of the intimate environment become even more obvious.[13] Because the possibility of alternatives reduces our vested interest in saving the relationship,[14] we indulge ourselves in an otherwise unavailable luxury—that of being extremely critical.[15] We have no need to keep reminding ourselves of the positive aspects of partner and relationship—a strategy that helps us to persevere when all is not well.

DISPLAYING DISCONTENT

As the initiator's discontent intensifies, the signs of it become more visible. The initiator displays it, to self and to others. Sometimes initiators display discontent to themselves by writing regular entries in journals, making lists of grievances, writing letters (some that get sent, some that don't), talking into a tape recorder, or spontaneously filling pages of scrap paper with outpourings about their partners and relationships that reflect anger, sorrow, confusion, and thoughts about what to do. Such actions reflect the intrapersonal struggle initiators experience as they attempt to define the problem. Regardless of whether or not initiators successfully resolve it, the effort itself has an important effect. By expressing discontent in these ways, initiators give their unhappiness tangible form—they make it public to themselves. They objectify it, acknowledge it, and confirm it. They work it through and make it real.[16]

Initiators continue to display their discontent to their partners, but with changed purpose. While from the start they have indicated dissatisfaction by both word and deed, their actions have been grounded in efforts to renegotiate the relationship so that it might continue. Now, however, the initiator raises complaints in order to convince the partner that the relationship is not only troubled, but perhaps unsaveable. The strategies for persuading the partner vary. The initiator may become more direct, or may cease lodging complaints entirely, continuing to express unhappiness in other ways: conveying mood in body language and manner, spending more time away from the partner, or finding ways to create distance when they're together.

The initiator also begins to display discontent to other people.[17] Although the display to self and partner is an elaboration of what has gone before, airing dissatisfaction before others is new. Through a variety of mechanisms, the initiator subtly but effectively relays the message to selected others that all is not well. In the partner's absence (and sometimes in the partner's presence), the initiator publicly demonstrates unhappiness.

> *Long before I separated, long before I knew I was going to do that, I let people know that I wasn't entirely happily married. Either never mentioning him at all, or mentioning little problems when appropriate that bothered me.* [MUSICIAN, AGE 32, DIVORCED AFTER 8 YEARS]

In the presence of others, the initiator may react to the partner in ways that reflect disinterest, disrespect, or dislike.[18] Some strategies are subtle—a failure to react, a frown displayed at the proper moment, innuendo, jokes, mimicry, hints—so subtle that the initiator cannot be accused of doing something unacceptable.[19] The lover arrives late at the bar—or the spouse comes late to a family gathering. The initiator fails to acknowledge the arrival, responds with a public denunciation and open quarreling, or heightens the appearance of fun and engagement she or he is having with someone else. In displaying discontent to the partner, the initiator also conveys a message to the others assembled.

Sometimes this display takes the form of asides that reveal the initiator's unhappiness to anyone in the vicinity. She announces angrily to herself as she arrives at the office, "Every morning I'm late to work because she can't get up in time to drive me there." He mumbles at a party, "She is so miserable at managing money that it's a wonder we have anything." Sometimes the displays are in the form of anecdotes, excerpts from the negative chronology of events the initiator is working on, that get cultivated and publicly recited, sometimes over and over—at parties, family gatherings, and other events where the partner is also present. We've all witnessed this. One partner goes on in not-so-loving detail about some characteristics or incident while those assembled laugh uncomfortably at this unsolicited and unwanted disclosure of the other partner's transgressions.[20] The discredited partner has several options: utter a denial, offer an excuse, join in the laughter, or become belligerent—none of which can overcome the fact that the initiator has introduced important information to others about the partner and the relationship.[21]

The initiator also displays discontent in intimate conversations with confidants.[22] This involves more than an occasional aside or revealing anecdote; it consists of in-depth disclosures about the partner and the relationship that are shared and assessed with another person, as the initiator works through doubts, ambiguities, and disappointments aloud.[23] Who initiators select as recipients of these feelings is significant, for their choice reflects the action they are contemplating. Initiators thinking of ending their relationships will talk to people who will listen without condemning. Some people, of course, are eliminated automatically from consideration because initiators can anticipate an unsympathetic response. A man simply does not go to his mother-in-law to complain about all the ways in which her daughter is failing him. So initiators approach someone they think will be supportive. The display of discontent is a way of testing others, of sending up trial balloons, and observing the stance others take in response.[24] Sometimes the initiator is surprised when an expected supporter argues in behalf of the partner, refuses to listen, or reacts in other ways that cause the initiator to turn elsewhere.

When I really started thinking seriously about leaving I tried to think, was there anyone that I could confide in? That I could work this out with? And I had to come up with a zero. There were a few people that I talked to about it. I talked to my Minister. He proceeded to just try and talk me out of it, brought up unconditional love and all that stuff to talk me out of it. I may have talked to my brother one or two times. He would say, "Hey, God put you two together." He wasn't condemning me, but he was very opinionated. So I didn't have anybody to talk to, to be open, and really hear me. I told the therapist about it and I really didn't feel that he was supportive. This is a pattern in my life that when I really get under the gun, I tend to pull in and to handle as much as I can by myself, if I can I'll do it myself, but when I'm drowning then I'll reach out. I never remember being in that kind of position before in my life, I was actually drowning. [SUPERVISOR, AGE 38, DIVORCED AFTER 19 YEARS]

Pushed away by real and imagined negative responses, the initiator is pulled toward people who are likely to be supportive, avoiding those with a vested interest in the relationship's continuance. Seeking affirmation that actions and feelings are correct, the initiator will choose a friend as a confidant, but not one who is a friend of the partner's or a friend of both. Some initiators confide in a relative, a friend from before the relationship, or a co-worker. Some share and explore their discontent with their children, as this woman did with her daughter.

I told her my negativism about her Daddy doesn't in any way mean that she ought to feel the same way. And that I'm not asking for her to agree with me when I'm spouting off, but just to hear me, because I need to spout off, but that I expect that she loves her Daddy, and that he's a fine Daddy, and that she should have a continued relationship with him, but that doesn't mean that I have to approve of everything he does, or that our relationship is necessarily good. Even quite recently, I had the courage to ask her if she would be very angry with me if I left her Dad. And she said, no, she would understand that. That she understands that our marriage is not fulfilling for me, and that if I need to make that decision sometime that she would understand me. [ASSISTANT PROFESSOR, AGE 37, DIVORCED AFTER 19 YEARS]

Some initiators choose a person whose relationship also is in trouble— a comrade in suffering—in whom they suddenly discover previously unrecognized compatibilities. They may renew or strike up acquaintance with single, separated, or divorced friends, whom they now see as having relevant expertise.[25] Some initiators may feel more comfortable soul-searching with a stranger: the passenger sharing the adjoining seat on a bus, the receptionist at the doctor's office, the person on the next bar-stool. Some initiators may feel safe only with someone who is outside their everyday social setting and therefore doesn't know the partner.

Other initiators, advantaged by a position in the business world and blessed with WATTS lines and travel allowances, may exchange their innermost thoughts with a business contact or a friend across the country.

In search of an outsider with no biases in behalf of the partner, some initiators may turn to a professional counselor as a confidant.[26] Often they go plagued by indecision, for their unhappiness in the relationship is counterbalanced by doubts and guilt.

> *I went to the Mental Health Center at the time to see if I could talk to somebody. It was the first person, I have to say, that I was really honest with. I told her everything. About sexual problems, about everything. I mean I was shaking. I told it to a woman, I said I don't believe I'm doing this and she said, "Well, have you made up your mind?" I said, "But what do I do?" She says, "Well, when you're ready to leave, you'll tell her." I said, "When's that going to be?" She said, "When the guilt gets too much for you, you'll be honest." I thought she was right.* [MECHANIC, AGE 28, SEPARATED AFTER LIVING TOGETHER 9 YEARS]

> *I needed to talk about it. I felt I had made a commitment when we moved in together, and making that commitment cost me a lot. I believed at the time that the commitment had a double edge. A commitment to her was also a public commitment to a lesbian lifestyle and I was only willing to do that, to be open about it, because I believed the relationship would last. I decided to go into therapy, and I did that for nearly a year, primarily about whether to leave the relationship or not. But I think I found out what I needed to know about my needs that were not going to be met in the relationship and about my ability to stay in a positive relation to her, whether or not we were together. But a lot of it was about whether I was ready to make the change or not and examining all the things a change would mean for me.* [LAWYER, AGE 35, SEPARATED AFTER LIVING TOGETHER 10 YEARS]

Some go for professional help not because of the relationship, but because they seek help with a problem child or because they are experiencing some personal problem, such as sleeplessness or depression. In conversation with a counselor, the initiator may come to view the problem in a different light. The child's behavior or the personal problem gets redefined as a relationship problem.[27]

FINDING A TRANSITIONAL PERSON

People do not make voluntary transition alone. From among those in whom they confide their discontent about the relationship, initiators find a transitional person: someone who will bridge the gap between the old life and the new. Traditionally, a transitional person has been thought of as a lover who is supportive but temporary, for the initiator and the lover uncouple sometime after the initiator's break with the partner.[28] The role of transitional person, however, is broader and more diversely played than thought. A transitional person is someone who comforts, supports, and, perhaps in addition, instructs the initiator through the end of the relationship and into a life apart from the partner. Providing support for a major part of the transition is essential. Consequently, the transitional person will be a confidant, but not every confidant will become a transitional person. This eliminates the occasional confidant as well as those who are one-time-only: the passenger on the bus, or the person on the adjacent barstool.

The relationship between the initiator and a transitional person will be based on an affectional bond. In contrast to traditional notions about a transitional person, however, sexual intimacy may not be a part of it.

You asked if I had anybody, there was one man who I believe was an angel that God sent. There was really no one I could talk to until I hired this 55-year-old Jamaican man as a postal clerk. He came into my life about maybe six months before Ann and I separated. He turned out to be more than a father to me. A Christian man with a lot of faith, and it wasn't long before I felt I could say anything to him and it would be OK, he would understand and he would have some advice to give me or just say it's going to be OK. Being able to confide in him helped me to remain sane and go through that whole thing with a feeling of being supported. He was like a life-line. [SUPERVISOR, AGE 38, DIVORCED AFTER 19 YEARS]

I finally found someone. I had a friend—someone I could talk to about my relationship with Ned. And little did I know how much I really loved this other man. He was a true friend, and I could confide in him and he would tell me, "Well, why are you staying with him? Why are you staying with this person?" He was important because I never really felt like I could do it on my own. I don't know—sometimes I wondered if I was really able to make life on my own. I always had those doubts and those fears. We never had sex together, but we shared this wonderful love between us. [CALLIGRAPHER, AGE 29, SEPARATED AFTER LIVING TOGETHER 7 YEARS]

Furthermore, the transitional person may or may not depart. For example, a professional counselor sometimes becomes a transitional person and the initiator develops an affective bond with the counselor. (Some initiators report a shift in commitment that further divides them from the partner and creates still another loss when the counseling sessions are terminated.[29]) The counselor provides support through a major part of the transition, but when the crisis has passed, the relationship ceases. On the other hand, the transitional person sometimes remains in the initiator's life. He or she may have been there all long, but becomes more important to the initiator when the trouble develops.[30] Then, when the initiator's life regains stability, the relationship resumes its former pace and emphasis. Imagine, for example, a boss and secretary with a congenial but impersonal business relationship. When the boss's home-life becomes troubled, the boss turns to and relies on the secretary for support. After the crisis dissipates, however, the relationship resumes its former style. Alternatively, the transitional person may stay on in a different role, becoming a permanent fixture in the initiator's personal life: the secretary (or therapist) may remain in the initiator's personal world by becoming a live-in partner or spouse.

Initiators may have more than one transitional person. They may turn to a lawyer, who guides them through the legal maze. They also may rely on a lover, and then recruit still another person in whom they confide their uncertainties about partner, lover, and lawyer. Often the transitional person is a role model: someone who has a lifestyle the initiator wishes to emulate or someone who has survived a separation. This reliance on more than one transitional person makes sense because we play multiple roles.[31] Changing one role as primary as our intimate connection often affects the others. Consequently, more than one transitional person may be useful because when we contemplate leaving a relationship, we must also take into account changes that will result in the addition, subtraction, or modification of other roles. Parents cannot give up their role as partner without modifying their role as a parent: the full-time mother who has never worked may take a job; the father who leaves home becomes a visiting father, or decides to abdicate his parent role; a spouse who is financially dependent on a partner either becomes employed or transfers that dependence to parents, to the state, or to a new partner. In short, initiators are contemplating not one transition, but several, which will require them not only to redefine themselves in terms of their partners, but also in terms of others. So they may seek support on more than one front, turning to more than one transitional person.

Finding confidants and transitional people is a complicated matter for initiators in homosexual relationships. Though publicly living together, homosexual couples usually reveal the true nature of their relationship to only a limited audience. Thus, when relationships get in trouble, both partners have fewer supports on which to draw—and drawing on them involves certain risks. Family members are likely to perceive breaking up as relinquishing the gay identity. Thus, while they may offer support, family members tend to celebrate uncoupling as a return to "normalcy": a heterosexual lifestyle. Consequently, initiators who confide their relationship problems to relatives risk possible loss of face ("You were wrong") and extensive negotiation in order to maintain their gay identity. Until very recently, professional counselors were not available to help in gay relationships, because "help" often came in the form of attempts to convert their sexual preference. Even now, counseling for gays is not universally available.

Within the gay community, finding a confidant or transitional person is no less complicated. The pool of eligible partners is small and competition is keen. A person whose relationship appears to be in trouble is perceived as a potential partner. Virtually all gay people have had the experience of uncoupling, but to be supportive and share this information risks the interpretation that this supportiveness is a "come-on." So some who could be friends do not offer their friendship. Those who do offer support are often interested in the initiator as a future partner and thus the transitional person is more likely to become a lover and new partner for gays than for heterosexuals. Initiators who are struggling to define and interpret their relationship problems have difficulty working them through without becoming involved in a new relationship—which increases the distance between the initiator and the partner.

As initiators display discontent about the relationship in conversation with a transitional person, the problems in the relationship become clarified and solidified. In the ongoing conversation, an idea often becomes transformed into a possibility.[32]

She was the first person I really started talking to about the problems at home, that seemed, at least at that time as I had figured out, to stem from working and trying to be a wife, too. I can remember one day that talking to her was really intense for me. The conversation wasn't that work was a problem. The conversation was, the marriage was a problem. That it was more basic than just that I wanted to work. It was more basic than just that she wanted to work. It was something more wrong. Somehow it was so resonant for me what she was saying. I think the significance was it made me realize the problem wasn't me. Together we sort of affirmed it was not us, either. We're not weird. It allowed me to deal better with my feelings that the marriage was troubled by not blaming myself for thinking it was just me, that I was somehow a personal failure or a personal freak, or something like that. I think the reason that the conversation was significant and the support was significant, was that that's the begin-ning—I think—as I can reconstruct it—of seriously thinking that I could alter the course I was on. [DAY CARE CENTER ASSISTANT, AGE 24, DIVORCED AFTER 4 YEARS]

I had decided we needed help, and that I just couldn't live with him. I was very hostile, very angry, and very upset, and I asked him to go to a counselor with me and he would not. He insisted it was my problem. So I went alone. And working through a lot of my own feelings with that counselor brought me to the point where I decided that I was no longer interested in making that marriage work. I was not ready for a divorce—I could not cope with the idea of being alone and financially taking care of myself. But I knew that I was no longer interested in beating my head against a stone wall. I would find my relationships outside of my marriage that would fulfill what I needed as best I could and I would prepare myself to live alone. [HOUSEWIFE, AGE 36, SEPARATED AFTER 12 YEARS[33]]

Such displays of discontent provide an outlet for the distress initiators feel. Whether in the form of asides, diaries and letters, anecdotes, or introspective musings with confidants and transitional people, these displays serve as safety valves.[34] This can be as functional to a relationship as a retreat from the battlefield which allows those under siege to go, bandaged and refreshed, back into the fray. When relationships end, however, this safety-valve function—the provision of temporary psychological relief—is counteracted by social consequences. These consequences, though unintended, widen the breach between the partners.

SOCIAL SEPARATION

By displaying discontent, the initiator begins to publicly dissociate from the partner. When we couple, we act in ways that publicly link us with the other person.[35] We demonstrate our connection to our partner by gestures of attention and affection. When we uncouple, we tend to demonstrate instead our disattention and disaffection. The initiator publicly dissociates from the partner not only by the content of the secrets revealed, but by the very fact that the initiator reveals them. Most couples collaborate to maintain a harmonic public image, in keeping with norms of privacy about the inner workings of relationships.[36] By revealing the discord to selected audiences,[37] the initiator signals an erosion of moral commitment to the relationship. A disavowal of the association is a way of leaving, of separating from the partner without physically separating. Thus, the initiator creates a public distinction, a public uncoupling—

one that happens for selected others before physical separation becomes a part of the public biography of the relationship.

In addition, the display of discontent validates the initiator's view of partner and relationship for people outside the intimate environment. Having a partner is socially acceptable. Getting rid of one is not.[38] This value is so ingrained in us that leaving—or considering leaving—someone who is still loving or dependent produces enormous conflict. When the partner has obvious good qualities, ending a relationship is even harder still. In order to violate the imperatives of the dominant social order—that people should come in two's, like the animals of Noah's ark—initiators transform partner and relationship, emphasizing the flaws.[39] They justify the leavetaking by stating to others the reasons why this case is an exception to the rule of togetherness. By so doing, initiators reduce the negative social consequences of uncoupling.[40] They create the possibility of exiting from the present relationship and at the same time avoid the appearance of condemning the dominant value system. Thus, initiators forestall social embarrassment should they later decide to take on a new partner.

A further divisive consequence for the relationship is that the display of discontent begins to change the social life of the couple. By showing unhappiness, the initiator alters the definitions others hold of the partner and the relationship. Moreover, others alter the way they define the initiator, relative to partner and relationship. These others respond in accordance with the changed definitions. Some people, kindred souls of the initiator, will respond to the initiator's display of discontent by approaching and offering friendship and support. By sharing secrets with confidants and transitional people, the initiator forms new relationships and strengthens some existing ones.[41]

But sharing secrets can also terminate bonds. Others, perhaps kindred souls of the partner, may withdraw. A pattern of public disclosure of negative sentiment about our partners violates others' expectations about how we manage relationships, and they will react to this breach of ethics.[42] While the partner who is the target of the discrediting may fall from grace with those who witness the initiator's display, the partner will not be alone, for in publicly discrediting the other person the initiator also risks discrediting self.[43]

Friends and acquaintances who are selectively exposed to this breakdown of the rules of relationship management will respond to the display of discontent in ways that lessen their own discomfort. A friend whose primary allegiance is to the maligned partner may cease doing things with the couple and continue to see the partner alone. A confidant of the initiator's may feel uncomfortable with the partner, consequently interacting less frequently or more superficially. Friends who are happily coupled may find the initiator's display objectionable or embarrassing and henceforth avoid the couple. Or they may change the pattern of get-togethers, opting to see the couple only when others are around to minimize the individual give-and-take, or arranging private activities in order to contain the unpleasantness. Some friends may feel the situation is threatening because they're having their own troubles. For that reason, they may withdraw as a couple, but perhaps one or both may establish a separate relationship with either the initiator or the partner. Others, unable to take sides, drop out of sight. A sifting and sorting of mutual friends has begun. These new arrangements confirm, not the coupled identity, but the separate identities of each partner.

Moreover, in displaying discontent to others, the initiator's own negative definitions of partner and relationship gain strength. Although others have the potential either to confirm, modify, or reject the initiator's emerging negative definitions, when relationships end, the initiator displays discontent in ways that *confirm* these negative definitions. The characteristics of confidants and transitional people make this automatically so, for initiators work their innermost feelings through with people predisposed to be sympathetic to them, whether out of loyalty, experience, distance, ideology, or profession.[44] By virtue of social location, these people are unlikely (or even, in many cases, unable) to argue in the partner's behalf.

The initiator's public disclosures result in ongoing conversations that validate the world view the initiator is creating—not only regarding the image of the partner, but that of the initiator in respect to the partner and the relationship.[45] As a result, the flaws in partner and relationship assume a reality they did not possess before.[46] Because of the nature of the chosen audience,[47] the initiator's negative definitions continue to develop with few obstacles: no one to disagree; no one to intervene. Through the process of "conversational liquidation," the initiator's image of the partner is transformed through talk.[48] Should the initiator turn to a counselor, the negative definitions gain additional confirmation in discussion with someone with professional credentials. The troubled relationship becomes "officially troubled."

Equally as significant for the relationship, the display of discontent initiates the social process of mourning. Mourning is essential to uncoupling, as it is to any significant leavetaking. Uncoupling is a transition into a different lifestyle, a change of life course which, whether we recognize and admit it in the early phases or not, is going to be made without the other person. We commit ourselves to relationships expecting them to last, however. (Some people, of course, expect them to last longer than others; nonetheless, there is always an expected duration,[49] otherwise we would not go to the trouble of merging belongings in the first place.) In leaving behind a significant person who shares a portion of our life, we experience a loss.

When we uncouple, we must come to terms not only with our loss, but with the possibility of our own contribution to it. We are face to face with our own shortcomings. Negative definitions of partner and relationship precede and accompany the leavetaking because the loss must be turned into an acceptable loss.[50] We justify our failure to ourselves by dwelling on the negative aspects of what we are leaving behind. By displaying discontent to self and others, we cope with failure and loss by privately and publicly mourning the object that was not what we thought it to be.[51]

So the initiator engages in obsessive review.[52] Parading discontent before self and before others, he or she develops an account of partner and relationship that makes uncoupling understandable and acceptable.[53] The initiator reorders the history of the relationship, those shared memories that bind two people together. In order to relinquish the relationship, the initiator must convert that history into one that's nonbinding— and thus constructs an unhappy history. Furthermore, the partner who is left behind must be an unsuitable partner. If a partner has erred deeply enough, leaving is socially legitimate.[54] Therefore, there is a necessity to dislike, to find the partner's failings unbearable. In the long run, it seems, we really cannot leave someone we like.

THREE

Mid-Transition

*U*NCOUPLING is more than a leavetaking. It is also a transition into a different life. This transition is marked by the coincidence of departure and arrival—the intermingling of going from and going to. By focusing on the negative attributes of partner and relationship, initiators begin to create something to leave behind. By exploring and investing in alternatives that are not shared with the partner, they start to construct a social location of their own. But the creation of a point of departure and a destination is not enough. In order to uncouple, initiators must make the transition from one to the other. They must take their leave and go on, physically and socially. Initiators actively participate in this transition; they respond to their unhappiness by making decisions, by acting. Still, the dynamics of uncoupling arise not from the actions of solitary actors, but from the interaction of the individual act with the social world. As initiators react to their personal discomfort, they trigger responses from others that propel them along their route, pushing them away from the old while at the same time pulling them toward the new.

But initiators do not abandon the security of the known for the unknown. Both the destination and the getting there must appear rewarding, familiar, and, consequently, manageable. While becoming coupled is somewhat ritualized and we all seem to have some intuitive notions about the transition, the same is not true for uncoupling. For many people, uncoupling means entering the unknown in a number of ways. Not all who uncouple return to some familiar lifestyle. Some have never been on their own before. They coupled immediately following high school or college and went from their parents' home (or college, acting *in loco parentis*) to life with a partner. Even for those who previously have spent time as a single independent adult, singlehood was accompanied by the expectation that eventually they would couple. Their singleness was consequently experienced as a preparatory stage—as a means to an end, rather than as an end in its own right. This time, the expectation that one must couple is not necessarily written into the experience.

EXPLORATORY SOCIALIZATION

Initiators who are unfamiliar with the path they are contemplating begin closely monitoring the world around them, exploring and considering information that allows them to anticipate the transition. Many sources of information are readily available. Magazines, such as *Playboy, On the Road, Ms, Gay Community News*, and *Cosmopolitan*, portray alternative lifestyles. Books, newspapers, and periodicals give details about separation, singlehood, and transitions. Movies, such as *Lianna, Shoot the Moon*, and *An Unmarried Woman*, vividly depict people in transition. Music often bears a poignant message to those in the midst of change. Television, which offers instruction on everything from the cosmos to cooking, from physical fitness to foreign languages, also teaches us about separation, divorce, and single life. From series about single parent families, from soap operas, from talk shows featuring authorities on these topics and celebrities known for their famous uncouplings, from documentaries about spouse abuse or children of divorce, we perhaps learn more than we want to know.

Some initiators report becoming fascinated with this information. They discover books, magazines, movies, discussion groups, and newspaper articles that are relevant to their personal situation. Some people have special opportunities to learn because their work is a source of information: counselors, divorce lawyers, social workers, or researchers who study uncoupling, for example. Some gather information in casual encounters with strangers.

> *I remember riding on the bus beside a woman who was getting a divorce. It was a lucky accident for me, because she didn't know me and so it was OK for me to ask her all kinds of questions about it. I remember it because it was the first time I ever said those things out loud.* [SECRETARY, AGE 38, SEPARATED AFTER 18 YEARS OF MARRIAGE]

Initiators make quiet observations. They notice how the woman upstairs deals with being a single parent. They watch how separated lovers behave toward each other in public. They record the reactions of parents and friends when discussing a local separation. When in the company of single friends, they pay attention to details of lifestyle. They make assessments: of those they know who have uncoupled, how many appear to be doing well? In choosing confidants and transitional people, initiators select their own agents of socialization. Often these individuals have made the same transition, or are in the midst of it themselves, and thus prove invaluable in illuminating the kind of "culture shocks" that may accompany uncoupling.[1] Initiators attend closely to talk of financial difficulties, living arrangements, batterings, property settlements, trashed apartments, and the finer points of divorce law and lawyers. They listen to stories of sexual encounters (or the lack of them) from the newly single. In exchanges with confidants and transitional people, they often are open and to the point.

I was one night paid a visit by a friend's husband. He was also a friend of mine by the way, which is what produced the complication. Anyway, he told me he needed to talk to someone, and I was one of the few divorced people he knew. He proceeded to tell me that he had been unhappy with my friend for a long time and had been seeing someone else. He had decided to end the relationship, but hadn't told her yet, and he wanted to know what I thought about it, what was a good way to do it, how did I like single life, did we go to a counselor, how did my ex- and I get along and all kinds of stuff like that. [HAIR STYLIST, AGE 29, DIVORCED AFTER 9 YEARS]

As initiators gather information, they compare and apply it to their own situation, weighing the costs and benefits of leaving or staying in the relationship: can they make it on their own, will the partner get violent, how will friends react, will the children suffer, what about money, is there anything better out there, what about loneliness?[2] Some may seek a lawyer to explore the legal ramifications of ending the relationship.[3] What they learn may lead to the conclusion that uncoupling is a venture into a strange land that looks neither familiar nor rewarding, and so they decide to give their relationship another try.[4] For those who uncouple, however, these inquiries not only give them information about the transition, but demystify it, building confidence that they can make the break.

I never conceived of myself as the type of guy who would walk out on his wife and kids. I mean, a commitment is a commitment, and I always keep my word. When Paul left his wife and kid, it showed me that, you know, hey, wait a minute, it's not all bad. You know, I could do it if I wanted to. [FINANCE OFFICER, AGE 33, DIVORCED AFTER 7 YEARS]

Thelma and I had been each other's support, or at least the most immediate source of it, all along the way. And so Thelma moved out, and I told Alvin Thelma moved out. And Thelma and I talked. And Alvin and I talked. Thelma's separation allowed me to drag up a lot of things with Alvin. You know, we had a couple talks that were good for me, when I sort of laid a lot of things on the table. I'd start out oblique-like, you know, Thelma and Tom's situation isn't much different from yours and mine. And he'd point out where all the differences were! Since Thelma was the immediate source of identification for me all along, if she could do it, then I could do it. She was the immediate source of the possibility becoming real for me, which made it the most natural thing in the world for me to do. There was absolutely no trauma for me when the time came. None. Because psychologically I was so much there already. [SECRETARY, AGE 25, DIVORCED AFTER 4 YEARS]

But initiators seek more than just information. They seek guidelines and legitimation. While knowing others who leave their partners demonstrates the practical aspects of how to manage (or not manage) the transition, the fact that they *do leave* also affects the initiator's ability to uncouple. Associating with other people who have uncoupled or are in the process of it adds normative legitimacy to leavetaking. Knowing others who leave exposes the initiator to an ideology of self: a belief system that emphasizes the importance of the individual over the group. The family is revered in this society as the site of love, sexual fulfillment, and self-realization.[5] To sever relationship ties is to violate assumptions about the priority of the coupled unit over the individual. In order to uncouple, the initiator must overcome social inhibitions about terminating the commitment to the partner. Those who end relationships develop a belief that responsibility to self takes priority over responsibility to the other person.[6] They come to view the relationship in pragmatic terms: since it is not intrinsically permanent, the relationship may be terminated when it no longer contributes to personal growth.

Knowing others who initiate a breakup encourages the initiator to do the same. People sometimes report a domino effect—the separation of one couple among several who are friends may be followed by the separation of one or more of the others. One man described such an occurrence in their couple's club: "The couple who founded our group announced they were getting divorced. We were all shocked to hear this because they were a bit older and seemed ideally suited and happy. We joked about it later because within the next two years all of us split up except one couple. I don't know what happened with the others, but I thought if two people like them decided they couldn't make it there wasn't much use in me struggling along with a bum marriage, and it was okay for me to throw in the towel, too.''

An ideology of self that legitimates leaving the partner can develop in other ways. For some initiators, this ideology seems to result from an independent experience that involves a dramatic shift from commitment to others to commitment to self.[7] The experience spawns a seeking-out of information and of other like-minded souls who reinforce and confirm the initiator's developing orientation.

> *I think it was my graduate school experience. I walked into a whole new set of ways of thinking about men and women. Sally was in leadership roles in clubs and other organizations and I began to feel angry about it. I felt angry and I also felt unfairly treated as the wage earner. Here I was working hard all day and she's out there playing. She hadn't changed, and she still hasn't changed. I did. Suddenly supporting her felt like such a burden. It was a relief to know that I didn't have to be totally responsible.* [TEACHER, TECHNICAL SCHOOL/WRITER, AGE 39, DIVORCED AFTER 18 YEARS]

One man told of going to his uncle's funeral.

> *I thought I was going to just another funeral. I cried. It changed me. I came home and I read Lynn Caine's* Widow. *I read Liv Ullman's* Changing. *I read about Paul and Hannah Tillich. I got in a T-group about the death experience. I finally found a counselor who gave me a rule to understand what was going on with me. He said, ''You've finally seen that you are going to die and realized that you don't have any time for any crap.''* [COMPUTER SALESMAN, AGE 35, SEPARATED AFTER LIVING TOGETHER 10 YEARS]

Some women report developing an ideology of self through the women's movement. Rather than viewing the idea of single as deviant or as a threat to family life, they come to see single as a positive state. Uncoupling, rather than failure or family breakdown, is reconceptualized as life transition and personal reorganization.[8] One woman showed me the following passage from Triere and Peacock's *Learning to Leave: A Woman's Guide*[9] which was particularly important in making her self a priority.

> *''Seriously, this is your life and it's the only one you've got for now. You don't have to apologize—even to yourself—for taking care of it. This is not a selfish position; it is a survival position. In the end, no one else is going to give you the concern you give yourself. This*

doesn't have to be exclusionary. You don't have to forget your children's feelings or your husband's sensibility. But for once, put yourself first.''

For some, acquiring an ideology of self is not a matter of picking up something new. Prior to becoming coupled, they may have had a lifestyle in which individual well-being took priority over a debilitating relationship. To uncouple, they simply reconnect with that former lifestyle, putting themselves back in touch with that ideology. The initiator may reconnect with the gay singles world by reintegrating into the social pattern of those without partners. Should the supporting ideology come from the family of origin, the initiator may reestablish family ties through visits home, letters, and phone calls.

PUSHES AND PULLS

In the discovery and adaptation of an ideology of self, the initiator inadvertently creates an audience with incorporated moral standards that reinforce and reward uncoupling—thus pulling the initiator away from the partner and toward others with sympathetic orientations. A related occurrence is that many initiators come to associate these standards not just with their immediate friendship network, but with a broader reference group (lesbians, single women, bachelors, gay men), thus creating a nonpresent but ideologically reinforcing audience for their activity.[10] The initiator progressively dissociates from the world the two inhabit as a couple, increasing the time, energy, and commitment invested elsewhere.[11]

In addition to being pulled toward the new, the initiator is pushed from the old. New associations grounded in common sentiments, experiences, and ideological bonds increase the initiator's estrangement from the partner. The initiator no longer feels "at home" at home. To minimize the unpleasantness, the initiator decreases interaction with the partner while in the intimate environment. Initiators escape by watching television, telephoning others, practicing a musical instrument, reading, devoting extensive time to the children, working, jogging, or going to bed early—or late. Some of these strategies not only isolate initiators from their partners, but also provide time to be reflective about the separate life they are creating. Hence, they are able, in essence, to be in two places at one time.[12]

These strategies do not represent an abrupt shift in the couple's behavior when at home together. They are a natural and accentuated extension of the decline in intimate conversation between the two over time. Again, the pushes and pulls of the transition appear. As a result of the initiator's unhappiness with the partner, the initiator experiences hostility and discomfort when the couple are together in their own space. The partner may react to the initiator's increased display of discontent by withdrawing, thus establishing a cycle of progressive alienation into the relationship;[13] by becoming increasingly attentive as the initiator reaches for independence; or by becoming angry, demanding, or seeking retaliation—in short, displaying discontent in return. Perhaps the response is some combination of these reactions. Whatever form the partner's reaction takes, it frequently has ironic consequences. The partner unwittingly feeds into the initiator's negative definitions by exhibiting unbecoming behavior that confirms the initiator's shifting focus. The partner's response highlights the poverty of the relationship in comparison to the self-validation that the initiator is finding (or that is promised) elsewhere.[14]

I mean there were some harsh moments, too, a lot of swearing and yelling and screaming and stuff. She used to do that to me at 3:00 in the morning when I was sleeping, in dead silence. I think she used to sit there and boil for about three or four hours and then say I'm gonna wake up this son of a gun and do it. She used to be like a mad woman. We didn't hit each other but she might as well have. That's when she used to get to me, when I was sleeping, I didn't know what was going on. It used to make me nervous. It scared the hell out of me. She could have knifed me to death, she was so angry. But that's when she would do it. Maybe that's when she felt stronger because, you know, I wasn't awake and active. [FINANCE OFFICER, AGE 33, DIVORCED AFTER 7 YEARS]

We had an active social life, with parties and group get-togethers regularly, but that started to not be fun for me. He would make me look bad in front of our friends. He would make little inferences about my emotional stability—that I was unreasonable, defensive, easily upset. Sometimes, he would goad me in front of them until I became everything he said, I would just lose it. [SALESCLERK, RETAIL CLOTHING, AGE 35, SEPARATED AFTER LIVING TOGETHER 2 YEARS]

The couple's shared activities and interests, which in the past provided common ground for discussion, are reduced.[15] Instead, the initiator has intimate conversations elsewhere, building bonds elsewhere, enjoying experiences with others, further reducing the quality of life with the partner. The partner spends more and more time alone.[16]

As things got worse, I wasn't with her much. I always went out with my friends and that wasn't necessarily every night of the week, but I did go out a lot. I'd go out to a local bar and I would have friends there and my friends came. Then I always felt I had to have days to myself—certain days, like Saturday was my own day—but it seemed to get more and more. [SECRETARY, AGE 26, SEPARATED AFTER LIVING TOGETHER 5 YEARS]

I was preoccupied by my affair with Karen. I was taking much more time away. For a long time I had gotten in the habit of robbing work time to be with Karen, so I would have to take some of the family time to pay back the work time. Weekends. I frequently would have to spend most of the weekend working. Well, that wasn't unusual for people in my profession but in my case it was clearly work that I could have gotten done if Karen hadn't been on the scene. My wife never knew that, but had become used to the pattern, as do most wives who have to give up a lot of evening and weekend time to work. I felt guilty about it because I knew why I was having to do that. [ADMINISTRATOR, AGE 44, SEPARATED AFTER 23 YEARS OF MARRIAGE]

I had myself very involved at that time in PTA and Cub Scouts to the point where—and I did that so I wouldn't have to spend the time with him actually. Oh, and I always read in bed every night. Yes, constantly I read in bed. And then I would hope he would fall asleep. [HOUSEWIFE, AGE 35, SEPARATED AFTER 11 YEARS OF MARRIAGE]

The result of this push-pull interplay is cumulative dissociation:[17] action and reaction feed into each other, widening the breach so innocently begun.

The growing estrangement between the partners is accompanied by estranged relations with others. Having needs met elsewhere, initiators reduce both the quality and quantity of time spent with people associated with the relationship.[18] They decrease the details they share with these others about their ongoing life because they have no need: they are sharing elsewhere. The initiator's interaction with friends connected with the relationship becomes superficial, as the initiator withholds important aspects of self. By so doing, initiators drive a wedge between themselves and the world that could become real for them.[19] The result is a decreased input from former intimates, giving them fewer shared experiences and consequently little common ground on which to interact. As the initiator's own social backdrop changes, she or he reperceives and redefines friends from the relationship. The initiator begins to see the incompatibilities and differences, focusing on the negative attributes of people associated with life with the partner. To the degree that the initiator reveals values contradictory to the norms of these associates, he or she further separates from that lifestyle by generating hostility, discomfort, or dislike.[20] The friends feed into the process by withdrawing or by reacting in other ways that make it easier for the initiator to leave them behind. The result, again, is cumulative dissociation.[21]

These weakened ties may appear to result from minor differences, such as preferences for child-rearing strategies, style of dress, political opinions, or leisure pursuits. But these are simply reflections of the true cause: the initiator's transformation of identity. In seeking more compatible alternatives, the initiator finds support for personal values—values not in harmony with the values of people associated with the relationship. Through new associations, these values gain strength and confirmation. Should the initiator demonstrate these values to people connected with the relationship who hold contradictory views, these people will interpret the initiator's actions as a sudden and undesirable shift in priorities. The more evident the initiator's values, the greater the objection of those who hold conflicting views. For example, for initiators who come from religious, social class, or ethnic traditions where commitment to family is deeply valued, the endorsement of an ideology of self often contradicts the teachings of the past. In order to leave the partner behind, initiators tend to shed other traditions that bind them to the relationship. Under these circumstances, uncoupling is often preceded or accompanied by a severing or weakening of ties to church or synagogue.

I now see my break with religion as a part of my developing individuality. At the time I was close friends with priests and nuns, most of whom have since left the church. I felt a bitterness toward the church for its definition of marriage. I felt constrained toward a type of marriage that was not best for me. [ASSISTANT PROFESSOR, AGE 37, DIVORCED AFTER 19 YEARS]

Two major changes in my life were occurring almost at the same time. Very close proximity. And that's something that really needs to be sorted out—that I really couldn't at this point do. I think it's almost too close to where I am now. To me it's easier to sort out what happened in the relationship than to sort out what is happening to me theologically because, like I said, I'm still interested in religious issues, religious questions, human life, human identity—I mean the whole—on a very general level. But as far as traditional church life and work, not at all. In fact, very alienated from that. With no interest in going back. And why that is—how the two are related—I mean, it's like a strand of rope and how those strands are related—the relationship and the church—I'm not clear on right now. [DIVINITY SCHOOL STUDENT, AGE 26, SEPARATED AFTER LIVING TOGETHER 1 YEAR]

You know how Catholicism works? In Catholicism, if you get a divorce, you commit a sin. And if you get remarried you commit another sin. As long as you're divorced, you're not eligible to participate in the sacraments. And if you remarry, you are excommunicated. Although they rarely go to the trouble of having a formal ceremony, that's the fact. I think saying "no" to being married was probably an indirect way of saying "no" to family, "no" to church, "no" to the whole environment that I grew up in, as well as "no" to Marianne. And she was just the unfortunate linking pin of all that. And I felt real bad about that. Took a long time to work it through. It seemed like that was real nasty. To be putting it all on her, [SALES ENGINEER, AGE 42, SEPARATED AFTER 18 YEARS OF MARRIAGE]

An open break with traditional religious ideals alienates friends and family members who hold fast to those beliefs.[22] Some may withdraw from the initiator, while others may stick around to argue or condemn. A strong negative response (or even its anticipation) may give the initiator pause, for leaving church or synagogue raises the spectre of losing still other relationships. Some initiators simply cannot do it, remaining coupled (at least publicly) both to the partner and to God. A few who left behind both partner and God believed that these two transitions were possible only because of another: the death of a loved one, a significant person whose opinion they cared about, who held fast to the traditions they were struggling to leave behind. Only then, when that person died, were they free to move on.

It was quite dramatic. The confrontations about religion had gotten more frequent. They often took the form of my being berated by other members of the family as being an undutiful son because I was not honoring my father by practicing the religion. He and I were much more straightforward about it. When he didn't like it, he told me so. I told him that I knew he didn't like it but that was too bad. It was a pretty straight confrontation but there were all kinds of ramifications. It's very hard for me to say this, then that, then that. These were all happening very much at the same time. It's clear that my intention to leave the church occurred to me before I knew my father was ill and before I knew I had to leave the marriage. How exactly all that fit together was very hard to dissect. I think his death probably freed me up in a very traditional sense—who I was separate from his rules and his culture. On my own emotionality, the effect was very profound, and that had a lot of ultimate effect upon the relationship. [SALES ENGINEER, AGE 42, SEPARATED AFTER 18 YEARS OF MARRIAGE]

Anticipating a negative response, the initiator may *not* discuss differences with those who would object.[23] Then, instead of risking being pushed away by the vilification of others, the initiator withdraws, either turning away out of discomfort, or continuing to interact but concealing differences. Like other secrets, this one separates the initiator further from the world created with the partner and strengthens ties with people who share the same world view. The result is on the one hand, a wedge; on the other, a bond.

Thus, the creation of new ties is accompanied by the termination of old, as the initiator leaves behind and is left behind by others associated with the relationship. These other ties atrophy because of the initiator's intentional avoidance, ability to redefine others in negative terms, and the tendency of certain others to similarly redefine the initiator. Children, although they do not necessarily espouse and openly argue family values or contest other changes in the initiator's life, may also be left behind. Simply by their existence, they represent the relationship. Children are a link to the past: past behavior, past ideas, past definition of self. Although we apparently cannot leave someone we like, and, as a consequence, redefine the partner and others in negative terms, the difficulty of going out the door remains when children are inside. In order to uncouple, some initiators also begin to separate from their children by spending less time with them, redefining them in negative terms, finding an alternative family, or taking other actions that neutralize the commitment and loss.[24]

Changes in the couple's social life become more pronounced. Rather than centering around the couple, friends now come from splintered sources. The separation of friendship groups is a reversal of what happens when two people decide to live together or marry. A new couple is drawn toward other couples and to groups that strengthen the new definition of themselves they are creating. The couple avoids associations that weaken this definition.[25] Uncoupling is accompanied by a rearrangement of friendship groups reflecting the two people's growing separateness.

But the socializing broke down because we really didn't have a group of friends that we could bring together that we both share. So the friendship things I think are symptomatic of our split. We never did have the same friends. We had friends that we brought to the relationship from different places before, but very rarely did she bring in somebody that I just didn't get along with. And the same was true of her. But we no longer felt comfortable with the same people. [NURSE, AGE 28, SEPARATED AFTER LIVING TOGETHER 3 YEARS]

She became very attached to girls that were divorced. Not the girls that were married. They used to come here. They were always bragging about how wonderful their life was. Who were my friends? Families, families. I'm involved with families, even now that I'm divorced. I'm involved with families with children. I love the setting of the family unit. [SOCIAL SERVICES WORKER, AGE 44, DIVORCED AFTER 19 YEARS]

Sometimes the separate friendship groups confirm not only the separation of identities, but the creation of a new partnership for the initiator.

Karen and I maintained an affair that went on for about ten years, which was fairly well known by a lot of people. At first we kept it a big secret, but that was hard on her. Because Karen was trying to keep it from even her closest friends, which meant she was very isolated the first couple of years we did this because she couldn't even have single women friends that she felt very close to without telling them what we were doing and that always gave her a problem. There were very few friends who knew us who also knew me as a couple in two different ways—virtually nobody. The friends that were Karen's that became ours were by nature and then by design simply not ones who I would ever have anything to do with my wife. So eventually it became known to more people, and you know, people tell other people. What everyone seemed not to do was to tell my wife. I'm convinced that she didn't know anything about it.

It was considerably less isolating when there were friends of Karen's that were brought into the affair. Single friends, and in a couple of cases, couples. Quiet dinners, or drinks at their houses, or occasionally we would have a weekend when we'd be away together, and sometimes we'd visit some people when we were away together. A couple of her friends who thought that this was a dead-end alley or stupid or/and immoral or self-destructive thing to do sort of parted friends with her. The ones she stayed friends with came to accept it. You know, this is the way you want to live, it's your life, and we have to admit that you seem a lot cheerier and a lot more productive, and who is to say its bad? But by the time it reached that public state, it must have been five years after it started, my wife and I, as a couple, really had very little social life. [ADMINISTRATOR, AGE 44, SEPARATED AFTER 23 YEARS OF MARRIAGE]

IDENTITY CONFLICT AND IDENTITY TRANSFORMATION

The transition is underway but incomplete. The initiator spends time in two worlds. Not yet ready to relinquish the old and plunge into the new, the initiator feels increasingly estranged from the old. Unable to leave, she or he is still required to participate—and this is not easy. The initiator has become an outsider: a person who, because of commitment elsewhere, no longer totally belongs. Having achieved some distance from the relationship, the initiator views the present situation critically. This experience is shared by every person who travels to a foreign country, or leaves home for an independent life. Difference, not distance, is the critical factor. Returning, the traveler evaluates the familiar with a newly acquired comparative ability. The result is often a disease, a sense of lack of fit, because the traveler has had an experience the others haven't. The traveler can perhaps describe it, but as an experience it is unshareable because it changed the traveler in ways not obvious to the others, and describing it will not similarly change the others.

Thus changed, initiators continue in the old paths with difficulty, no longer willing participants, but uncomfortable and critical ones. These changes are reflected in diminished participation in the relationship, in what they are no longer willing to do, or refuse to do.[26]

> *I think at the point that I completed that counseling that I really knew what it was I wanted to do, I had somehow already begun separating myself from him. I no longer really was investing. I wasn't building toward our being partners. If we were together and it was pleasant, fine, but I did nothing to make it happen. I didn't do anything to encourage our relationship. I didn't do anything sexually. We were still sexually relating to each other, but I didn't do anything to make it better. I was not at all concerned. I didn't like going out socially. If he wanted me to do something, he asked me to go to a social event or something with him I'd do it if it didn't interfere with anything that was too serious for me. And that was basically the way we lived. I had become very selfish about my needs.* [STOCKBROKER, AGE 35, SEPARATED AFTER LIVING TOGETHER 12 YEARS]

They hesitate to engage in activity that would perpetuate the link with the partner: having children, for example. They instinctively feel that a child would close a circle within which they would be nearer the partner than they are inclined to be.[27] Other mutual endeavors that would bind the two together for a long period are similarly avoided: redoing a room, buying season tickets, taking out a loan. Initiators often express discomfort with being linked to the partner even for situations of short duration—for example, public appearances. Alternative resources have in many ways replaced the relationship as the initiator's main source of identity and sense of being comfortable with self and with the world. Yet other people respond to them in public as a couple, exchanging anecdotes and initiating conversations based on taken-for-granted assumptions of a shared history and a shared future. Because initiators doubt there will be such a future, public appearances are a painful reminder of their increasing marginality in the world they live in as a couple.

Ironically, certain types of public gatherings can be a welcome relief from the tensions at home. Uncomfortable at being linked with the partner when out with close friends, and uneasy when the two are at home, the initiator may find formal social get-togethers easier to manage because the characteristics of the group, the setting, or the reason for the gathering allow the initiator to interact with the partner in a superficial way. Two people can attend a large party, a movie, or go to a bar (if the music is loud enough) and never talk to each other from the time they walk in the door until they leave.

Most difficult to manage are public situations in which the initiator and partner must interact. Especially troublesome are traditional celebrations that confirm the dominant value of togetherness: family assemblages at holidays or birthdays, weddings, baptisms, anniversaries. Even get-togethers where everyone present is coupled are experienced as couple-confirming rituals. While the event publicly accentuates the bond between the two, for the initiator it emphasizes the contradictions between self-concept and the partner role. At the same time, the event calls for the initiator not to let these contradictions be noticed by others. Initiators sometimes get through these conflict-producing situations by isolating themselves in some way.

> *Thanksgiving seemed like the longest day in the world. My life was so different from what everyone in the room thought it was. And there was no way I could begin to tell them. I felt like a stranger with my own family. I found I isolated myself even further by thinking about things at work. It was the only way I could get through it. I could be there and not be there at the same time.* [SALES REPRESENTATIVE, AGE 36, DIVORCED AFTER 11 YEARS]

Some initiators' sense of separateness is so extreme that they are unable to continue the custom of sending Hanukkah or Christmas cards because they no longer can bring themselves to link their names with the partner in so public and permanent a way.

The initiator's transition is sometimes revealed symbolically. It may be reflected in the initiator's removal of the wedding ring ("I seem to have developed an allergy to the band," or "It slips around all the time and I'm afraid I'll lose it."). It may be reflected in a changed attitude toward other inanimate objects that represent the relationship.

I used to worry about the house. Now I have very few people in this house. I do not entertain, the only people that come over are very close friends of mine—and if they don't like the way I keep house, that's tough. When his mother was coming, I used to shovel up the place. They were up this weekend and I didn't even bother shoveling it—if they don't like it that's tough too. I get a great deal more fulfillment outside and this house is not a reflection of me. [INSURANCE CLAIMS ADJUSTER, AGE 35, DIVORCED AFTER 12 YEARS]

In all we didn't spend money on much furniture. Partially, the problem for me was first, an emotional one. If I buy furniture, am I making a commitment to the relationship? Two, a time commitment, it takes time to pick out furniture, and I didn't want to waste my time on that. Third was the money. [MEDICAL ILLUSTRATOR, AGE 26, SEPARATED AFTER LIVING TOGETHER 2 YEARS]

The initiator's entrenchment in two worlds may be reflected in an insistence on a separate checking or savings account, a move to a separate bed, or by the desire, if the initiator is a woman, to revert to her maiden name. It may be reflected in physical changes. A man may grow a beard or mustache. A woman may lose weight or change her hairstyle. It may be reflected in the initiator's speech, as "we," "us," and "our" are replaced by "I," "me," and "mine."[28]]

Changes occur in the couple's pattern of intimacy. Some are subtle, and may go unnoticed for a while.

After she had gone, it occurred to me one night that she had long ago stopped coming to the door to kiss me hello when I came in for supper. I don't even know when it happened. [INSURANCE TRAINEE, AGE 28, DIVORCED AFTER 4 YEARS]

Even changes in bedroom intimacy may occur so gradually that the partner does not identify them as symptomatic: changes in who initiates the lovemaking; changes in its frequency, duration, and intensity; changes in the tenderness of the exchange; changes in what is exchanged.

Along about the time he began thinking in terms of himself, what he wanted to do with his life, there were also changes in our sex practices. He was thinking more in terms of satisfying himself. [CARPENTER, AGE 23, SEPARATED AFTER LIVING TOGETHER 1 YEAR]

Bedtime was a problem. I was so involved with Sarah that I felt making love to my wife was disloyal. I would find all kinds of ways to get out of it, like taking work home from the office and not pulling my briefcase out until ten at night. [BANK MANAGER, AGE 58, DIVORCED AFTER 36 YEARS OF MARRIAGE]

We were still having sex, but I could only do it by pretending she was someone else. [FREIGHT HANDLER, AGE 24, SEPARATED AFTER LIVING TOGETHER 4 YEARS]

One thing that was never good for us from some point after we were married was our—we had a lousy sex life. I suppose we can't go through the history without getting into that. Connie was never into it that much to begin with, and as the relationship grew older, she just grew not into it at all and I stopped being able to turn her on. [SALESMAN, AGE 30, DIVORCED AFTER 3 YEARS]

As the initiator grows increasingly autonomous, these signs of change begin to threaten the partner. Deep commitment to other than the relationship—to career, to a cause, to education, to a hobby—reflects the altered commitment to the relationship. The partner begins to note these changes and feels excluded.

He went home with somebody last weekend. That hurt me so bad. I'm totally in love with him. I can't understand how he can do that. My friends tell me he's just too attractive and has a big sexual appetite that must be satisfied. [FLORAL DESIGNER, AGE 28, SEPARATED AFTER LIVING TOGETHER 4 YEARS]

She developed some of her own friends. I think it was worse, because I began to be a little suspicious of what her friends were telling her. Once I met the friends that she had, I became nearly paranoid as to what they were really like. In some instances, she had some male friends, and I would not know exactly what their intentions were, and if she had female friends, they may be telling her things that would be harmful to our relationship. Do they like men or do they hate men and that also becomes a problem. I really became a little paranoid of the influence that other people have on the relationship. [SOCIAL SERVICES WORKER, AGE 44, DIVORCED AFTER 19 YEARS]

He started to buy different things, and it was for himself. "This is mine," he would say. He used to redecorate all the time, but without including me in it, whereas we used to do everything together, plan it for hours, do it on paper, and talk and talk about it. He was taking advice from another friend who became very close to him. He no longer liked the things I like. We used to both like classical music, and conservative traditional art was another thing. And now he was getting much more "west coast"—and I know it was his new friend's influence. [STUDENT/SERVICE COORDINATOR, AGE 28, SEPARATED AFTER LIVING TOGETHER I YEAR]

Despite feeling excluded, the partner does not react to the initiator's behavior as a threat to the relationship. Nonetheless, the initiator already has left in a number of ways. The initiator has acknowledged that the relationship is troubled and has made this fact public. In so doing, he or she has begun mourning the loss of the relationship and has redefined the situation so that the loss is acceptable both to self and to selected others. The initiator has found other resources, developed support, and considered and confronted the possible consequences of uncoupling. The initiator has undertaken something tantamount to a rehearsal, mentally and, to varying degrees, experientially, of a life apart from the partner.[29] All these responses have a cumulative impact: publicly and privately, the initiator has been redefining self as a person separate and independent from the partner. In direct contrast to the oblivious state of the partner, the initiator is keenly aware of this transition.

I was really feeling very ambivalent about the marriage, and what I should do. It seemed to me that rationally I belonged to Karen and that if I don't go with her I'm going to lose her, and yet it wouldn't be fair to my wife, either, if I go back to my wife and the kids go away and the two of us haven't got anything. When I'd come back from being with Karen I'd spend at least two days wondering whether I should tell Annette we should get a divorce. Also it meant we couldn't plan anything. I really didn't want to plan a vacation next summer when I thought by then I might have decided I have to leave her and go be with Karen. I couldn't plan anything with anybody. I literally couldn't think beyond the next weekend. I probably looked a little crazy. My wife wanted to plan a trip with the kids spring break and I wouldn't. I couldn't even explain to her why. I wasn't even sure why, but I knew perfectly well I couldn't tell Karen I was thinking about leaving my marriage and at the same time tell her I was thinking about a family trip in the spring. At the same time I couldn't tell Annette I would definitely do anything either. I really got so that there was just a black wall in front of me. [ADMINISTRATOR, AGE 44, SEPARATED AFTER 23 YEARS OF MARRIAGE]

I was embarrassed to introduce him to my friends. It was more comfortable to be with him with our old friends, until I got to a point of being embarrassed to be with him, even with them. [LEATHER CRAFTSMAN, AGE 42, SEPARATED AFTER LIVING TOGETHER I2 YEARS]

There was tension, before we were ever married, there was tension between who I was when I was myself, just, you know, without him, and who I was with him. But somehow I was holding on to that old me. You know, I can be married but I don't have to lose my own identity. What it really came down to be was that was I going to be a Cosgrove or was I going to be a Murphy. I thought I could be both. About the time I started thinking of taking my name back and wanted my name back, part of what I was feeling is that I didn't like the person I was and I wanted to be Patty Cosgrove again. I really liked Patty Cosgrove and I had begun to very much dislike Patty Murphy. And I wanted to be Patty Cosgrove again, and the name was just a symbol of that. [GRADUATE STUDENT, AGE 26, DIVORCED AFTER 4 YEARS OF MARRIAGE]

For the partner, however, the relationship is still central to life and, therefore, identity. The partner continues to be committed to the relationship. He or she has not turned to others for support, has not endorsed an ideology that legitimates ending the relationship, has not considered and explored in any serious way what life without the other person might be. In short, the initiator has begun a transition out of the relationship. The partner has not. The initiator has begun accumulating the resources to negotiate that transition. The partner has not.

FOUR

❧ ─────────────────────────────

Signals, Secrecy, and Collaborative Cover-Up

*H*OW is it possible, when two people live together, for one to slip so far away without the other's noticing and acting?

Partners often report that they were unaware, or only remotely aware, even at the point of separation, that their relationship was deteriorating. Only after the other person is gone are they able to look back and recognize the signals. One man, married 20 years, spoke to me two months after his wife left him and was still trying to piece together what had gone wrong. He had come home from work to find a note from his wife on the kitchen table. He brought the note to the interview. It began, "I care for you, but can no longer live with you." He expressed shock and dismay, saying that he had no reason to suspect she was unhappy. Yet as he began describing their relationship, it appeared (to me) that she *had* given some clues that all was not well. For instance, he said, "She asked me a couple of times to go with her to family counseling. Now I figured if she was having trouble with the kids, that was her problem, not mine. If she had said 'marriage counseling,' I would have gone." He remembered that the morning of the day she left she walked him to the door and hugged him, which she didn't usually do, and she was crying. He said, "I just figured it was something with the kids or a friend. She often cried about things. You know, I didn't even ask her what was wrong."

Initiators, however, tell a different story.

I tried early on talking about breaking up. It's amazing. We would sit down and I would say to him, "I don't think this is going to work. I think we're just too different and I'm going to have to go one way and you're going to have to go another way." He would counter with things like, well, he never reacted much. He would say, "I think we can work it out," or something like that. "You couldn't make it on your own anyway," he would say, or "You don't mean that," things like that. [ACTOR, AGE 32, SEPARATED AFTER LIVING TOGETHER 5 YEARS]

And I told my husband, I said, "Now, why don't you take this seriously? I've said this a hundred times. What do you think this is, I'm feeling unhappy today or something?" When I told him I wanted a divorce, he said "What do you mean?" He was shocked. And I had been yelling and nagging and complaining about the quality of the marriage for years. It's like he didn't have ears. [SEAMSTRESS, AGE 36, DIVORCED AFTER 16 YEARS]

The obvious contradiction between these statements of initiators and partners forces us to consider the possibility of some enormous failure in communication. How fascinating, yet how ironic, that when we begin relationships we develop a sensitivity that allows us to pick up on the smallest cue. We are intent on discovering and knowing the other person. So much is understood on a nonverbal basis: a look across a room, a slight smile, a downcast glance, a frown. We are so tuned to each other, constantly exploring, checking, and testing the nature of our bond. Given this early attentiveness, what causes the failure of communication, especially when what is at issue is so central to the life and identity of both partners?

To speak of a communication failure implies a breakdown of some sort. Yet this does not accurately portray what occurs. In truth, communication difficulties arise not from breakdown but from the characteristics of the system itself. Despite promising beginnings in our intimate relationships, we tend over time to evolve a system of communication that suppresses rather than reveals information. Life is complicated, and confirming or disconfirming the well-being of a relationship takes effort. Once we are comfortably coupled, the intense, energy-consuming monitoring of courtship days is replaced by a simpler, more efficient method. Unable to witness our partners' every activity or verify every nuance of meaning, we evolve a communication system based on trust. We gradually cease our attentive probing, relying instead on familiar cues and signals to stand as testament to the strength of the bond: the words "I love you," holidays with the family, good sex, special times with shared friends, the routine exchange, "How was your day?" We take these signals as representative of the relationship and turn our monitoring energies elsewhere.[1]

As intimate relationships begin to deteriorate, this shorthand method that we've evolved for tapping the health of the union tends to obscure change and can prevent the sending and receiving of new information— even when the partners are expending every effort to do one or the other. When relationships get in trouble, however, neither partner's approach is characterized by such singlemindedness. A direct confrontation is an exchange in which the initiator reveals secret feelings, thoughts, and acts with sufficient clarity so that the partner acknowledges the relationship is deeply troubled. Only when both partners admit the seriousness of the situation can they begin to negotiate. For several reasons to be discussed, both partners will avoid direct confrontation. Instead, they take advantage of the established communication system. They convert it to their own purposes, using it as a welcome barrier behind which they each can hide for as long as the other will let them. Together, they orchestrate the revelation and suppression of facts in an interplay that results in concerted ignorance. It's a collaborative effort: one tells without telling; the other knows without knowing.

THE INITIATOR'S CONTRIBUTION

Consider, again, the display of discontent. In the beginning, initiators keep their unhappiness secret. A major part of uncoupling, after all, is internal, and thus invisible—private contemplation, brooding, quiet assessment.[2] While this goes on, the initiator continues to participate in the routine aspects of life with the other person. As unhappiness grows, the initiator begins to reveal it to the partner. The initiator's discontent at this point is often vague and ill defined and its display bears the same characteristics.

Early attempts to communicate dissatisfaction take the form of complaints directed toward changing the other person or the relationship. These complaints are aimed at the partner's daily failings—the mundane aspects of life with the other person. For example, the initiator may criticize how the partner spends leisure time. "Why do you watch TV so much? Why don't you turn it off and do something else?" But television watching may not be the real issue. The initiator may be questioning the partner's level of commitment to the relationship, or the appropriateness of a partnership with a person who values such an activity.[3]

The initiator expresses discontent by dwelling on an isolated incident or behavior and thereby veils the real issue, which is that being in the relationship conflicts with the initiator's sense of self. Not that this is intentional. The initiator may not, at this point, be able to articulate the deeper problem of identity conflict. Nonetheless, the partner responds in terms of TV watching. A variety of responses are possible, none of which will eliminate the initiator's unhappiness. The partner may, indeed, stop watching TV—usually a temporary measure. The partner will turn off the set, but resume a place in front of it the next night. Even if the partner miraculously and permanently gives up TV, this response is likely to miss the deeper target of the initiator's complaint. A more likely response, however, is that the partner will regard the complaint as trivial and ignore it.

The initiator's early reflections on the quality of the partnership do not always surface as complaints, but may be expressed in other ways: sullenness, anger, a decrease in intimacy or relatedness. Having always brought a gift, the initiator may bring an inappropriate one or a thoughtless one. The report of daily events usually exchanged at dinner gets more and more brief. Naturally, such signals are subtle and thus difficult for the partner to detect.

The display of discontent becomes increasingly bold, however, as the initiator comes to view the relationship not simply as troubled, but as unsaveable. Other interests get more attention, and the energy the initiator devotes to restoring the relationship dwindles.[4] Correspondingly, discontent no longer is expressed to improve the situation, but to convince the partner that the relationship is not working. Though the initiator's purpose has changed—and with it the frequency and intensity of the display of discontent—the signals often remain indirect and subtle.

> We didn't argue that much. I think now, I think a lot of it was communication. We never really talked about it. I never told her I was unhappy. Yeah, superficially you know. She might say, "What's the matter?" and all that stuff, and I'd say, "I'm not into it today," or something, but I never really got into it deep enough. [RECEPTIONIST, AGE 27, SEPARATED AFTER LIVING TOGETHER 5 YEARS]

> Oh, I would comment on girls walking down the street. Just little things to get your digs in if you can't get them in any other way. I would go to work out at midnight. She didn't get the message. No, she took it as reasons to get mad at me. It was never what I might be feeling, it was always her reaction to what she thought, never to what I thought. She never asked what I was thinking. [PRODUCE MANAGER, AGE 36, DIVORCED AFTER 11 YEARS]

> I used to try to tell her with humor: "You've heard the one about the guy who went to the drugstore and never came back? Well, someday

I'm going to do that." [TEACHER, TECHNICAL SCHOOL/WRITER, AGE 39, DIVORCED AFTER 18 YEARS]

I could only talk to him when I was drunk. I would get drunk, then tell him the important things. Later, of course, he would always discount it, you know, because anyone who's drunk never means what they say. [BANK TELLER, AGE 23, SEPARATED AFTER LIVING TOGETHER 3 YEARS]

Even initiators who try hard to articulate their unhappiness acknowledge the difficulty of direct confrontation.

Prior to last spring, when I began to feel like I was reaching a point of being sure myself that it was going to end, I tried in so many ways. I tried, I was giving him clues, but yet I've done it many times with such subtleties that it's almost like a feeling of I want him to know, but yet I don't. Saying something very symbolically, or making an analogy to him that appears very simple, but yet if he really thought about it, it would have much more significance. And I don't know why, I never came out just blatantly and said, "This is how I feel." But how can you tell another person in words, it's impossible to tell another person in words, the depth, the seriousness of what you feel.
   For example, relying on the tone of voice. If I've been hurt by something, I would say to him. "That really hurts me," and look him directly in the eye and say, "What you said an hour ago, that really upset me," and, you know, like I would feel totally crushed on the inside. And he would say, "Oh, I'm sorry, I won't do that again." In other words, approaching him on one level with a lot of feeling and emotion, trying to convey it but not really knowing how to convey it as strongly as I would want to convey it, and have the response given in almost a flippant manner—you know they haven't made the connection. The more frustrated I became, the less cues I was willing to give. Then I just started building a wall. But it wasn't very obvious because the distance that existed was like throwing an emotional block to protect me from becoming more and more hurt. It wasn't as obvious as being verbal and things. Because he didn't really recognize the wall as emotional distance. I mean that wall existed in other forms, for other reasons, so he didn't really recognize that wall. . . . So I found it self-defeating, in a sense, for while I thought he would notice the wall or miss my presence, what went on was he got more comfortable, I guess because he thought the problems had disappeared. [MUSIC TEACHER, AGE 28, SEPARATED AFTER 6 YEARS OF MARRIAGE]

Initiators have several reasons for these subtle, indirect signals. They often avoid direct confrontation because of their own uncertainty about their life direction and their ability to leave the relationship. Swapping the familiarity of evils known for (perhaps) evils unknown is risky. No relationship is all bad. Moments always exist when the partners are brought together in an experience that is sometimes surprising in its meaningfulness: the birth of a child, a visit from a shared friend, a spontaneous and wonderful love-making, the passing of a mutually beloved parent. At such times, both partners recognize the importance of the bond and the shared history that led to that moment. For initiators, such experiences interject contradictory information into the negative definitions they've been constructing. As a consequence, they are forced to acknowledge the positive aspects of life with the other person. Perhaps the relationship is not as bad as they thought. Furthermore, a disappointment at work, a quarrel with a new lover, or a feeling of loneliness while traveling away from home can introduce contradictory information of another sort. Not only may the relationship not be as bad as they thought, but the alternative lifestyle may not be as good as they imagined. As long as initiators are plagued with uncertainty, they cannot afford to be unrelentingly blunt in their efforts to convince the partner that the relationship is unsaveable. They may, after all, stay. So they raise their complaints, but not too strongly—not too consistently.

Many times, the initiator may feel protective of the partner, and does not want to hurt, to witness the suffering, or live with the guilt. Concern for the other person's feelings and fear of the possible consequences at first ties the initiator to indirect methods.

I made decisions. My only reluctance to be more honest and more open with him, which in the long run meant a sort of torturing, was in part because I know I didn't want to hurt him. [STOCKBROKER, AGE 35, SEPARATED AFTER LIVING TOGETHER 12 YEARS]

Well, what happened, I just was afraid to talk about it. I just didn't want to open it up then. I wasn't ready to open it up and there were times when she just needed a whole lot for me to open up. She would prod me but I was afraid if I really said to her, "I don't love you. You know, you're a wonderful person, I can't fault you anything, but I have no sexual attraction for you, and sexual intercourse is unfulfilling for me. I'm not intellectually stimulated by you, I don't feel a sense of home and companionship that I really feel like I need and like I've had in other relationships and I want out," that's what I was feeling, and I was afraid that I might say it and that would really, really crush her. [SUPERVISOR, AGE 38, DIVORCED AFTER 19 YEARS]

Others soften their display of discontent, not only to protect the partner, but to protect themselves. Some initiators fear that revealing the depth of their discontent will result in arguments or possibly retaliation. Others, although finding the relationship unrewarding, may not be ready to give up the partner completely. They may hope that the bond can be transformed in some way that makes staying in touch possible. Direct confrontation raises the possibility of total loss, and the initiator may not be ready for that.

So the cues that, if given, would cause the partner to redefine the situation as serious are withheld. The initiator may say, "I'm unhappy," not "I'm unhappy . . . and I'm seeing someone else." In addition, constant negotiation is, as one person said, "a drag. It creates a hassle, takes energy. Maybe it gets results short-run, but not long-run. We make a point, or a complaint, and eventually give up on it." Trying to get the other person's attention is not only tiresome, but stressful. No matter how unsatisfactory, the daily routine does offer at least the comfort of being routine. So the initiator may persevere for a while, then fall into a passive acceptance of the status quo. The result is an on-again, off-again effort.

> I tried for better than a year to persuade him I was unhappy. And I never know—like right now we are in a lull—and we just don't discuss it. I don't know if you have experienced this or not, but we will go from saying it's awful, I can't stand this marriage, to not mentioning it for months. We just go on like there is nothing wrong. We talk about the kids, we eat dinner, we go places. [HOUSEWIFE, AGE 36, SEPARATED AFTER 12 YEARS OF MARRIAGE]

Even when the initiator's signals become so bold and direct that the seriousness of the situation would appear (from the telling) to be patently obvious, the effect is diminished by the context: they are interjected into a daily routine full of established signals with taken-for-granted meanings that represent the well-being of the relationship. For example, every couple evolves a style of conversation unique to their relationship. Some initiators report that their relationship was so congenial for so long that when trouble began, no model existed for discussing it. The couple's exchanges were characteristically so nonargumentative and accommodating that some initiators found it hard to interject complaints, and, when they did, it was done in a nonargumentative, accommodating way. Others complained of the opposite problem. Lodging complaints was as much a part of their relationship as turning off the lights at night. Signs of discontent were obscured because conflict and antagonism characterized their every exchange.

The display of discontent can also get buried in the daily schedule. A negative signal can become simply a deviant event that momentarily mars the smoothness of the ongoing routine.[5] For example, in addition to the initiator's conscious attempts to convince the partner that the relationship is not working, other signs of change appear. As time passes, initiators tend to exhibit characteristics anticipating their transition: changes in forms of talk, friends, intimacy, humor, taste for music or food, leisure pursuits, reading material, or even physical appearance. The number and frequency of these signs tend to grow as the "other life" grows. They are visible and certainly alter the terrain of the relationship. Nonetheless, these signs of change appear slowly. While they would surely catch the partner's attention if they came all at once, the same is not true when new signals are introduced slowly amid others that indicate stability. A series of discordant signals can accumulate so slowly that they become incorporated into the routine; what began as a break in the pattern *becomes* the pattern.[6]

We'd have some kind of incident everyday. Everyday I came home from work she had something on her mind. I didn't this, I didn't that. I just stopped listening. Who wants to hear that crap all the time? [ELECTRICIAN, AGE 62, DIVORCED AFTER 39 YEARS]

I think we drifted away from affection. We drifted away from me giving her a kiss in the morning and at night. I would say, over a period of maybe 3 or 4 years. And I think, probably we drifted away sexually too. Not as often. I think it reached a point there where probably we didn't have sex any more than twice a month, which, you know, as you read these books, is not very much. At our age I think it's probably sometimes once a week or something. I found that happening. I did complain, early on when I thought we should have more sex and everything. I think it's funny that—I can't really think of the reasons but—I wasn't alarmed. Because when we finally did have sex, it was good sex. You know—it was good. It was prolonged and—but it became more infrequent. [PRODUCTION MANAGER, AGE 52, DIVORCED AFTER 25 YEARS]

Not only do the initiator's negative signals tend to become incorporated into the existing routine, but, paradoxically, the initiator actively contributes to the impression that life goes on as usual. Even as they express their unhappiness, initiators work at emphasizing and maintaining the routine aspects of life with the other person, simultaneously giving signals that all is well. Unwilling to leave the relationship yet, they need to privately explore and evaluate the situation. The initiator thus contrives an appearance of participation,[7] creating a protective cover that allows them to "return" if their alternative resources do not work out.

Our ability to do this—to perform a role we are no longer enthusiastically committed to—is one of our acquired talents. In all our encounters, we present ourselves to others in much the same way as actors do, tailoring our performance to the role we are assigned in a particular setting.[8] Thus, communication is always distorted. We only give up fragments of what really occurs within us during that specific moment of communication.[9] Such fragments are always selected and arranged so that there is seldom a faithful presentation of our inner reality. It is transformed, reduced, redirected, recomposed.[10] Once we get the role perfected, we are able to play it whether we are in the mood to go on stage or not, simply by reproducing the signals.

What is true of all our encounters is, of course, true of intimate relationships. The nature of the intimate bond is especially hard to confirm or disconfirm.[11] The signals produced by each partner, while acting out the partner role, tend to be interpreted by the other *as* the relationship.[12] Because the costs of constantly checking out what the other person is feeling and doing are high, each partner is in a position to be duped and misled by the other.[13] Thus, the initiator is able to keep up appearances that all is well by falsifying, tailoring, and manipulating signals to that effect. The normal routine can be used to attest to the presence of something that is not there. For example, initiators can continue the habit of saying, "I love you," though the passion is gone. They can say, "I love you" and cover the fact that they feel disappointment or anger, or that they feel nothing at all. Or, they can say, "I love you" and mean, "I like you," or, "We have been through a lot together," or even "Today was a good day."

The normal routine also can be used to cover up something that *is* there.

I had already established the habit of working late, and often would go to the computer room down the hall, so she couldn't reach me by phone. It was a simple matter to use these evening hours to be with someone else. [COMPUTER PROGRAMMER, AGE 27, SEPARATED AFTER LIVING TOGETHER 4 YEARS]

The partner is confronted by a mixed array: the initiator signals that all is well while at the same time signaling all is not. As one person said, "It's like the sound of the wings of a bee. You think that you hear a faint buzzing, but you're not sure." But maintaining secrecy is collaborative—the partner also has a hand in it.[14]

THE PARTNER'S CONTRIBUTION

We approach social situations with a frame of reference constructed from integrated sets of assumptions, expectations, and experiences.[15] Everything is perceived on the basis of this framework. The framework becomes self-confirming because, whenever we can, we tend to impose it on experiences and events, creating incidents and relationships that conform to it. And we tend to ignore, misperceive, or deny events that do not fit it.[16] As a consequence, it generally leads us to what we are looking for. This frame of reference is not easily altered or dismantled, because the way we tend to see the world is intimately linked to how we see and define ourselves in relation to the world. Thus, we have a vested interest in maintaining consistency because our own identity is at risk.

We do not surrender easily the worlds we create; we tend to disavow knowledge contradicting our existing frame of reference. We may puzzle over contradictory evidence, but usually succeed in pushing it aside—until we come across a single piece of information too fascinating to ignore, too clear to misperceive, too painful to deny, that makes vivid still other cues we do not want to confront, forcing us to alter and surrender the world view we so meticulously have constructed.

The partner's frame of reference includes expectations about the range of signals the initiator might convey. It also includes expectations about the duration of the relationship.[17] Typically, partners comment, "I believed that once you're married, you're married," "The idea of divorce never occurred to me," or "I was sure I was going to be married the rest of my life." These statements reflect not just individual sentiments, but socially expected durations—assumptions generally held about the length of time an individual is expected to occupy a given status. Recall that, in order to uncouple, the initiator reduced vulnerability to social expectations about commitment. The initiator has redefined partner and relationship in ways that legitimate uncoupling, and endorsed a belief system in which personal well-being has priority over commitment to another.

The partner's frame of reference affects interpretation of the initiator's signals.[18] The partner fits the initiator's behavior in with personal expectations about the duration of the relationship, and within the range of signals that he or she has learned to expect from the initiator.[19] When a new signal does not fit—"I packed your lunch." "Did you pack a gun in it?"—the partner will not take it seriously since it falls outside the frame of reference. But the partner will hear, "I love you," because the words affirm the partner's existing world view.

Why did I not pick up on all this? Because this man, amongst all of this rubble, the ironic thing is this man came home every day and told me he loved me and told me what a wonderful . . . I mean in between all this bull shit, oh "You're the most wonderful wife anyone could ask for. I love you." It was crazy. Verbally he fed me what I needed. [SECRETARY, AGE 38, DIVORCED AFTER 10 YEARS]

The initiator's signals may, indeed, be vague, intermittent, and hard to detect. But the other side of the story is that the bad news may be so inconsistent with the partner's sense of self and the world that it is heard but denied. The partner collaborates in the secret-keeping by self-deception. The initiator is not the only one with secrets, for, as Bok notes, "it is secrecy that lies at the center of such self-deception: the secrecy that is part of all deception. In deceiving ourselves, according to such a view, we keep secret from ourselves the truth we cannot face." [20] The communication of discontent clearly has two aspects: the difficulty in relaying bad news to the person with whom we have shared a period of our lives, and the difficulty (if we are the partner) of receiving that bad news. So partners select the good news, not the bad, for to do otherwise might force them to alter their world. [21] They sift through the mixed array of signals, selectively incorporating ones consistent with their ongoing frame of reference and discounting those that challenge it.

And I felt like he was away a lot. And I felt like, you know, what is it that's keeping him away so much? There were nights when he would be on duty and that would be like, you know, I wouldn't hear from him. And then there were times when he would even go away like on a Saturday, you know. He'd say, "I'm going out for a trip." And oftentimes it was to go out and buy books and he would go on long journeys kind of like, wandering around looking for books and antique books and stuff like that cause that was his hobby. But sometimes he didn't come back until really late and I was beginning to really suspect that something was going on. And that was awful for me. I didn't say much. I felt, "Oh, Sandra, you're just imagining things" and then I would feel like, "No, you're not imagining things." You know, I just argued with myself a whole lot.

It wasn't articulated. That was what was so funny. He never said to me, "I'm not happy with the way that we don't have fun." Or, "I'm not happy with the way that things are." He didn't ever let me know that. But I could say that there were cues because he would come home and he wouldn't say very much. At the time it just seemed like that's who he was. A lot of—he was managing our family—you know, he felt a lot of responsibility about managing the family, man-

aging the finances, making sure that things got handled. He was good about that. He had a lot of things that he didn't do good but, you know, he sort of was in the driver's seat for our family. So I felt like he was doing a fairly—I felt like he was taking responsibility so this was a sign that things were OK still. [SOCIAL SERVICES ORGANIZER/ TEACHER, AGE 40, DIVORCED AFTER 12 YEARS]

The partner wards off information in order to preserve or maintain the status quo, postpone a difficult choice, or avoid a threatening situation.[22] The partner gets to hang on to a life with the other person. But in the long run, by collaborating to help the initiator keep secrets, the partner precludes the possibility of doing something to avert or alleviate the potential danger.[23]

Partners may deal with the mixed array of signals in still other ways. Instead of denying that trouble is brewing, partners will sometimes acknowledge the negative signals—but reinterpret them, allowing their frame of reference to remain undisturbed. For example, partners may view negative signals as positive and couple-confirming.

Our sex life wasn't great but when we did have it, it was good. It was sort of infrequent. We made love on our vacation and it was fantastic and that was only a year ago. I mentioned that to her and how we made love there and everything and walked the beaches and she said that was simply sex. That was saying to me she didn't love me, but how can you separate the two? [PRODUCTION MANAGER, AGE 52, DIVORCED AFTER 25 YEARS]

Some partners acknowledge the negative signals, but define the problems as a normal part of being coupled and, therefore, nothing to get alarmed about.[24] Their existing frame of reference includes ideas about what is normal and what is deviant in relationships and they diagnose theirs accordingly.

I was a person who thought that one suffers through and that throughout life certain sufferings happen and that's just the way it is. And I thought that as a woman I should really feel so lucky that I was married to this bright man who a lot of people thought was witty and I had these two beautiful children and I had a nice house and I had what seemed to be a glowing possible future. Why in the world, even though if one looked one might see that I was not happy, why in the world would I ever want to change that? I mean, I never saw my mother happy. Why should I assume that I should be happy? You know. Happy, what's that? Really, I know that's where I was at. I don't think I've ever really felt a kind of happiness in life until more recently. I didn't know about happiness. I knew about laughing. But I didn't know about a feeling of satisfaction. [SOCIAL SERVICES ORGANIZER/TEACHER, AGE 40, DIVORCED AFTER 12 YEARS]

Some of these notions seem to be drawn from a sort of folk wisdom: "All marriages have trouble. Ours wouldn't be normal if we didn't." "After a while, all couples lose their interest in sex." "Oh well, everybody has their ups and downs." "We had some arguments, but, you know, all couples have their arguments." Their relationship doesn't seem to fit cultural stereotypes of a relationship in trouble: arguing is *not* constant; breaking up or divorce is not mentioned (except during an argument, when it is taken as situational, rather than part of the ongoing relationship).[25]

Partners often draw conclusions that their problems are normal and thus not to be worried about without knowing how their situation actually compares to other peoples' relationships. Traditionally, many family matters are kept private. The display of discontent, remember, is reserved for select audiences. Usually, couples work together to present a harmonious front when appearing publicly.[26] (In testament of our skill at this is the frequent comment, "What! But they were such a perfect couple!" uttered by others when hearing of a break-up.) Unlike initiators, who have been confiding in selected others, gathering information about alternative lifestyles, and developing a standard against which the relationship is measured, partners usually have acquired little comparative information by which to judge the relationship.[27] What knowledge they have gathered is likely to be from people who share their world view, thus confirming their own frame of reference. The situation of partners is comparable to that of young children who are routinely abused. These children frequently assume everyone's family operates like their own, until they go off to school, make new friends and visit other families. Only then do they discover that other children are not physically abused, and that their situation is the exception, not the rule.[28]

Another way the partner may cope with negative signals is to see them as signs of a temporary dilemma: this too shall pass. The partner may interpret the initiator's discontent as the result of some external social circumstance. As soon as it clears up, the relationship will run smoothly again.[29]

I think that at the point I may have gotten into a lot of denial, you know. I had this power to only see the things I wanted to see, and in many instances John would lie about things and I would catch him in lie after lie and then I would say . . . Well, things are going to get better. Once we get married it will be OK. I really believed that. I

really thought that he was going to change. Marri
solve everything because he was under so much pre
about us living together. He was unhappy, but once
all that would change. [SECRETARY, AGE 38, DIVORCEI

In a way it was kind of a tumultuous time. Both of ou
near the end of the semester. We weren't spending as much time
together but I didn't see that as a problem at the time just because
we had other commitments and had to get that done. But then once
the work was done, I expected that everything would be back to nor-
mal. There was one other time when she broke down into tears and
it really at the time didn't seem to make sense. She said how much
she really cared about me and wanted us to be together and wanted
to work things out between us. I said that's fine, I want to work things
out. I love you and care for you. I know we can—at the end of the
semester as we get over this tumultuous time with the finals and all,
things will work out and be back to normal. We can spend more time
together. [MEDICAL STUDENT, AGE 25, SEPARATED AFTER LIVING TO-
GETHER 4 YEARS]

Partners may attribute the negative signals not to some temporary external social circumstance, but to a physical or mental affliction they think
temporarily has beset the initiator.[30] And this—not the relationship or
themselves—is the source of the trouble. Almost like an evil spirit, this
temporary affliction possesses the initiator, causing uncharacteristic actions.[31]

He was going through this "middle-age" panic that a lot of men go
through, where they see their careers at a standstill and are afraid
they are getting old and need to prove themselves. I knew he was
seeing a lot of women but I thought most men do this and it will
pass. [HOME SALES REPRESENTATIVE, AGE 45, DIVORCED AFTER 10 YEARS]

But I never gave up hope. Probably part of it was the change of life.
She had just turned 50 and my brother-in-law said she had been hav-
ing hot flashes and for a period of time I was blaming it all on that
and just figured that sooner or later she would see the light.
[PRODUCTION MANAGER, AGE 52, DIVORCED AFTER 25 YEARS]

As a consequence, the partner believes the source of the trouble lies not
in self or relationship, but in the initiator.[32] The partner suggests the
only obvious solution—the initiator should get professional help.[33] If
the initiator argues for joint counseling, the partner may make a few
courtesy visits, then drop out,[34] or refuse to get involved, suggesting

d that the initiator go alone. (After all, it is the initiator's prob-
l.) In part, the suggestion is made to de-fuse the situation, with the
idea that the counselor will no doubt set the initiator straight and all will
be peaceful again. Ironically, one possible consequence is that the initiator follows the partner's suggestion and, alone, does turn to a counselor. With the counselor, the initiator works through the difficulties.
Issues crystallize. Problems become identified with the relationship or
with the other person, rather than with the initiator. Because the partner
is not present to collaborate on the definition of the situation, the initiator continues redefining partner and relationship negatively without in-
terruption or contradiction. Should the counselor become a transitional
person, the initiator may gather not only professional support, but also
the information and confidence to go it alone.[35]

THE COVER-UP: A COLLABORATIVE ENDEAVOR

Ironically, though separated in many ways, the partners remain full-
fledged partners in one endeavor: suppressing information about the status of the relationship. Whether the partner responds to the mixed array
of signals by disavowing signs of trouble, defining them as normal and
therefore not serious, or defining them as temporary, the results are the
same. Despite warning signals, the partner's response is *not* the response of one who sees a fire and drops everything to run and put it
out. Even when the partner begins to question the initiator, the questions
at first tend to get asked in gentle ways. It's hard to pose questions
when we suspect the answers may cause us to rearrange our lives, even
temporarily.[36] So the partner, too, avoids direct confrontation.

*He experienced my friendships with other people as a wedge, for
sure. One of the problems I guess that he had—one of the few things
he ever talked about—was the feeling that I was getting "too close
to other people." I was spending more and more time with friends
and he always used Todd and Joe. "You spend more time with Todd
and Joe than you do here." He'd never say "with me," but he would
say "here." He never expressed it as a problem that my affections
were going to other people and not going to him.* [OWNER, USED BOOK
STORE, AGE 36, SEPARATED AFTER LIVING TOGETHER 8 YEARS]

*We had sort of been doing this long distance romance for about a
month and a half because our families would get together about every
two weeks and we would be making eyes at each other and breathing
heavy around the corner, that sort of thing. And sure, nobody knows!
Well, how can anybody miss that? Nobody can miss that. Now I re-*

alize and I feel bad when I think of it. I don't think he missed it. Going home in the car one time—he said—"If you ever had an affair, would you think about having it with Hank?" And I am so damned honest. I said, "Yeah, if I ever had an affair, he'd be the first man I'd think of." That was the truth. I mean, I could do nothing but answer his question. But that was all he said. He didn't follow it up. [LEARNING DISABILITIES TEACHER, AGE 49, DIVORCED AFTER 23 YEARS]

Should the partner become bold enough to try to engage the initiator in a direct confrontation, the initiator may continue the cover-up.

This woman called to arrange a meeting with me. And he told me he wasn't seeing her anymore. And basically I wanted to say, "I don't want to talk to you," but there was something—I had to know what she wanted, you know. So I told her I'd meet her—I worried about what she was going to say to me. And so she met me afterwards in the cafeteria and she said, "Why don't you give him up?" This kind of thing. So I really still thought maybe he wasn't having an affair with her. It was just she, you know, that wanted to—so I told him about it and he said, "No, don't pay any attention to her. Everything's all right with us." But then when he finally did leave, he did run away with her. [BLOOD DRAWER, AGE 38, SEPARATED AFTER 4 YEARS OF MARRIAGE]

It got so that she was gone so much. We hardly ever had time to ourselves anymore. I asked her about it. I said, "What's going on, are you staying away for some reason?" She would say it was just work. But I missed her. So as she continued to be away pretty consistently, I got upset. She would avoid conflict. She would say she was sorry, be home a few nights then be gone again. She would cut the conversation whenever I got upset, and then go ahead like she was. [FURNITURE RESTORER, AGE 32, SEPARATED AFTER LIVING TOGETHER 9 YEARS]

It was the loss of the best friend status, I became just the mate, not the mate and best friend. And that was about when we stopped having sex, around that time. I think it was mutual. He withdrew first, then I, to protect my own ego, withdrew also. We discussed it some, and he would say, "I'm just not into it. I'm going through a non-sexual stage. I'm going through a time when I don't feel like having sex. I don't know what I'm doing." [STUDENT/SERVICE COORDINATOR, AGE 28, SEPARATED AFTER LIVING TOGETHER 1 YEAR]

Both partners respond in ways that suppress information. Their responses are guided by a key principle of everyday interaction: in social encounters, we avoid embarrassing the other person.[37] We cooperate to help each other save face. The initiator helps the partner save face by refraining, when confronted, from delivering the critical piece of information that would cause the partner to lose dignity[38] and which also, by the way, would lead the partner to the unavoidable conclusion that things are in bad shape. The partner helps the initiator save face by accepting the initiator's responses to questions instead of probing relentlessly, exposing the initiator's subterfuge.[39] The two partners' collaborative secret-keeping is not solely altruistic, however, for both have something to lose in a direct confrontation. The initiator will not risk losing the relationship until he or she has created what seems to be a secure niche elsewhere. Initiators will reveal all to the partner only when the costs of staying in the relationship are outweighed by the benefits of leaving. Until then, the initiator will continue to tell without telling. The partner will acknowledge the discordant signals and confront the initiator directly only when the situation becomes so costly in terms of emotional energy, tension, and human dignity that the partner has more to lose by suppression than by revelation. Until then, the partner will continue to know without knowing.

FIVE

The Breakdown of Cover-Up

T HE collaborative cover-up eventually breaks down as a result of interaction between the two partners which is so subtle, so complex, so volatile, so dynamic that using words to describe it imposes an order contradicted by reality.[1] The initiator controls this moment, for the partner will not admit the relationship is in serious trouble until the initiator displays discontent with sufficient clarity and force so that the partner can no longer avoid this conclusion. To get the partner's attention, the initiator increases the frequency, intensity, and visibility of signals previously unnoticed—or else interjects new ones sure to do the job.

DIRECT CONFRONTATION

One new signal is a direct confrontation in which the initiator reveals secrets in full, clear, and painful detail.[2]

> *The violent part was all during a two week period. Actually, it had been the month before that we stopped sleeping together. He never really came out and said he no longer loved me till the violence broke out. He would scream out, "I can't stand you. You bore me." [FLORAL DESIGNER, AGE 28, SEPARATED AFTER LIVING TOGETHER 4 YEARS]*

> *My then-husband came home for dinner. He had been acting very quiet for weeks and I had been asking him what was wrong. He had*

79

a very responsible job and was under a lot of pressure and I assumed that it was because of his work that he was just so quiet, and he kept telling me it was just work. Well, he came home for dinner with some kind of downtrodden look on his face and I said to him, "What is wrong?" We were all assembled at the dinner table and he asked me to come upstairs, said that he just couldn't stand it any longer. So I left the children and went up into the bedroom and he closed the door and he told me he loved somebody else. Just whamo. So he was very confused. What was bothering him was that he really thought that he loved me, too. He just didn't know what to make of it. So I was trembling all over. He said then he wanted to tell me and he wanted to go to her right then. [TEACHER, AGE 35, DIVORCED AFTER 11 YEARS]

We finally started talking about it and got the cards on the table and I could tell her, "Look, I love you but I don't feel sexual love toward you, and I can't explain why. I know it's my fault and so forth, but I may leave." And you know, she began to cry a little bit, but she held it together until we got back in the house. It was like we talked about it a little bit and she said, "You want a divorce? You don't want a separation?" I said, "No, I think I want a divorce, you know, we can always," I didn't really mean it, but I started to placate her a little, "we can always remarry down the road, but I really think I need to be a single man again and to discover some things." [SUPERVISOR, AGE 38, DIVORCED AFTER 19 YEARS]

The initiator directly confronts the partner not only with negative feelings, but with the wish to end the relationship. Taken together, these two messages are so powerful that the partner is forced to alter the frame of reference that she or he has held on to so dearly—though by attempting to break the news gently, the initiator sometimes still clouds the issue by giving mixed signals even now ("No, I think I want a divorce, you know, we can always," I didn't really mean it, but I started to placate her a little, "We can always remarry down the road." "So he was very confused. What was bothering him was that he really thought he loved this other person, but he thought he loved me, too"). The initiator who follows up this speech by simply and spontaneously walking out the door or by insisting that the partner leave gives a powerful signal, however.

Initiators directly confront the partner only when absolutely certain about their feelings.

I gave him a lot of years. I could never see an end to it. But I did come to that point where I knew I wanted it to end. I could no longer take jealousy. I could no longer take children constantly in and out of my life. I mean, you know, you live so many months in your gay relationship and then bang! Christmas comes and you have to live an entirely different life and then summer comes and you have a different life again. [CALLIGRAPHER, AGE 29, SEPARATED AFTER LIVING TOGETHER 7 YEARS]

Many speak of a precise moment when they "knew the relationship was over," when "everything went dead inside," when "I walked through this house and felt none of it was mine," when "I realized I didn't belong there anymore."[3] The partnership is clearly incompatible with the initiator's own sense of self, life, and values. Being in the relationship now unambiguously *detracts from and stands in opposition to* the person the initiator has become. Initiators experiencing this moment of certainty sometimes say that it is accompanied by the feeling of being a guest or a stranger in familiar surroundings. Others remember it as a moment when it was not themselves, but the partner who seemed to be the stranger.

One man described the sudden illness of his father-in-law. In the long hours and days that followed at the hospital, his wife became embroiled in arguments with other family members focusing not on her father, but on what the husband considered petty conflicts. He was thunderstruck by her decision to let him go to the hospital in her place so that she would no longer have to deal with her other relatives. His conclusion: "I listened to her with disbelief that she could treat her father this way. How could she do this? What kind of values did she have anyway? She was someone I no longer knew. How could I have gotten hooked up with such a person?"

The initiator's certainty results not only from the recognition that he or she no longer belongs in the relationship, but also from a sense of belonging elsewhere. Self-validation is now coming from other sources. The relationship has been replaced with something else that confirms the initiator's sense of self, and this resource now provides stability— the sense of being "at home." The initiator finds the differences between worlds so clear and so great that not only is no remedy possible, but continuing in the relationship is out of the question.[4] Although the initiator has experienced this conflict between individual identity and the identity bestowed by the relationship all along, these feelings are now sharply defined and keenly felt. More important, the initiator identifies and articulates this conflict as the source of unhappiness.

Often the initiator's moment of certainty occurs after the initiator has had an intense experience elsewhere, then rejoins the world shared with the partner. Perhaps the initiator returns from a reunion with family or old friends, a business meeting in another city, a stolen weekend with a lover, or from a satisfying time alone. The juxtaposition of the two worlds creates a "re-entry shock," as the initiator experiences the home environment with the other experience freshly in mind. One woman who had just completed a strenuous and exhausting work assignment was faced immediately with weekend visitors who were friends of her husband. Though she wanted to rest, she felt pressure to respond to the expectations of her husband and his friends that she spend the weekend cooking and entertaining. She did, but the experience led her to conclude that she could no longer continue in a relationship based on traditional notions about women's roles that were so contradictory to her personal beliefs.

Once convinced of feelings about the partnership, initiators no longer dwell on the question of whether or not to go. Instead, they begin to think about *how* to go.[5] Uncoupling has many costs. Many people remain in unhappy relationships because of their unwillingness to suffer the economic, emotional, and social costs of leaving: loneliness, disruption, a decreased standard of living, the loss of other relationships, the misery of the partner, the astonishment and anger of parents or in-laws, the sorrow of children, the condemnation of the Church, the holier-than-thou attitude of friends who "have had trouble too, but we stuck it out." Initiators who immediately confront the partner with their wish to terminate the relationship do so because they believe they can manage these other costs of the transition.

Planning

Not all who experience certainty about the partner act immediately, however. Unable or unwilling to endure the costs of leaving, they plan instead to confront the partner when some future event occurs that decreases these costs: "after Tommy starts school"; "when I get the raise"; "when Dad dies"; "when I finish the degree"; "when the kids are gone"; "when I get a job"; "when his health improves." I am reminded of an old story about a couple in their eighties who filed for divorce. The judge questioned the partners extensively about their mutual wish to end their relationship so late in life. Finally convinced that they both were deeply unhappy and had been so for decades, he asked, "Why have you taken so long to do this?" They responded, "We were waiting for the children to die."

For some initiators, the plan to end the relationship in the future may remain a fantasy, a rehearsal for something that never happens. This fantasy may even become the alternative that allows them to continue in the relationship. Fantasies about leavetaking are not restricted to those who arc uncoupling or wishing to uncouple. The happily coupled also indulge. A miserable experience with the other person may trigger images of being somewhere else with someone else—or even alone. But it remains a fleeting notion, unacted on. For those whose discontent is longstanding however, the fantasy is more than a passing thought. It is regularly incorporated into the initiator's life, and evokes thoughts about leaving that assume an organized, means-ends character, eventually leading to action. Planning becomes serious business and initiators become very efficient about it.[6] They consider the financial implications of a separation.[7]

> I had started to think about living someplace else on my own. The thought came into my head—financially, how do I do it. I would find myself going to work . . . I did my thinking while driving, and adding up column A and column B and seeing if I could make it, you know? And if I couldn't have financially done it then, I probably would have stayed on until I could. But I had made up my mind, yeah, prior to leaving, and when I did that was one of my thoughts. [POTTER, AGE 32, SEPARATED AFTER LIVING TOGETHER 9 YEARS]

They may start a secret savings account or juggle finances, either hiding assets from the partner or taking steps to assure that the partner will be secure. They may consult a lawyer about the procedures and consequences of separation and property settlements. They may consider alternative living arrangements. Occasionally, there is written evidence of planning. Initiators sometimes jot down lists of things they would do or need if on their own. They write letters, confiding their plans and feelings to a transitional person. One initiator reported beginning a journal with full knowledge that something unusual was happening in his life, and he wrote to record it as it unfolded.

> When I switched jobs, I knew it was my year of revolution. I started keeping a journal, which I titled just that: "My Year of Revolution." I wrote so later my kids would understand and would know who I was. She doesn't exist on paper. If you looked at that, you would never know my wife was in my life at the time. [TEACHER, TECHNICAL SCHOOL/WRITER, AGE 39, DIVORCED AFTER 18 YEARS]

Although writing is a means of making thoughts and ideas concrete, and thus a mechanism by which the initiator makes discontent public to self, sometimes it also becomes the catalyst for a direct confrontation. When initiators are ready, they may reveal feelings to their partners by, in effect, reciting what previously has been recorded in the journal or leaving the journal or correspondence in a place where their partners are sure to see and read it. In one direct confrontation, the initiator read aloud to the partner from a journal.

> *One day she bought a notebook. Every night, we go to bed, she writes in the notebook. One night, we went to bed, and she pulled out the notebook. And she said, "I've been evaluating you and I've been evaluating myself, and I want to read to you the findings of my evaluations." I said OK. And she said, "You are my enemy and you are my oppressor." And then she goes on and evaluates good points and bad points, and they were very accurate, very accurate.* [SOCIAL SERVICES WORKER, AGE 44, DIVORCED AFTER 19 YEARS]

Some initiators' plans include preparing the partner to live alone. Initiators can decrease the cost of leaving by decreasing the partner's social, emotional, and financial dependence on the relationship. Consequently, initiators sometimes encourage partners toward alternative resources of their own. Earlier in the transition, initiators may have urged partners in these pursuits to make them more attractive and thus improve the relationship. Now the urgings have a different thrust.

> *The way I defined being a good wife and the way John defined being a good wife were two different quantities. He wanted the house to look like a hotel and I didn't see it that way. He couldn't see why I couldn't meet his needs. . . . When he first asked for a divorce and I refused, he suggested I go back to school. I remember a man who worked with John who sent his wife back to school so she could support herself, so he could divorce her. I asked John if he was trying to get rid of me. He didn't answer that. He insisted I go, and I finally went.* [ART TEACHER, AGE 45, DIVORCED AFTER 16 YEARS]

> *When we first become lovers, we stopped doing the bar scene. It is such a threat. Everyone is looking and it's almost like a game there to try to take a lover from someone else, so we just didn't go. People are so desperate for meaningful relationships, you know. After I started seeing Paul, I wanted to go again because Scotty is a great dancer and he always attracts a lot of attention, so like I thought if we started going to the bar again, Scotty would meet someone and then I could be with Paul.* [ACCOUNTANT, AGE 29, SEPARATED AFTER LIVING TOGETHER 3 YEARS]

> *For a long time we had had sexual problems. We went to the doctor and he told me, "You know, your wife operates in a delicate way, and things have to be just right between you or she won't be able to respond." Well, she kept refusing to have sex and finally she suggested I find it somewhere else. I was very upset at this. She said*

"You're a strange man, you know, all the men would be delighted to get a wife like that." I said, "I'm not delighted, I'm hurt. It's one thing that a man falls in love outside a marriage, you know, head over heels, it's one thing. But it's another thing when the wife says it's OK for you to go outside and find sexual satisfaction with another woman and doesn't care. I'm supposed to be your first love, your first priority." [SALESMAN, AGE 30, DIVORCED AFTER 3 YEARS]

As the planned date of confronting the partner approaches, initiators may turn their attention to tying up the loose ends of living with the other person. They may announce their departure after completing some commitment the partners have made together, after they have the house in good repair, or even after a thorough cleaning. Not only do they get the house in order, but also themselves and their belongings: having shoes or car repaired, visiting doctors or dentists for check-ups, getting braces on the kids, sorting through clothes, documents, or keepsakes. They suggest to a friend that they may suddenly need to move in for a few days. Some look for an apartment, or even rent one.

The initiator's planning often culminates in a precise moment when, according to schedule, resources at hand, and with a well-rehearsed speech, the initiator confronts the partner about wanting to end the relationship.

It was all planned like Omaha Beach or something. Down to the last lifeboat. I'd been planning it for two years. I wasn't going to fuck it up. I must have rehearsed the speech a thousand times. It began, "I am going to say something to you that in the short run will hurt you and upset you, but in the long run you will be much better off." I didn't want to tell her before Christmas, though I knew being with the family would be hard for me. I would rather be off alone someplace. In fact, I thought about how good it would be to not have Christmas but to be off in a room by myself, reading a good book. But telling her then would just destroy things for everyone, so I decided to wait until the kids were back in school. So that's what I did. I chose Friday night, because that would give us the weekend. We would have Saturday and Sunday to work through this, she could get used to the idea, then I would move out Sunday night. Monday would be business as usual. It didn't quite go like that, I mean I knew she would be upset, but her response really devastated me. I did deliver my speech, but the rest of it just went to smithereens. [LAWYER, AGE 50, SEPARATED AFTER 25 YEARS OF MARRIAGE]

She had a good friend coming to stay with us for the weekend, so I thought that would be a good time to tell her. I told my sister and made arrangements to stay with her until I could find a place of my own. I made dinner that night and was so nervous I was nauseous. The minutes dragged. It was awful. I kept thinking, "This is it. If I don't do it now, the timing will probably never be so right again." Also, I had told my sister, so that meant I really had to go through with it. We had dinner. We talked about our days. We cleaned up. After dinner, it was her habit to have coffee and read the paper. I sat down beside her. I said, "You know that I haven't been truly happy for sometime now." She put her coffee down and looked at me. I went on. I got through it. [SECRETARY, AGE 26, SEPARATED AFTER LIVING TOGETHER 5 YEARS]

Changing Plans

Life, however, usually does not allow us to be quite this orderly. The initiator's carefully thought-out plan is often changed because of some unforeseen event that shifts the costs and benefits of leaving or staying. The leavetaking can be delayed again and again, or instead occur precipitously. The initiator may alter the scheduling of the announcement because, unexpectedly, the cost of staying in the relationship dramatically increases. The initiator loses an important resource and in its absence, tension between the partners escalates. Perhaps a close friend moves away, a project is completed, a love affair dissolves, or a parent dies. With the resource gone, the relationship seems unbearably bleak and, in fact, intolerable. Then, disregarding inadequate preparation, the initiator directly confronts the partner before the planned date.[8]

Usually, the initiator not only drew self-validation from the now-absent resource, but also gave it time and energy. As a consequence, the initiator spent less time with the partner. With the loss of the alternative (unless the initiator quickly finds a substitute), interaction between initiator and partner increases, exposing incompatibility and generating conflict. A change that increases the initiator's leisure time can contribute to the decision to confront in another way. Social disruption is one of the costs of uncoupling. The initiator may have delayed bringing matters to a head before because work or other commitments did not leave time for the predicted disorganization that would follow. The alternative commitment absorbed time, and the initiator now has time to spare.

Sometimes it's not the real loss of some resource but the *threat* of loss and the *potential* of increased interaction with the partner that causes the initiator to confront earlier than planned.

It was terrible. I realized that without the kids here to come home to, I was really lonely. The first week or so I was really happy. You know, I'd come home and I did what I wanted to, and I just enjoyed the peace and quiet. But then I started thinking, my God, I can't wait for them to get home. I want to find out what they're doing. I want them to tell me what they're doing and I want to tell them what I'm doing. And then I realized, my God, in two or three years they are leaving. They are going to go away to college. And I've always believed this, you know, you raise children to leave you—you don't depend on your children. And I decided at that point I had better start making some moves, because it was going to be just so awful without them. On a Saturday night when he and I are here alone, it's just awful. It just feels so hollow to be here alone and have nothing. It's better for me when he is away. I don't hate him so much. Because I don't expect anything from him. But when he is sitting right here in this same house and there is nothing, I feel angry at him, and angry at myself. [ASSISTANT PROFESSOR, AGE 37, DIVORCED AFTER 19 YEARS]

We had been seeing each other for some time, when all of a sudden this man moved in next door to her. They started in right away being friends, and I thought nothing of it. Our plan was to marry when my kids were grown, at that time it was three years away, then I would divorce Madge. And she seemed comfortable with that idea. But then the shock came. She started talking about how her kids needed a father and one night I was over there and she said Bert (that's his name) had offered to come across with a ring right then. I moved fast. I went out and got a ring of my own and took it over there, then told Madge I wanted out. [DIVISION MANAGER, AGE 54, DIVORCED AFTER 19 YEARS]

The cost of staying also may increase because of events affecting the partner's life. Perhaps the partner begins some transition that promises to change the couple's lifestyle in a way that is not in the initiator's best interest.[9] The partner makes a choice—or contemplates making a choice—and the initiator acts.

We moved out of state so he could do his residency. We bought a house, and he was ready to establish a permanent life there. After four months, I told him I didn't want to be with him any more and I was going to law school. In the years he was in medical school, I had developed a lifestyle without him, and the move took me away from everything that had kept me comfortable. [LAWYER, AGE 36, SEPARATED AFTER LIVING TOGETHER 6 YEARS]

He suddenly decided that he would be around more. He started talking about changing his work so that he could spend more time with the family. My major complaint throughout the marriage was that he was gone all the time. But, meanwhile, in his absence I had restructured my life, I had gotten very involved politically and was away a lot myself. Suddenly after all these years he's saying, "Let's do things together. I'll be home all the time. I'll take care of the kids, you can do your activities, but I'll be home." The offer came too late. The destruction had already occurred. Not only did I no longer want to do things with him, but his being around would be a problem. There would be the expectation that we do things together, and I would either have to cut back on my outside involvements, or go ahead with them and there would be constant conflict. I really couldn't face that. [POLITICAL ORGANIZER/VOLUNTEER, AGE 58, DIVORCED AFTER 24 YEARS]

Perhaps the partner experiences some loss: becomes seriously ill, loses a job or a close friend. As a consequence, the partner's dependence on the initiator increases. Initiator and partner spend more time together with the result that the couple's incompatibilities become more obvious, causing the initiator to act before the scheduled confrontation.

The initiator may confront the partner earlier than planned because an unexpected event makes life apart from the partner seem more appealing and manageable. Consequently, the benefits of leaving increase. Although accumulating resources all along, the initiator discovers that some critical gap is suddenly filled, providing the catalyst for departure. Some find a transitional person. Some have a new opportunity in their job or a sudden financial windfall. Others describe a brief romance that did not offer a promise of anything permanent, but gave them the courage to confront because of increased self-confidence, or the suggestion that something better might be out there waiting for them.

Many initiators are prepared to cope with all the costs of leaving except one: the social consequences of being responsible for the breakup. How will the partner respond? Threats, crying and pleading, violence, suicide? If there are children, how will they react? Will they be so hurt and angry that the initiator can only end the relationship at the cost of losing the children's affection? And what about friends and relatives? While the potential negative repercussions can never be completely avoided, initiators often try to reduce them. One way is to relocate, and, when settled, confront the partner. Clearly, relocation does not alter the response of others, but geographic distance can delay it and lessen the initiator's susceptibility to it. This strategy is an elaboration of an earlier theme: as the initiator becomes increasingly unhappy, the initiator decreases the amount of time spent with critics, potential or real. This earlier decrease in interaction, however, is usually unplanned, resulting from the need to shift to a social location more in keeping with self-concept. Once certain that the relationship can no longer continue, however, the initiator acts deliberately.

When we moved from Boston to the Midwest, I knew I was taking Carrie there so I could dump her. [ASSOCIATE PROFESSOR, AGE 35, DIVORCED AFTER 9 YEARS]

I knew there was no way she would stick around California if we were to get divorced. I also knew my mother would have an absolute fit, which she did. I think that my reason for moving to California was to make the divorce possible, because I wouldn't have to face my mother. She'd be out of the picture and I would only have to make a phone call, which I could handle easier than face to face. [SALES REPRESENTATIVE, AGE 36, DIVORCED AFTER 11 YEARS]

Some initiators reduce uncoupling's social consequences by taking advantage of a move planned for two and converting it to a move for one.

I couldn't go through the separation in my own country. So I look to this country like my salvation. The two families were quite old-fashioned. Divorce . . . I guess I was the first one in the two families. And I would never have any support from anybody. He was very well liked by my family, too. And I was liked in his family. So the pressure would have been very great. I would never have done it there. I don't think it was possible. I came here to school with that idea, that he would not join me and I would never go back to him. [SOCIAL WORKER, AGE 54, DIVORCED AFTER 15 YEARS]

What really precipitated my leaving when I did was I was accepted in the training program. I knew that I would be moving out of New York City and there would be a big change. That's when, I said, that will be the time. I took a weekend and went to visit my brother. I spent 4 days on the beach, you know, with a book and just looking out at the ocean. This was my big decision time. I was going to come back and either be in that relationship or not. I knew before I left what my decision was going to be. I just hoped that I had enough courage to tell her. We took a walk and I told her that I decided that I wanted it to be over. [POTTER, AGE 32, SEPARATED AFTER LIVING TOGETHER 9 YEARS]

By relocating without the partner, the initiator not only avoids negative reactions but, in addition, advantageously couples this natural dismantling of social ties and separation of belongings with those of ending the relationship. A similar result is achieved when the partner makes the move, expecting the initiator to come later. After the partner has gone, the initiator tells the partner not to expect company. Sometimes the partner may be away only temporarily. Taking advantage of this absence, the initiator may let the partner know by phone or letter that the relationship is over—or, on returning home, the partner may discover the welcome mat gone and the door barred, often legally.[10] Or perhaps the initiator quietly moves out while the partner is away.[11]

> *We had been living separate lives for the last several months. She had gone to visit a friend on the coast for a week and I felt very good about being on my own, and there was something about being in the apartment without her, a feeling of being in the past, I guess, and I thought if I don't leave now, I never will. It was easier with her gone. Not as messy.* [LICENSED PRACTICAL NURSE, AGE 28, SEPARATED AFTER LIVING TOGETHER 3 YEARS]

Although these latter tactics are not likely to deflect the response of interested outsiders, initiators do reduce some social consequences by removing themselves from the full brunt of the partner's response.

Some initiators are so paralyzed by potential social repercussions that they are simply unable to confront their partners. Despite being prepared to end the relationship in every other possible way—a secure alternative, certainty about the poor state of the relationship, a keen sense of belonging elsewhere—they are overwhelmed by the anticipated response of the partner and others. Some skip a confrontation with the partner and just leave, perhaps only delaying rather than avoiding negative repercussions. Some put behind partner and community permanently.

Some initiators never go. They remain in the relationship, hoping for fate to take the matter out of their hands. One woman, regretting the years spent in a marriage she felt bound to by her religion, told me she was so unhappy and so desperate to get out that she used to pray for her husband to die. Others wish for fate to intervene in a way somewhat more beneficial to the partner:

> *I keep hoping—with Stan traveling—I had one friend who offered to seduce him, just to show him that it was all right—that he will meet somebody else, that he could do it, and maybe he would look around. Some cute little secretary would be perfect for him.* [HOUSEWIFE, AGE 42, DIVORCED AFTER 24 YEARS]

But fate can be not only slow but unreliable, and the fact remains that the initiator is unhappy. The visible signs of discontent increase. As a result, instead of directly confronting the partner or unambiguously leaving, the initiator gets the partner's attention through equally effective but more *indirect* means.

INDIRECT METHODS: SHIFTING THE BURDEN

The partner responds to the increasingly visible negative signals by redefining the relationship as troubled. A confrontation results, but not because the initiator takes responsibility for it and directly reveals wishes and feelings. It happens because the initiator displays discontent so that the responsibility for the confrontation is shifted to the partner. Confrontation has the potential to change the course of the relationship in unpredictable ways. By transferring the blame for it, the initiator also transfers potential negative consequences to the other person. These indirect methods are not new, by the way. They have been part and parcel of the initiator's expression of unhappiness all along. Though they do not necessarily occur separately, I will distinguish them.

Fatal Mistake

The partner responds to the initiator's escalating display of discontent by committing some grievous error. The initiator seizes on it, confronts the partner with the wish to terminate, and points to the partner's behavior as the reason for all the ills in the relationship. The initiator confronts, but the partner's failure is the reason the relationship has come to this crisis. The partner admits to this failing and concedes its consequences. Not only does the partner redefine the relationship as troubled, but the partner assumes the responsibility for the problems—and the confrontation. The partner's fatal mistake can occur several ways. A partner may respond to the initiator's discontent with unprecedented reactions that reinforce the initiator's negative opinions:[12] creating angry scenes, becoming demanding and interrogative, withdrawing from the initiator, bestowing suffocating attention, becoming physically abusive, refusing or insisting on sex, exhibiting hysteria, destroying furniture or belongings, or taking a lover. With this evidence of discrediting behavior at hand, the initiator confronts the partner: how could the initiator possibly continue living with someone who behaves in this manner?

The partner can make another kind of fatal mistake. He or she fails by virtue of some longstanding characteristic. Previously a source of minor complaints, the irritating trait now becomes a major stumbling block, for as tensions increase between the couple, the objectionable characteristic has a tendency to occur despite the partner's best efforts to control it. Not only does it occur, but it occurs more often and is more exaggerated. Suppose the initiator has always objected to the partner's drinking. The partner tries to control it, but in response to mounting tension and personal unhappiness goes on a binge. This episode becomes the last straw. Or suppose the initiator is disturbed by the partner's emotional highs and lows. In a discussion in which the initiator lists all the ways in which the partner fails, the partner seethes with rage, then becomes hysterical. The initiator scores the point. Or suppose the initiator complains that the partner is an unsatisfactory sex partner. Under pressure to perform, the partner becomes frigid or impotent. The initiator points out the flaw. The partner makes the fatal mistake of displaying the characteristic one more time. The initiator then confronts the partner, justifying the wish to terminate on the basis of the partner's obviously unremediable failing—in essence playing a trump card held all along.

The partner's fatal mistake may be an error of omission, rather than of commission. The initiator asks something of the partner that the initiator knows in advance the partner cannot do. The idea of making someone an offer he or she can't refuse is reversed: the initiator makes the partner an offer she or he can't accept. For example, in one relationship where the partner valued monogamy, the initiator suggested that the couple's relationship be expanded to include other sex partners.[13] The partner found this solution impossible and could not agree to the arrangement. In another, the partner was a woman who could not bear children. The initiator complained that her infertility (formerly viewed as beneficial) was a source of unhappiness. The partner conceded her inability to meet the other person's needs and the initiator made his point.

Decreased Interaction

A second indirect method initiators use to force partners to redefine the relationship as seriously troubled is to gradually decrease time spent together. Initiators are likely both to withdraw psychologically while in the home and to disappear more and more into the outside world. They've been doing this all along, of course, but as their unhappiness increases, their absences become more prolonged. Initiators may do this in order to provide time out from the relationship and its consequences (conflict, boredom, displeasure, fear) or to pursue more pleasurable activities elsewhere.[14]

Initiators may even use short separations as a test of their own ability to operate independently. They may try a weekend away or a vacation by themselves. They may visit relatives and friends: one week increases to two, and two increases to six. They may take a job, work late, or extend their other activities so that the couple's time together is reduced. If presented with the option, initiators may increase the amount of traveling they do on the job, stay overnight with a friend in the city occasionally, or the more affluent may even take an apartment in town. Sometimes the separation is of even longer duration. The initiator may take a job-training course in another city, sign up for the armed services, or engage in a lengthy period of education at a distant school.

If you want to see what a man loves, Oscar Wilde notes, observe how he spends his time.[15] Whatever the initiator gives as the rationale ("big push at the office," "my friend is having a crisis"), the fact is that the couple is spending less and less time together. Their interaction diminishes to the point where the partner eventually gets the message that something is amiss. The partner accepts the unwanted solitude for the negative signal it is, and confronts the initiator about the status of the relationship.

Rule Violation

A third indirect method involves violating the rules of the relationship.[16] The initiator breaks some rule (either spoken or unspoken) about proper conduct toward the partner and the initiator's behavior is so contrary to expectations that the partner is shocked to attention. A person who cares would not behave this way. The transgression is a breach of trust so great that the partner's self-concept is put in jeopardy; personal dignity is challenged to the extent that the partner cannot continue in the relationship without losing face.[17] The costs of ignoring the initiator's display of discontent now overwhelm the benefits. Compelled to acknowledge that the relationship is in serious trouble, the partner confronts the initiator, demanding an explanation.

The initiator may violate rules about kindness and respect shown to loved ones.

I came home early and Peg came in and she just kind of yelled at me and said, "What are you doing here?" You can't believe the change in her when she finally let it all out, she became like a different person, really. It was frightening. She treated me with contempt, hate, bitterness—would not speak to me, she just spoke through me. She talked to the kids and would be nice to them, as though nothing had happened but her treatment of me was unbelievable, she treated me like dirt. Everything she had been keeping in just came out. Nothing

I could say or do would affect her. [TYPESETTER, AGE 38, DIVORCED
AFTER 14 YEARS]

The initiator may violate the rules about sexual intimacy with the partner.

*I really wasn't physically attracted to him because this was a person
that not only did I not love him, but by this point, I did not like him.
But I went through with sex anyway. And never clearly telling him. I
just gritted my teeth in the dark and went through with it. Finally,
when things were their worst, I said, "I just don't feel that I can,"
and he said, "Why? I support you, I dress you, it's my house, you
know." I said, "What does that have to do with it?" And he said,
"You owe it to me." And I say, "OK, take it." That's basically our
last conversation over this thing. I don't love you, we have nothing
together, you have threatened me, you expect me to trust you and
love you after that. Do you want it, go ahead, I'm here—and he
never approached it from that time. Saying no then was the first thing
that got through to him.* [HOUSEWIFE, AGE 48, DIVORCED AFTER 24 YEARS]

The initiator may violate the rules that accompany being entrusted
with a partner's secrets. In an argument, the initiator may strike out
verbally at the partner saying or doing something that can't be undone.
Drawing on intimate knowledge of the other's history, the initiator at-
tacks the partner's most vulnerable point. From the shared past, the
initiator draws a wounding weapon: "You're just like your mother!";
"You're a lousy lover!" The initiator may violate the rules about re-
specting the other person's possessions, attacking objects that symbolize
either the partner or the relationship.

*She began throwing all my books out the window. Obviously, it wasn't
the books she wanted to throw out.* [STUDENT, AGE 22, SEPARATED AFTER
LIVING TOGETHER 2 YEARS]

*He and a friend did a midnight raid on the apartment. He destroyed
the furniture and stuff that we had gotten since we'd been together.*
[FLORAL DESIGNER, AGE 28, SEPARATED AFTER LIVING TOGETHER 4 YEARS]

*She slashed the tires on my car. She knew that would get me. She
even told me she was going to.* [SALESMAN, AGE 30, DIVORCED AFTER 3
YEARS]

He put a knife through my face in our wedding picture. [CLINICAL
PSYCHOLOGIST, AGE 36, DIVORCED AFTER 8 YEARS]

The rule violation may involve physical assault. The sudden onset of
abuse in a relationship, or a change in the pattern of abuse in a relation-

ship where it is taken for granted can cause the partner to act. In a marriage where "a slap every six months or so was standard operating procedure," a fight in which the initiator tried to choke the partner to death was the catalyst. Even in the face of such flagrant rule violation, the partner may choose not to confront. Acknowledging that the relationship is in trouble, but fearing that discussing the situation might hasten the relationship's decline, the partner does nothing.

> When he began to physically abuse me, I could figure out some way so he wouldn't do it. It's incredible when I think of it. But it seemed to me often, I mean, I would just sit and say, "It seems like he's doing everything he can for me to end this marriage." I had a feeling he was trying to make the marriage fail. But he didn't really want it to. And I sort of instinctively knew that if it failed, I would be the one who ended it and he would be the one to blame me for ending it—but he really wanted it, but he would never let himself or anybody know that he wanted it to end. But something about him wanted it to end. Or else—it was either he wanted it to end or else he wanted me to prove again that I loved him despite the fact that he kept pushing me to end it. But then I didn't end it, so it would reinforce his dependency on me. But it was OK to be dependent because I wouldn't go away. No matter what he did, I wouldn't go. He was like a naughty little kid. [ASSISTANT EDITOR, BOOK PUBLISHING, AGE 32, DIVORCED AFTER 8 YEARS]

The partner's threshold for tolerating these rule violations, these assaults on dignity and identity, sometimes depends on how much the violations become public. Although we may lose face before the person we live with, the indignities we suffer may still be tolerable because no one else knows (or we *think* no one else knows). Should the initiator's rule violations become visible to others, the partner will usually act to avoid social embarrassment.[18]

The violations that are most public, and thus most likely to move the partner to confront the initiator, are those pertaining to sex with other people.[19] By their very nature, they are public at the most fundamental level.

> He didn't tell me. That's what made me angry. Up to then we had a fairly open relationship. We were seeing each other, sleeping together, living together, but if we really wanted to see somebody else, as long as it was, "I'm going to do this, I won't be in, and do you like this person," it was OK. I have this philosophy. I do not own anybody's body, I maybe want your soul, which is what I wanted, but I don't own your body, and as long as you—I told him this, we

told each other this—as long as you come back to me, and as long as I'm first, do what you want. Then he started an affair with a woman named Darlene but he didn't tell me about it. He started sneaking around like we were married to one another and he was some 40 year-old man going through his second childhood. It was very insulting and it made me very angry and very upset. I thought about killing myself a couple of times, like what am I doing wrong, what could I be doing that he could do such a rotten thing to me? Because it was a pretty damn rotten thing to do, not having the consideration to at least tell me, which I think is what hurt most of all. [STUDENT, AGE 21, SEPARATED AFTER LIVING TOGETHER 2 YEARS]

And what happened is they had made plans to go into New York early one morning and didn't come back until the wee hours of the next morning with all kinds of explanations—I didn't even ask for explanations. That's what made me start to think. He started telling me how bad the driving—you know, all this sort of stuff. I half listened. Then a hotel receipt just happened to be in this folder of things he brought back from New York. He wanted me to see these things and I said, "What's this?" And he said, "Where'd you get that?" I said, "It was right here." He doesn't know to this day, he said, how it got there but, like my brother said, "Every thief eventually leaves evidence behind and they usually want to get caught." He denied it because he didn't want to implicate this person. [DANCE INSTRUCTOR, AGE 28, SEPARATED AFTER LIVING TOGETHER 4 YEARS]

I started looking for him at the party and I had the suspicion that he was actually, you know, hanging out with some woman. And I found him, you know, like making out up in this dark attic space with a woman. It was terrible. I couldn't believe it—it was like I just all of a sudden knew where to go look. And there he was. It was like I just knew that he might be there and I opened the door and there he was. And I'm sure it was really kind of shit for him too, to be caught. So then I came downstairs. I said something so he really knew who it was, in case he didn't know. And so I went downstairs and I was like standing there kind of angry and I think I probably had had wine so I was a little drunk and people were all sort of around me doing whatever they were doing and he came down and he just sort of laughed and, you know, and I said, "I want to go." So we left. At home I was so angry at him, I was so angry at him, I was like hitting him. And it was like we just had no verbal agreement about this kind of thing, that we could go to this party and each person for him or herself. You don't take your wife to a party and sort of ditch her. [SOCIAL SERVICES ORGANIZER/TEACHER, AGE 40, DIVORCED AFTER 12 YEARS]

But the breakdown of cover-up is, as we have already seen, likely to be avoided by either or both partners. Even when the partner picks up on the negative signals, becomes deeply alarmed about the relationship, and energetically, persistently, and directly confronts the initiator, the initiator may take still another turn at obfuscation.[20]

Something he had said before going to bed finally struck me, what he meant. He said, well, I'm doing such and such and you aren't. I realized I was not included, or that there was no way possible I could be included in the way it was set up. I woke him up at 5 o'clock in the morning to just scream and argue about it. Just nothing that I did seemed to sink below the first level of his consciousness. I could not seem to communicate to him. I wrote him notes, I wrote him letters, I called him on the phone at work so we could talk. In person the argument seemed to get too screaming sometimes, so I never really accomplished much in person. I cried, I got angry, I extended myself more to him thinking he needed more from me, I pulled myself away from him thinking that he didn't deserve me at all. Anything that came into my head I tried because I was in a panic. This relationship was not anything at all that was making me happy. He knew—he knew for sure there were problems in the relationship. He wanted to split. He wasn't telling me. I think what he was doing was behaving in a way that I would ask him to leave. When I would say this is a problem, I want to talk about this . . . he would say I'm tired, I want to go to sleep. [MEDICAL TECHNOLOGIST, AGE 30, DIVORCED AFTER 9 YEARS]

I said, "I need to talk to you. I think I'm gonna go out of my mind." And I said, "What's going on between you and Frank?" And he said, "What do you mean?" I said, "I'm not crazy. I know there's something going on between the two of you. Let's talk about it. Are you having a problem, a sexual problem?" And he said, "What! You know you're talking about me! What are you implicating?" I said, "I don't know but I know I'm not crazy but I feel like I'm going crazy" because I just, you know, and he just reversed it and I was the one who was wrong and "You better think about what you're saying," and hung up. I was crazy, and right after that he came home that night and he said, "You know I've been thinking about what you said all day. It does seem that way. I didn't know how to deal with it either. He has been getting on my nerves lately, too. He is a pain in the ass," and you know, it was like I'm hearing what I want to hear, but I don't believe it. [CO-OWNER, HAIR STYLING SALON, AGE 33, DIVORCED AFTER 13 YEARS]

Partner as Detective

The partner picks up on the signals and confronts, but the initiator does not open up to the partner. Thwarted in the attempt to get to the bottom of things, the partner finds the signals of trouble too strong to ignore. Propelled by a suspected infidelity, the partner assumes the role of detective, searching for evidence to confirm the status of the relationship—whatever it may be.[21]

One day, I was emptying the trash. I think this was probably in the bedroom where the waste basket had a piece of paper torn up into a dozen little pieces and it intrigued me, so I put them together and it turned out to be a receipt from a florist for some flowers that had been sent to a girl in care of a dentist's office. So I called the dentist's office and asked for the girl and she got on the phone and I asked her if she knew Ronnie Sacco, and she said, "He's a patient here," and I said, "Well, this is his wife and I was wondering why he would send you flowers." [EXECUTIVE SECRETARY/SUPERVISOR, AGE 34, DIVORCED AFTER 9 YEARS]

I found rubbers in his pocket, that's what it was. One night his wallet fell out on our sofa and I went to pick it up and I saw this funny shape and, you know, when you used to buy three packs . . . that's in the olden days, you know. I was already pregnant, and I said to him, "See this?" "Yeah?" "What is this?" "None of your business. What're you looking in my wallet for?" I said, "You don't need these with me. What're you carrying them around for?" I started crying. He wouldn't answer me. He just sat there. "You had no business going in my wallet." I said, "You have no business carrying those things." I became insane. I was obsessed with finding out what was going on. I began spying on him. I would see who he left work with. I mean I sat with binoculars with my next door neighbor because I didn't want my car to be seen and my next door neighbor borrowed a car and I sat there watching for him. [SECRETARY, AGE 38, DIVORCED AFTER 10 YEARS]

I believed she was seeing someone. I also believed that if I confronted her, she would probably deny it and proceed more carefully. At first I tried to woo her back, but this only convinced me that my first intuition was right. I got worried about how long this might have been going on and how serious it was—probably serious, I thought, because I couldn't imagine her involved with someone she cared nothing about. Whatever was going on, I wanted it to stop. But I needed evidence. I must tell you that at the time I was absolutely crazy with fear and grief, and yes, jealousy, or you would never understand why I did this, but I hired a detective to find out what was going on. [DOCTOR, AGE 64, DIVORCED AFTER 24 YEARS]

Sometimes the initiator's rule violation comes to light not through the partner's own detective work, but because someone else sees the initiator in some setting or engaging in some activity that is suspicious and uncharacteristic. Perhaps a friend observes an intimate lunch in an out-of-the-way restaurant, or a neighbor catches a glimpse of a quick embrace at a group outing. Those who witness this evidence bear a heavy burden. What to do? The heaviest burden often falls to those living in the same household who have loyalties to both partners: the child, who is taken on an outing as camouflage for one parent's Saturday lunch with a lover; the child, who witnesses a frequent visitor to the house when one parent is away; the child, who picks up an extension phone and hears a whispered conversation not meant for other ears.

Witnesses often remain silent, unburdening themselves only after the couple has separated. But occasionally, moved by the obvious breach of conduct and a connection to one of the partners or to the couple, a witness steps forward, presenting evidence. The partner may deal with this news of the initiator's transgression as with previous negative signals: by ignoring, misperceiving, or denying the information. Indeed, the partner may discredit the witness and cut ties with the bearer of bad tidings. Sometimes the news triggers the partner's search for evidence of confirmation or contradiction. When the information comes from a third party, the partner is often moved to act because what perhaps had been only a vague doubt gains legitimacy due to the observations of another person. Moreover, the partner's actions now have a witness. Someone else has evidence of the initiator's rule violation, and what the partner previously chose to ignore can no longer be overlooked. To save face, the partner must do something.

When partners engage in a search for evidence, the search becomes all-consuming. Their preoccupation is total, as they devote large portions of their thought and energy to confirming the status of the relationship. The initiator's denials only serve to spur the partner on. The following is an extraordinary instance of undercover detective work, in which two partners joined forces to disentangle the mixed signals they each were receiving from their spouses.

Despite her husband's evasiveness, the woman mentioned previously who watched her husband through binoculars from her neighbor's car was convinced her husband was seeing someone else. The family's telephone would ring several times every evening. If the wife answered, the party would hang up, then call back repeatedly until the husband would answer. When the husband answered, the wife would hear him say, "You have the wrong number." Once the husband answered the phone, the calls would cease for the evening. If he didn't answer, the calls continued until the wife was driven to take the phone off the hook. This went on for several months. The wife again and again accused the husband of having a lover. He repeatedly denied it. Throughout this period, he told his wife that he loved her. The wife began searching for evidence. She narrowed the field to two women with whom her husband might be involved.

> I finally decided I had nothing to lose so that every time my phone would ring, I picked it up and dialed two phone numbers, one call to each of them. Each time my phone rang, I made two phone calls and hung up when they answered. I said that every time I get upset, someone else is gonna get upset with me. One day I got a phone call and a man said, "Are you Mrs. So-and-So?" and I said "Yes," and he said, "Is your husband Steve?" and I started crying and I knew who he was and I said, "Oh my God, tell me what your last name is." And he said, "My name is Johnson" and it was the husband of the first woman I pegged and I said to him, "Do you know what your wife has done to my family, do you know what she's done to my household?" and he said, "Lady, I know what she's done and I'm sorry," and he said, "But I have to talk to you." And he came up the following Saturday.
>
> He was just as devastated as I was. So what was happening was every time she was calling me I was calling his house and he was thinking it was a man calling and finally he tapped his telephone and he put in an elaborate recording system that ran for eight hours a day when he went to work. He played back the tapes for me and I could hear the bitch calling me and and me answering the phone. Then he's talking, my husband's talking, to the woman on the phone. All of these denials. It was crazy but we were on top. It was crazy but good because they were conspiring up and down the line and had all kinds of plans to do all kinds of things. And we finally had them.
> [SECRETARY, AGE 38, DIVORCED AFTER 10 YEARS]

When the detective work leads to evidence that is incontrovertible, the victory is scarcely sweet. The partner is forced to acknowledge the worst.

there are ads, you read the newspapers, you see what the qualifica-
tions are that they want, you try to re-do your resume to fit the ads,
and you keep trying to find work in your area.

The partner may try to change his or her appearance by dieting or
taking greater care with clothing and hair. The partner may eliminate
habits that annoy the initiator, or inject creativity and passion into the
couple's sex life. Courtship patterns are reinstituted with a newfound
intensity. There is a desperation and hence an unnaturalness about them,
for now the rituals of courtship are concentrated efforts to stave off an
unwanted loss. The partner may try to bring romance back into the relationship: candlelight dinners, conversations about happy times in
the past, a vacation or weekend away, doing more things together. The
partner may attempt to become more interesting to the initiator, perhaps
by some program of self-improvement, perhaps by becoming involved
in an attention-getting affair. The partner may demonstrate a greater
interest in the initiator's activities. If the initiator likes horseracing, the
partner may start going to the track; if the initiator paints, the partner
may take up watercolors. Often, the partner becomes fascinated with
magazine articles or books on how to improve relationships.

In addition to changing self in ways that will appeal to the initiator,
the partner may try to change the relationship, again following the initiator's earlier path. The partner may suggest a change in the rules of
the relationship. ("If you need more freedom, how about a night out?"
"I've always been monogamous, but if you want to start bringing people home, we could try that.") The partner may suggest a shift in the
division of labor. ("I'll get a job." "I'll go 50–50 with you on housework and childcare." "I'll stop working so much and be around more.")
Perhaps, this time, it is the partner who suggests changing the structure
by adding a new member—a baby.

The partner also tries to change the initiator. Intuitively on target, he
or she tries to reshape the initiator's interests and alternatives. The partner may insist that the initiator stop seeing a lover; drop out of school;
spend less time with single friends; devote less energy to work. In place
of these alternatives that separate the two socially, the partner suggests
activities that reinforce identity as a couple: spending more time with
the children; engaging in a common hobby; rebuilding a shared social
life. The partner may urge the initiator to consult a counselor, minister,
or social worker in the hope that a professional will help restore the
errant initiator to a proper place in the relationship.

And the partner just may manage to save the relationship. The initiator may find that the direct confrontation and the negotiations that fol-

In a direct confrontation, the partner reveals the initiator's secrets, exposing the subterfuge—and the impoverished state of the relationship.

For initiators to use decreased interaction, the fatal mistake, and/or rule violation rather than assume the responsibility for confrontation themselves seems not only to be the coward's way out but, if intentional, also unspeakably cruel. Consider, for a moment, the question of intent. An initiator is a person caught in an unhappy situation. Wanting to make the break and unable to directly confront the partner or to leave, the initiator's unhappiness finds expression in other ways: irritability, drunkenness, rudeness, displays of temper, absences, silence, withholding love.[22] Negative signals increasingly appear or—perhaps more accurately—the little symbols of civility and affection we reserve for our beloveds disappear. These signals are, in part, a reflection of the tension and stress initiators are experiencing.[23] They are weighing whether to stay or to go, and showing the agitation that normally accompanies making any major decision. In addition, concern about how to approach the partner also produces stress and changes in behavior.[24]

Further tension results because initiators are engaged, to varying degrees, in two different lifestyles and the strains eventually begin to show. As initiators become increasingly involved elsewhere, the signs of their transition—changed habits, conversation topics, new interests, physical changes—become more numerous. Controlling all the signals becomes more difficult. In addition, initiators are no longer as committed to maintaining the cover-up as they once were.[25] All these factors combine to exacerbate the display of discontent. As a result, initiators challenge the partner's definition of self and of the relationship. And while initiators may not deliberately set out to create such dissonance for the partner, they nonetheless realize their actions will provoke it.[26]

I could never have left Julie. She was so vulnerable, I just could not do it even though I didn't love her anymore. But I started disappointing her in lots of ways. I realized I was becoming someone that I knew she couldn't like. [HIGH SCHOOL TEACHER, AGE 26, SEPARATED AFTER LIVING TOGETHER 4 YEARS]

I remember this distinctly only because it really happened in the span of a couple of weeks. Two or three weeks in a row—it wasn't done on purpose. But when I look back I wonder subconsciously if I did. I came home at 4 and 5 in the morning, from whatever I was doing and I forgot my keys and it's stupid, but I did this, like two or three weeks in a row. I mean I'm no idiot, but I was doing this, and I had to wake her up. She always would let me in, you know. [FINANCE OFFICER, AGE 33, DIVORCED AFTER 7 YEARS]

It was at the point, I think, where I had almost totally decided myself and there was no real turning it around. It was more a question of how do I deliver the message? How do I discuss the possibility? I don't think I tried to persuade her. I think I just slung ultimatums at her all the time in the form of behavior and I didn't apologize for it or try to excuse it. I disguised it for some reason but I didn't deny it. She knew I was seeing other people, but then I got caught a lot. Call it whatever you want. It's not clear to me whether I wanted to get caught or not. I still don't know. We talked a lot about how I was unhappy. And we weren't having sexual relations. And it wasn't, you know, I wasn't saying, "I've got to get out of here," all the time. But I really can't recreate that dialogue very well. I'm sure that for me it was mostly nonverbal and mostly negative. Just hiding out. Going back to the study and shutting the door. Leave me alone was the message. And just not initiating anything that was at all mutual. I suspect more of it was just responding to my own feelings than it was a calculated display of negative. So how did I deliver the message? I think mostly behaviorally. Just withdrawal and absence and passivity. [PSYCHOLOGIST, AGE 44, DIVORCED AFTER 12 YEARS]

Although many factors contribute to the indirect methods described, the question of the initiator's intent remains a difficult issue to sort out. Sometimes, initiators retrospectively question their actions. Did they intentionally act to get their partners to assume the responsibility for changing the course of the relationship? "I didn't think so at the time, but now I wonder if I took my lover out publicly so my wife would catch me at it." On the other hand, some initiators admit they knew their actions were intentional. Initiators deliberately resort to the fatal mistake, rule violation, and decreased interaction when they not only no longer love the other person, but more commonly no longer like the partner. Interest in their own well-being overrides consideration for that of the partner. The security initiators derive from their alternatives and their desperation to be out of the relationship combine to create a situation in which the end justifies the use of any means to attain it.

In sum, when initiators shift the responsibility for the confrontation to the partner through these indirect methods, we cannot say that intent is always present, or that it is always absent. If we want the answer to this question, we must look carefully at the details of the individual case. Even then, we may not resolve the question, for many initiators do not know the answer themselves.

SIX

Trying

*C*ONFRONTATION creates the possibility of negotiation. Once the cover-up breaks down and both partners acknowledge that the relationship is deeply troubled, they're able to negotiate and to try. They enter into these negotiations differing in several important ways. For initiators, the transition has been in progress for some time. By the time confrontation occurs, their chosen alternative has often replaced the relationship. They have thought about life without the other person; they have considered it, learned about it, and, to varying degrees, experimented with it and moved into it. Moreover, they've concluded that the relationship is unsaveable and they can no longer continue in it. Partners, on the other hand, typically are still deeply invested in the relationship. They have not seriously considered the possibility of life on their own nor do they have a lifestyle that now fortuitously stands as a ready alternative to the relationship.

Of the many ways the two partners differ as they begin trying, a telling difference involves trying itself. Initiators feel that they already have tried.[1] They tried earlier when they first concluded the relationship was seriously troubled. They attempted to communicate their unhappiness and to change the partner and the relationship to better meet their needs. Failing, the initiator moved in other directions. Now the partner is ready to try. Oblivious to the advanced stage of the initiator's transition, the partner does not acknowledge the initiator's early efforts to save the relationship.[2] Thus, for the partner, the solution is simple: if both people try, they can succeed. The partner argues for another chance.

I'm not a quitter. It never occurred to me that if I did everything I could, if I was fully trying, that I could not save the relationship. [PSYCHOLOGIST, AGE 36, SEPARATED AFTER LIVING TOGETHER 6 YEARS]

I was hurt deeply. I was panicked because I needed him so much. And I still thought that I could pull it through. I had enough confidence in myself, I guess all the way through this that if I tried hard enough, I can save this relationship. So I started saying why don't we go for counseling, why don't we do this, or do that. [MEDICAL TECHNOLOGIST, AGE 30, DIVORCED AFTER 9 YEARS]

Sometimes the partner doesn't get to try. In the direct confrontation, the initiator refuses to negotiate—the decision to go is final. The incident that finally succeeds in getting the partner's attention may be the initiator's departure. If not already out the door, the initiator may be on the way.

I just said, "I've had it." And I knew that if I stayed, I would not survive. It was very painful to have to face the end of something. And I felt somewhat like a failure. Did I try hard enough? And I realized, well, I tried the best that I could. I did as much as I could with the resources I had and maybe I could have done more but that's all I could do at the time. [STOCKBROKER, AGE 35, SEPARATED AFTER LIVING TOGETHER 12 YEARS]

She said she never had a vacation and we didn't go out any place by ourselves, without the kids. What could I say? I said, I'm sorry—that was just my way. I meant nothing by it. It was just my way and I like to travel too. I was just locked into a lifestyle but I meant nothing by it and said I wasn't trying to be mean to you or anything like that, I was happy around the house and we should have gone out more often. She said, "I've had enough. I want to go places and do things," and I said, "I do, too, let's start." She said, "It's too late now." [PROCESS INSPECTOR, AGE 41, DIVORCED AFTER 19 YEARS]

The partner, left alone, protests that the initiator never tried.

I think she made a mistake, as I see it. I don't like the fact that she did what she did without wanting to fight for the marriage. I'll never change my opinion on that. Things could have been worked out if she was willing to try. [ELECTRICIAN, AGE 62, DIVORCED AFTER 39 YEARS]

I was surprised. I didn't realize that she saw a problem in the relationship and mostly I expressed my shock. I told her that I was also irritated and angry that she didn't tell me that there was a problem, that she, in a sense, wasn't giving me a chance to work things out with her. She's just saying there's a problem—she's clearly saying there's a problem now but there's no chance to work it out and try to see if we can change things for the better. She's just saying there's a problem, I'm leaving. Goodbye. [FURNITURE RESTORER, AGE 32, SEPARATED AFTER LIVING TOGETHER 9 YEARS]

DIRECT CONFRONTATION AND CHANGE

But sometimes the partner does get to try. A direct confrontation can have an unexpected effect. The two interact, perhaps with an intensity that has long been absent. This sudden intense exchange can remind the initiator of the other person's good traits and the ties that exist between them. In addition, the partner, perhaps for the first time, has the opportunity to present details about the couple's life together that the initiator has underplayed, forgotten, or ignored. (The initiator charges, "You never tried to be a parent to Michael." The partner responds, "But you never let me. You always took charge. You never let me do anything alone with him. You never gave us a chance to become close.") The partner poses alternative explanations that contradict the negative history of partner and relationship that the initiator has been constructing.

In stating the case to the initiator, the partner draws on his or her own experience of the life they've shared. Faced with possible loss, all the partner can see is the good in the relationship. While the initiator has taken a relationship mixed with good and bad and emphasized the bad, the partner now responds by focusing on the good. It is as if both partners were sifting the same sand through separate sieves and each retaining different grains. For every negative point the initiator presents as substantiating evidence, the partner calls forth examples that support an opposite definition of the situation. The partner focuses on the bond; the initiator on its disintegration. The partner recalls the good times; the initiator remembers the bad. As a result of the confrontation, the initiator sometimes becomes confused.

During a particularly bad evening, which turned into a weekend confrontation, I realized what I had been doing. I realized I had been putting things in categories of black and white. They were really more gray. I needed to deal with her and with the relationship in terms of the gray. Thinking in terms of black and white makes it too easy to leave. [JOURNALIST, AGE 32, SEPARATED AFTER LIVING TOGETHER 3 YEARS]

What happened next was that Annette and I did nonstop thinking about our problems. I told Karen that during this time I couldn't see her.

Annette and I were closer than we had been in years. And in fact, there were an awful lot of tears, an awful lot of guilt, an awful lot of recriminations and so forth, but we found that having this to talk about was consoling, in some ways. It was a certain amount of relief for me in being able to explain all of this, and a certain amount of relief for her, bad as it was, worse than she had anticipated, and also we found we were making love with each other and enjoying it, and that hadn't happened for a long, long time. [ADMINISTRATOR, AGE 44, SEPARATED AFTER 23 YEARS OF MARRIAGE]

The confrontation stimulates a deep probing of the past. As a consequence, the initiator's negative definitions of partner and relationship may be challenged and shaken. For the sake of the children, for the sake of a bond once deeply felt, for the sake of a partner who wants the relationship to continue, for the sake of self-respect, for the sake of failed hopes, for the sake of an unexpected tug at the heartstrings, for the sake of doubt, guilt, or faltering courage—for some or all of these reasons, the initiator agrees to try.

The partner rises to the occasion. He or she treats the relationship as a priority and devotes energy to it, working to make the other person stay.[3] The partner channels efforts in directions that repeat the steps the initiator took earlier. Having now acknowledged that the relationship is troubled, the partner tries to change self and the relationship in ways to better meet the initiator's needs. The partner's work is already laid out, for the initiator has been pointing out traits that need correcting for some time.[4]

He had no desire and it was all my fault. I was overweight, which didn't bother him in the slightest for 5 years, but all of the sudden it bothered him. I was at first flabbergasted and went on a diet, but if it wasn't that it was something else. I honestly couldn't lose 60 or 80 pounds overnight. It would take a while, anything I did, but it just wasn't good enough for him. Why should I sleep with you? You're this, you're that. This is after 5 years of being very close when all of the sudden, I could do nothing good enough. [TRAVEL AGENT, AGE 27, SEPARATED AFTER LIVING TOGETHER 6 YEARS]

The partner responds to the initiator's complaints by trying to become someone the initiator can once again love. As a clinical psychologist told me:

It's like finding a job. If you thought that there were no jobs out there and you were not going to be able to do what you wanted to do, you'd quit trying, right? You'd do something else. But as long as

there are ads, you read the newspapers, you see what the qualifica-
tions are that they want, you try to re-do your resume to fit the ads,
and you keep trying to find work in your area.

The partner may try to change his or her appearance by dieting or taking greater care with clothing and hair. The partner may eliminate habits that annoy the initiator, or inject creativity and passion into the couple's sex life. Courtship patterns are reinstituted with a newfound intensity. There is a desperation and hence an unnaturalness about them, for now the rituals of courtship are concentrated efforts to stave off an unwanted loss. The partner may try to bring romance back into the relationship: candlelight dinners, conversations about happy times in the past, a vacation or weekend away, doing more things together. The partner may attempt to become more interesting to the initiator, perhaps by some program of self-improvement, perhaps by becoming involved in an attention-getting affair. The partner may demonstrate a greater interest in the initiator's activities. If the initiator likes horseracing, the partner may start going to the track; if the initiator paints, the partner may take up watercolors. Often, the partner becomes fascinated with magazine articles or books on how to improve relationships.

In addition to changing self in ways that will appeal to the initiator, the partner may try to change the relationship, again following the initiator's earlier path. The partner may suggest a change in the rules of the relationship. ("If you need more freedom, how about a night out?" "I've always been monogamous, but if you want to start bringing people home, we could try that.") The partner may suggest a shift in the division of labor. ("I'll get a job." "I'll go 50–50 with you on housework and childcare." "I'll stop working so much and be around more.") Perhaps, this time, it is the partner who suggests changing the structure by adding a new member—a baby.

The partner also tries to change the initiator. Intuitively on target, he or she tries to reshape the initiator's interests and alternatives. The partner may insist that the initiator stop seeing a lover; drop out of school; spend less time with single friends; devote less energy to work. In place of these alternatives that separate the two socially, the partner suggests activities that reinforce identity as a couple: spending more time with the children; engaging in a common hobby; rebuilding a shared social life. The partner may urge the initiator to consult a counselor, minister, or social worker in the hope that a professional will help restore the errant initiator to a proper place in the relationship.

And the partner just may manage to save the relationship. The initiator may find that the direct confrontation and the negotiations that follow are reminders of the good in the other person or in the relationship and the two define the relationship as both worth saving and saveable. Both people try, and they succeed. But those who claim victory are a select group. Most often, even if both people are willing at the outset, trying fails.

OBSTACLES TO SUCCESS

The couple is working against almost insurmountable odds. The initiator's transition has been in progress for some time, with shifts in ideology, friendship groups, commitment, and lifestyle. The result is social relocation and, with it, a transformation of identity. The initiator is, in a very real sense, a different person. Nowhere is this identity transformation more dramatically revealed than in the telling words many initiators eventually utter, "You don't know me anymore." Saving the relationship requires the initiator to again engage in redefinition of self, other, and relationship. These alterations are as extensive as those that preceded the confrontation. They take time. Obviously, people do save relationships.[5] But success is seldom quickly achieved as a result of the efforts that immediately follow confrontation.

Even with both people acting as willing participants in the effort, trying usually results in cosmetic changes that do not alter the fundamental social changes that have gradually occurred throughout the initiator's transition. Trying, for both people, at this point means trying to be someone they are not. Such changes, artificially imposed, are difficult to maintain.

> I was very upset, hurt, crying, but at the back of my mind I thought well, maybe this too will change if I can continue to play—play, that's an interesting choice of words—play this open, warm, loving type of person, that maybe I'll get her back, still, and not be too angry or hostile at her. So I probably kept a lot of that inside which would be a more natural reaction. I wanted to be so solid and reasonable and open and communicative and all these good warm things so as not to lose her. I definitely felt a mix of feelings, but it was a controlled reaction. I thought about the best way to face this, to understand what's going on, what's going to help the relationship, help me get what I want—those sort of ruminations. [FURNITURE RESTORER, AGE 32, SEPARATED AFTER LIVING TOGETHER 9 YEARS]
>
> I saw a movie with Lee Remick on TV—the story of her divorce or something and it shows her buying nightgowns and trying to be nice and you spend all that time doing those things because you think that

that's gonna solve everything. I did 'em all. Oh, I never raised my voice anymore. I mean, after I found out he was in the affair everything was—you know, he'd say, "I'm sorry," and we'd sit at the fire at night, drinking wine and talking about it. [TEACHER, AGE 35, DIVORCED AFTER 11 YEARS]

Both people come to sense that the period of trying is a result of the confrontation, and that what is going on is not the relationship, but something else. The partner wishes things were back to normal. The initiator may long for stability, but "back to normal" is not the direction the initiator wants the relationship to go. Efforts to change things remain superficial, tending ultimately to break down. The necessary social change—redefinition of self, other, and relationship—does not occur. The situation may improve, but it is usually temporary.

I decided to make a try for it, but it was after the first two weeks the relationship settled back down to what it had been. The first two weeks, I could do no wrong, she would listen attentively, never disagree, and instead of Hagar the Horrible, there was a pussycat around. It was like a totally different person. I mean there was no vestige. She would say, "I'm going to do this, is that all right?" instead of just doing it, which is what she usually would do. I think perhaps my dissatisfaction brought her to panic. The fact that I had threatened to leave and physically left, even if it was only for six or seven hours, showed that I would really do it. I think that there was a little bit of panic in her reaction from that day forward as to just how stable our relationship was. It wasn't a comfortable situation to work within. [DIRECTOR OF DISTRIBUTION, AGE 36, DIVORCED AFTER 11 YEARS]

The next few weeks, I overreacted. I took her up to see a concert and I started doing a few things around the house, so I would do some of the things she was complaining about and her response to that was, she just laughed and said, "It's obvious it won't last. It's too out of character," but that was her reaction to it, that it wouldn't last. [PRODUCTION MANAGER, AGE 52, DIVORCED AFTER 25 YEARS]

When the immediate crisis came up, we became very close and were very good together, but that dissipated fairly quickly. We never really got it all together again. We were sitting around on tenterhooks and worrying about things, but the crisis that had driven us together wasn't holding us together. It was kind of keeping us bumping into each other from afar. [ADMINISTRATOR, AGE 44, SEPARATED AFTER 23 YEARS OF MARRIAGE]

The phrase ''bumping into each other from afar'' is an apt description of two partners who, while inhabiting the same physical location, inhabit separate social spaces. Now they are interacting with heightened frequency and intensity. The differences, the disharmonies, come into sharp focus.

I think I came to the conclusion that it wasn't going to work after the counseling attempt and I don't think we ever both focused on trying together after that. What he calls trying is a matter of meeting some of my demands. It isn't really changing the nature of the whole relationship. He is not going to change into a person that is interested in the kinds of things I am interested in. And I got to the point where I thought, well, what right do I have to demand that of him anyway. I don't expect to change into the kind of person that he would rather have. [OWNER, USED BOOK STORE, SEPARATED AFTER LIVING TOGETHER 8 YEARS]

We tried to find some activity that we could share. She suggested we start a garden, and I never liked gardening. I suggested we take a bridge class, but she wasn't good at cards. I suggested sex, but she didn't think that was funny. The real trouble was that she was never really good at that, either. We discovered that about the only thing we had in common was eating, so we decided to go to dinner once a week. The idea was that we would have an evening all to ourselves that was special, but either we didn't have anything to say, or what we did have to say just created an argument. The whole thing was a disaster. It just confirmed for me how little we had in common. [TEACHER/TECHNICAL SCHOOL/WRITER, AGE 39, DIVORCED AFTER 18 YEARS]

Trying is further undermined by the power imbalance in the relationship. The partner is at a distinct disadvantage. The initiator enters negotiations with a social world the partner is excluded from. Even when the initiator forswears alternatives in order to try, he or she nevertheless knows these alternatives exist and are (in most cases) still available. The initiator realizes that self-validation can be found elsewhere, and alternatives, real or imagined, create power.[6] It was, after all, the existence of alternative resources that brought the initiator to confront the partner or to behave so that the partner initiated a confrontation.

The power imbalance between initiator and partner is made vivid by the initiator's readiness to withdraw, potentially changing the partner's life regardless of personal wishes about how that life might proceed. The initiator thus becomes the decision-maker. By stating complaints, the initiator sets up the conditions for trying. Though initiator and partner both agree to try, the partner assumes the burden of saving the relationship. While striving to meet the initiator's needs, the partner constantly seeks evidence of progress in the initiator's response to every word, every action. As Rubin notes, "If I have to ask for acknowledgment of my status, I am already in a singularly disadvantaged position."[7] The harder the partner tries, the more the disadvantage compounds. Though hoping to regain the initiator's love, the partner tries to maintain a performance knowing that failure means losing the relationship. Partners complain of their lack of control, their sense of powerlessness.

I had lost my identity somewhere along the way. And I kept losing my identity. I kept letting him make all the decisions. I couldn't work. I wasn't able to be myself. I was letting someone else take over. I didn't have any control over it. I didn't know how to stop it. I was unsure that if anything really happened, I could actually make it on my own or not. [GRADUATE STUDENT, AGE 30, SEPARATED AFTER 12 YEARS OF MARRIAGE]

Understandably, partners are not at their best under these circumstances. When they most want and need to be attractive, their confidence is undermined, their ego in disarray. Moreover, in their attempt to fix things, partners tend to devote less time and attention to other activities.

She said I never was interested in her work, so I started reading the books she had laying around. [STUDENT, AGE 24, SEPARATED AFTER LIVING TOGETHER 4 YEARS]

I was so afraid I would lose him that I stopped going out with my girlfriends and I tried to plan things for us to do together—you know, to bring the romance back. [SECRETARY, AGE 30, SEPARATED AFTER LIVING TOGETHER 3 YEARS]

They react by withdrawing from other social settings that enhance a sense of self, and instead invest increased energy and time in the relationship. This strategy may sometimes improve the situation, yet in relationships that end it has ironic consequences. First, partners tend to become less interesting to initiators, with less of a life of their own to bring to the relationship. Second, the longer trying goes on, the greater the investment in the relationship and the greater the renunciation of rewards and opportunities from other sources.[8] Should separation occur, the relationship is gone and they have diminished other resources they may have had.[9] The partner gives up self to gain self—and loses.[10]

I had to exhaust myself thinking of ways to make this man and my marriage work and never once thought of putting demands in, hey, you know, so that I would constantly be going crazy trying to find out what makes him happy, what does he like, and I had this fear, even though the relationship was unhappy, you know, of losing him, so my whole life became concerned with making this guy happy and I never knew me. I'm just starting to know me now. [SOCIAL SERVICES ORGANIZER/TEACHER, AGE 40, DIVORCED AFTER 12 YEARS]

I think I spent so much time trying to please her that I wasn't even myself anymore. I was always trying to accommodate whatever she wanted to do. I gave up everything else. I did it because I wanted to be with her at all times. I wanted to do stuff with her. The more rejected I felt, the more I gave up. [SALESMAN, AGE 30, DIVORCED AFTER 3 YEARS]

There is still another obstacle to success. Trying has its own cost. It takes energy, dedication, and concentration, and in the rush of daily life other demands are constantly being made. Habits develop because they are comfortable, and once stability is again achieved in a relationship (i.e., the crisis appears over), those habits usually reappear. We try, perhaps succeeding for a while, then fall back into the previous routine.

Many couples engage in repeated cycles of trying. Often, both partners hesitate to sever ties. The relationship may vacillate between active trying and passive acceptance of the status quo, because of the failure of each to pull the other to a common definition and the inability of either to make the break.[11] Such cycles not only drain the participants emotionally, but contribute to the relationship's demise. The initiator, who perhaps entered skeptically but willingly into negotiations with the partner, may conclude that the original intuition to end the relationship was correct. Furthermore, repeated failures gradually chip away at the partner's belief that the relationship can be salvaged. Despite the willing participation of initiator and partner at the outset, trying and failing tend to convince both that the relationship is unsaveable.

Some partners try, however, and keep the relationship going despite all obstacles. Out of desperation, fear, anger, or unhappiness, these partners respond to the potential loss of the relationship by shifting the initiator's costs and benefits of uncoupling. Partners draw on their own resources, making every possible effort to hang onto the relationship.[12] Initiators stay, but not because they once again find self-validation in the relationship. They stay because they can no longer afford to go.

Some partners hold the relationship together by making life more comfortable for the initiator, thus increasing the benefits of staying: reducing the initiator's household chores, catering to particular wishes, allowing free pursuit of alternatives, giving attention or granting solitude—whatever it takes to keep them in the fold. Other partners respond in ways that increase the initiator's cost of leaving. Some become deeply disorganized or depressed, exhibiting weakness or self-destructive behavior. They may attempt suicide. Others may threaten to withhold resources—the children, financial support, joint property. Sometimes partners try to keep the initiator by acting in ways that reduce whatever resources the initiator has.[13]

I went over where she worked and told her to leave my guy alone. [STUDENT, AGE 21, SEPARATED AFTER LIVING TOGETHER 2 YEARS]

He had been counting on an inheritance from his mother, and I figured he wasn't going to be able to support two separate households without it, so I went to his mother—we had always been close—and told her what was going on and she reacted just like I thought. She wasn't going to give him the money if he left. [HOME SALES REPRESENTATIVE, AGE 45, DIVORCED AFTER 10 YEARS OF MARRIAGE]

This man she had been seeing was married and lived in Denver. She met him at a meeting, and after that he would arrange his business and come here to see her. After she told me about it, I called this man's boss and made an appointment to go out there and talk to him about this executive of his who was running around. I had found out some other things about him that would not have benefited the company had they gotten out. As it turned out, the president was very glad I had come. [LAWYER, AGE 38, DIVORCED AFTER 12 YEARS]

Some partners may abuse the initiator physically or destroy property. Some threaten to destroy the other person's future—even their life—if they leave.

Initiators may stay, but for all practical purposes, they are gone. Life, meaning, and self-validation have not been reconstituted in the relationship and initiators continue to derive their identity from alternative resources. Should they lose those resources, they will find another social niche allowing them to sustain their identity apart from the relationship. The alternatives from which they might draw self-validation are many and varied, as described in Chapter 1. And the niche may not always be one others would view as self-validating, for sometimes people find identity in what appears to be a loss of it: for example, depression, drugs, alcohol, or the pursuit of many lovers.[14] Whatever the choice, initiators find sustenance for themselves, staying on, "in" but not "of" the relationship. Even at that, the partner's success may be temporary. Some unexpected change in resources may shift the balance of power and the partner's apparent victory turns out only to temporarily delay the initiator's departure.[15]

TRYING AS A TERMINATION STRATEGY

Trying may take yet another form. The initiator agrees to try. But, despite the partner's promises, arguments, pleas, and reminiscences, the confrontation has not changed a thing. While the partner defines the relationship as saveable, the initiator does not. The initiator's goal is to terminate the relationship and separation is an important step in that direction. For the initiator to leave (and, as we will see, for the partner also to go on), the partner must not only conclude that the relationship is in serious trouble, but that it is unsaveable. So the initiator will continue to display discontent until the partner comes to this conclusion. The initiator agrees to try, but only in order to convince the partner the relationship is over. The initiator's idea is to try, but to fail.

> Yes, I do really feel that he might have finally at long last listened to what I was saying. It was too late. I no longer cared what he did for me. I had drifted by then. I had drifted so far away. I think he tried. I really do think he tried and I just didn't care anymore. No matter what he did, it wouldn't have helped. It was too late. It was past the point where everything was gone. [LEATHER CRAFTSMAN, AGE 42, SEPARATED AFTER LIVING TOGETHER 12 YEARS]

> I think earlier I tried with the marriage and all, but I found myself getting away from it. What I mean by getting away from the marriage is that after a while I didn't try anymore because I felt I had a different sexual preference. There was no way the marriage could work. What I had to do was convince Leslie it wouldn't work without telling her why. [FINANCE OFFICER, AGE 33, DIVORCED AFTER 7 YEARS]

The initiator grants the partner the opportunity to try, but not to succeed.[16] He or she tries in order to gradually ease out of the relationship, allowing the partner time to adjust.[17] By overcoming the partner's potential objections of "but you never tried," or "but you never let me try," the initiator hopes to get the partner to agree that the relationship is over. Sometimes initiators agree to try to convince themselves that they have given the relationship their best effort. Some try for other reasons, of course. They may try in order to prove to other people that they have done everything they could to work things out. Obviously, if both partners have tried and failed, and if both agree the relationship is over, the potential negative social consequences are reduced. In addition, some married initiators agree to try to gain some recognition from the court that they have made a legitimate effort to do something about the relationship before abandoning it.[18] But ambivalent, they are not.

Subsequent negotiations are thus at cross-purposes. The initiator sees the relationship as unsaveable. The partner views it as saveable. Trying is characterized by the efforts of both partners to pull the other to accept their definition of the relationship.

I was being deceived and tricked and she knew very clearly, and I stated very clearly, that I did not want to bring another child into the marriage. See, that was where we were at odds. I'm talking divorce, and she's talking having babies. [ADVERTISING SALESMAN, AGE 38, DIVORCED AFTER 8 YEARS]

I went to the library and I got myself a lot of books. I read a lot of books about marriage, you know, books dealing with marriage and marriage problems. On the other hand, she was reading different materials. Materials dealing with the women's liberation movement. She was reading books like Take Care of #1, *you're the most important person. I say, well, what about commitment, what about the demands of the family on yourself and on me, what about the kids, and we have to make adjustments for the kids if we want to stay with them as a family. And that isn't what it says in your book. And she got very upset about it. And this thing that she came up with, "You're my enemy and oppressor" was based on material that was boring to me. I said, you know, that's not what we said when we got married. I say we are a family, we can do a lot of things as a family. We can be a family and enjoy it.* [SOCIAL SERVICES WORKER, AGE 44, DIVORCED AFTER 19 YEARS]

While the partner tries to save the relationship, the initiator tries to get the partner to accept an unwanted transition: uncoupling. This is not easy, for the partner is fighting not only to save the relationship and preserve identity, but to save face. When our status as a partner is threatened by the decision of the other person, not only do we question our own competence, but we fear that others too may question the competence with which we have carried out that role. To loss of substance is added loss of social honor,[19] which explains a partner's wholehearted tendency to try to save the relationship, even when, by personal admission, the relationship "hasn't been that good."

Initiators must appear to try and simultaneously convey the message that trying is not working.[20] When the goal is separation, initiators cannot afford the luxury of sentiment. They can't make the break if they allow themselves to be moved by the partner's pleas, fears, attractiveness, or threats. If they are affected—even momentarily—they dare not show it, for the partner would take even the smallest signal as a possible change of heart. Initiators cultivate a stance toward the partner that is sufficiently angry or benevolent or detached to allow them to proceed toward physical separation, insulating themselves emotionally from the partner's efforts.

> So many times we would stay up all night long arguing and saying, this is it, this is it and then fall asleep and then the next day, oh well, let's try. In other words we had gone through it so many times that it was really hard to say I'm going to go and then to go. There was something really different about it this time. I didn't get upset at all. I didn't cry once over it and it was kind of like I really knew I had to just keep that kind of facade. I had to be serious, I couldn't change my mind, I couldn't break down, you know, because if I broke down, then I probably would not go through with it. Putting on this cold facade was really painful and really hurt, but I knew from the past that if I had not done something that we would have ended up in the same cycle again. We would have both gotten real upset with each other and started looking at the negative side of it and the scareyness of it, and then probably I would change my mind. [MUSIC TEACHER, AGE 28, SEPARATED AFTER 6 YEARS OF MARRIAGE]

> I made up my mind that I was going to follow this through and get out of it as delicately as I could without harming the person. I guess I'd been out of love with the person for about a year before I broke up. But the person wasn't ready. Really couldn't understand it, really couldn't believe it. We talked. Didn't want to hear it. I wasn't getting through. So I had to deal with it in other ways. I had to change attitudes. I had to learn how to deal with myself, I had to learn how to be patient, I had to learn how to pull myself out and look at things, and I had to stop loving—to really say I can't love anymore like this because I'm going to be used, so I just have to get this over and done with. Then I have to help this person in order to get them out of here. Because I don't want any hassles with the relationship. I don't want any animosity, I don't want any hard feelings, and I want the best type of "get out" that I can. And it took me about six months to do that. When I finally decided—hey, I don't need this—I could deal with it on a different basis, and I could look at things, and I could actually be on the outside, still be in the relationship, and still deal with it. [X-RAY TECHNOLOGIST, AGE 35, SEPARATED AFTER LIVING TOGETHER 4 YEARS]

The initiator, socially and psychologically absent from the relationship for some time, is in a tough spot. Often the partner has turned to no one for comfort about the relationship. Unlike the initiator, who has confided in others, the partner hesitates to take this step, for fear that talking about it will change things, or from a belief that the crisis is a temporary one that will be resolved—then no one will ever have to know. Having always had the responsibility for taking care of the partner, the initiator is keenly aware that the partner especially needs taking care of now. Some initiators feel an obligation to fulfill their role as caretaker at the very moment they are trying to put that role behind.[21] They face the competing demands of leaving the partner, while at the same time preparing the partner for the loss.

Some initiators, sensitive to the partner's need for consolation and unable to provide it, encourage the partner to turn somewhere else for comfort and emotional release.[22] They may secretly solicit someone to befriend the partner, handing the partner's emotional care over to one who can be counted on to listen and provide emotional support throughout the coming events—a neighbor, an older child, a relative, or friend of the partner.[23] Other initiators, out of concern for the partner and secure in their own resources, simply withdraw from certain relationships they value, thereby leaving a mutual friend or loved one free to respond to the partner. Such actions not only ease the initiator's departure, but also exhibit a concern for the partner; they serve to mitigate the pain of uncoupling for both. The result, though kind in intent, is nonetheless expeditious. By recruiting a resource person for the partner, the initiator supplies a confidant (or possibly even a transitional person) with whom the partner will share secrets about the relationship—a necessary step in the partner's transition.

The initiator may suggest that the partner see a professional—in effect, hiring someone to be responsible for the consolation process.[24] Seeking professional help may even be the partner's idea. In an effort to save the relationship, the partner suggests counseling. The initiator agrees.[25] The initiator goes a few times, participates superficially, then drops out, complaining that the counselor is ineffective, the proceedings are biased, or that the partner is obviously the one who needs help—so why should they both go? The initiator abandons the proceedings, leaving the partner alone to develop a supportive relationship with the counselor.[26] The partner has a person who provides an emotional outlet and solace—functions normally supplied by a spouse.[27] Moreover, by dropping out, the initiator makes the point that trying didn't work.

Counseling and Definition Negotiation

Alternatively, the initiator may agree to or suggest counseling in order to use the counseling sessions to convince the partner that the relationship is unsaveable. Under these circumstances, joint counseling—though entered into with apparent common purpose—becomes another arena in which partners attempt to negotiate. They have opposing goals, however, and these conflicts sometimes cause great difficulty in choosing a counselor. Partners will push for a professional whom they believe will be committed to saving the relationship: the person who married them, a counseling center that represents their religious denomination, or a rabbi, priest, or minister. Initiators, on the other hand, will lobby for a counselor with no apparent bias toward keeping relationships together. Once a counselor is selected both go, expecting the counselor will side with their individual positions. Both compete for the support of this third person who has now entered the fray.[28]

While counselors can describe the general trends they observe among their clients, like sociologists, they are unable to predict what's going to happen in the individual case. Counseling may act as a safety valve to diffuse tensions, in effect allowing relationships to hold together, although the difficulties remain unresolved. All things are possible, from reconciliation to termination. Nonetheless, counselors note that in most cases by the time a couple seeks counseling, it is too late. They report that although two partners declare in each other's presence that they both want to explore the situation objectively and save the relationship if at all possible, in private the two frequently reveal their opposing goals.

> *I've gotten so I can usually tell whether or not it's a dump-job on the first phone call. The person will say, "Listen, I'm bringing in so-and-so" and then proceed to detail the situation a little, putting so-and-so in a bad light, and how bad things are, and then goes on about how so-and-so needs support, and finally gets around to how they need to be brought to understand how bad things are. Sometimes they are very direct, telling me they have someone else who is waiting and they need my help to get this over with.* [SOCIAL WORKER]

> *She took me aside and said, "I want to divorce him, but haven't told him yet." And he took me aside and said, "I used to be an alcoholic but I've reformed. I want to be a good husband. I really love this woman and I want to do everything I can to save this relationship."* [CLINICAL PSYCHOLOGIST]

Sometimes a counseling session allows the initiator to reveal what she or he has not been able to say before. Encouraged by the presence of the counselor, the initiator directly confronts the partner, giving vent to feelings previously unexpressed: "I want a divorce"; "You disgust me''; "I never loved you''; "I'm gay''; "I've wanted out of the relationship for five years''; "You have never satisfied me sexually''; "There's somebody else.'' With the disclosure of this news, the partner realizes, for the first time, that the relationship is past all hope. The words, uttered before a minister or therapist and perhaps other family members bring not only despair and resignation, but public humiliation, as the counseling session is transformed into a degradation ceremony in which the partner's failures as a partner are publicly proclaimed.[29]

We had one session with the counselor, with the whole family there. It was a disaster. Everyone ended up crying, except me, I didn't have any tears, and she said, "I just don't love him anymore, I used to love him, but I just don't love him anymore.'' She said it earlier, too, when it was just she and I in front of the counselor. That was one of the things that came out and I asked her if I just couldn't try to make it work and she said, "If I had feelings for you, I would, I just don't have any more feelings for you.'' This hurt. I said, "How do you think this makes me feel now, when I'm just told I'm a failure as a husband?'' but it didn't make any difference. I was a complete loser. It was pretty much like in the counseling she just wanted to say it again. She wants out, she doesn't love me, and it was almost like the finale. We were altogether as a family and she just pronounced me unloved and announced she definitely wanted out and wanted to have her freedom. While the kids were there. It ended up with him asking them to give us all a big hug and kiss and they were crying and we were crying and it was obviously the end. [PRODUCTION MANAGER, AGE 52, DIVORCED AFTER 25 YEARS]

But a direct confrontation, even with the counselor's supportive presence, may not yet be in the initiator's repertoire. The initiator may continue to hope that the counselor will say the relationship ought to end, or that the partner will draw that conclusion from the proceedings. Counselors report that initiators sometimes manipulate the partner by dropping information a little at a time until the partner finally says what the initiator never could: "Sounds like you don't love me'' or "Sounds like you don't want to live with me any more.'' Some counselors report that in family therapy it is often the children who finally suggest that the relationship ought to end.

Sometimes no one says it. The initiator is unable to make the disclosures that would bring about an anguished but speedy reversal of the partner's hope that the relationship can be saved. The dilemma goes unresolved, as each partner continues to work unsuccessfully toward separate ends. In frustration and fatigue, they abandon counseling for a while, only to resurrect it periodically, along with renewed bursts of trying. The couple may find that seeking professional help fails for an unexpected reason.

> *After a year of counseling we were still sitting there screaming at each other—they gave us plenty of time. We had co-therapists and they would give us two hours if we needed it and often we did. We had a male and a female therapist, so there were 4 every time, which we really needed because we took sides and we wanted to get people on our side and we were very competitive and this way at least somebody was on everybody's side. At least you could feel like they were all the time. But after a year of therapy we would go in and scream at each other the whole time until one time the male therapist stood up and said, "I'm not coming anymore. I don't care what you do. I'm just not going to sit here and listen to this anymore." And he walked out. So that was the end of the therapy. I felt like, well, that was the end of that.* [LEARNING DISABILITIES TEACHER, AGE 49, DIVORCED AFTER 23 YEARS]

Regardless of what transpires between counselor and clients, counseling can have unintended consequences for a relationship. Though people often seek professional help in an effort to keep their troubles private, in reality they're making their secrets public to another person. Bringing in a specialist to deal with the relationship affects the partner's definition of the relationship. How can the partner deny the seriousness of the situation if the couple seek the advice of an expert? Furthermore, if other people are aware that the couple are seeing a professional, they will react in ways that create additional changes in the couple's social life. And should counseling fail, or be abandoned without resolution in either direction, the relationship's troubled status gains additional confirmation.[30]

Separation

The initiator may suggest a temporary separation as a way of trying. The initiator says: "I need some space"; "Perhaps we ought to see other people for a while, so we can see how we really feel about each other"; "I have to find myself and figure out what I want out of life"; "We need some time to think this through"; or, "I'd like to try being on my own for a while." At some time in our lives, we all have either heard these words or said them. Again, the initiator's concern for the partner appears. Not wanting to hurt, the initiator encourages the temporary separation as a further means of bringing the other person to accept the idea that the relationship is unsaveable, to shift the partner to rely on outside resources, to initiate the physical breach gently.[31]

> *Even at that point, at initial separation, I wasn't being honest. I knew fairly certainly that when we separated, it was for good. I let her believe that it was a means for us first finding out what was happening, and then eventually possibly getting back together.* [ARCHITECT, AGE 34, DIVORCED AFTER 8 YEARS OF MARRIAGE]

Separating "temporarily" is not without its benefits for the initiator, for the physical break can be managed with as little ill will as possible. The benefits to the partner are questionable, however. Separating temporarily as a way of trying is undoubtedly easier for the partner to accept than a separation that clearly signals the beginning of the end. Yet a separation that occurs under the guise of trying does not cause the partner to redefine the relationship as unsaveable. The partner continues to hope and to try, investing energy in a relationship that, for the initiator, is over.

But separation can give a clear signal that trying has failed. Unable, by more gentle and gradual methods, to bring the partner to agree that the relationship is unsaveable, the initiator may abandon the pretense of trying. The initiator leaves, catching the partner off-guard.

> *We were having a tenants' meeting at our apartment. I came home from work to straighten up and discovered that her things were gone. Everything had been going so well for so long that this possibility had not even crossed my mind. I was totally confused. So I called her at her office. She said she had left me, that she just couldn't do it anymore. I started crying and said, "Well, can't we just talk about it?" And she said, "I've tried, but it didn't work. I've got nothing more to say. I'm sorry about the meeting, but I just cannot be with you anymore, even for that."* [TEACHER, AGE 31, SEPARATED AFTER LIVING TOGETHER 4 YEARS]

Moving out is a public act. The person responsible for catapulting the couples' problems into the public eye bears the brunt of the social reaction. When the partner still wants the relationship to continue, the responsibility for breaking up is never an easy burden to assume—and, in fact, most initiators don't.[32] Instead, they continue to display discontent to convince the partner that the relationship is unsaveable. Separation eventually occurs because the partner responds to the initiator's display either by initiating a separation or by behaving so that the initiator has legitimate reason to do so.[33]

The result is the fascinating but false impression that the partner is the initiator, and the social responsibility for the separation falls to the partner.[34] But appearances often deceive. Although partners sometimes act in ways that cause others to attribute the responsibility for separation to them (and, indeed, partners often lay this unwelcome burden at their own feet), they do not assume the role of initiator as I have defined it: the person who first begins a social transition out of the relationship. The partner's actions are precipitated by the initiator's display of discontent, and occur, for the most part, without benefit of a social transition similar to the initiator's, which would prepare the partner for the physical break.[35]

Separation results from the same indirect methods discussed earlier: a fatal mistake, rule violation, or decreased interaction. The fatal mistake can be the catalyst for separation—a partner cannot correct the flaw that, if corrected, would allow the relationship to continue. The initiator not only sets the criteria for whether or not trying succeeds, but sometimes also establishes a deadline. The passing of that deadline serves as notification to the partner that the effort has failed, justifying separation.[36]

> *It was over for me. I was aware when that happened because I knew when I got involved with this woman that there was no hope at that time for my marriage, and I thought this was a very clear message to me that we didn't have anything going for us. But what happened in the meantime, I had said to myself, this was six weeks before Christmas, that if things don't drastically change in the next six weeks that will be it. So six weeks before Christmas I told her. We sat down and we talked and I said this is it. I said that in six weeks if she didn't change, which I knew she wasn't going to, that I was going to separate.* [ADVERTISING SALESMAN, AGE 38, DIVORCED AFTER 8 YEARS]

Physical separation occurs, but the initiator points to the partner's behavior as the cause of it. No matter who leaves, the partner assumes the social responsibility for the separation.

The partner may order the initiator to leave, threaten to walk out, or actually do it as a response to the initiator's decreased interaction.

> *I wanted out of the marriage, but there was no way she would ever go for a divorce. I decided I would treat her as if we were divorced. You've heard of these do-it-yourself divorces? Well, that's sort of what I did. I slept on the couch, I never spoke to her, pretended she wasn't there. Just lived my own life. Finally, she threw me out.* [PRODUCE MANAGER, AGE 36, DIVORCED AFTER 11 YEARS.]

The partner may initiate the physical separation because of the initiator's rule violation. In a moment of anger, no longer able to bear the conflict or tolerate the ambiguity, or simply when dignity is at its lowest ebb, the partner suggests—or even demands—separation.[37]

> He knew I was monogamous and that I wanted him to be. We had talked and talked about that, because I didn't think it was fair that he should see other people and because of it, I risk getting AIDS. Then that night I walk into a bar—his bar—and there he was with someone else. I couldn't believe it, after all our talk. I just walked out. I told him when he called the next day that I didn't want to see him for a while. [SALESCLERK, RETAIL CLOTHING, AGE 35, SEPARATED AFTER LIVING TOGETHER 2 YEARS]

When the partner initiates physical separation, the expected outcome is reconciliation. The partner takes this step either to relieve tensions or possibly as a threat that may lead to reform. The initiator takes advantage of the suggestion, however.[38] The initiator either beats a hasty retreat or holds the door while the partner does the same. Later, the surprised partner finds the way back into the relationship blocked.

Displaying discontent until separation occurs as a result of some fatal mistake, decreased interaction, or rule violation is an indirect method for terminating relationships. Because initiators are often unable to be direct—to express a wish to separate or leave—they react in ways that achieve the same result, but shift the responsibility. Again, these indirect strategies give us pause. In the last chapter, we considered the initiator's indirect strategies and the question of intended consequences. Let us reconsider them now, focusing instead on unintended consequences.

While the fatal mistake, rule violation, and decreased interaction have a similar result (the partner takes the blame for the separation), they raise different issues. Consider, first, the fatal mistake. Relationships end because something is irritatingly and irretrievably wrong. The potential for a fatal mistake is always present, because fatal mistakes are, after all, grounded in behavior. The question worthy of pursuit here concerns the dynamic of a particular form of fatal mistake: once a flaw has been pointed out, it has a tendency to become routinized rather than reduced; exacerbated rather than excised. For a relationship in trouble, the consequences of repeatedly noting an irritating characteristic can affect negotiations in unanticipated (and fatal) directions.

This paradoxical but unintended result is not peculiar to relationships in trouble. Once a behavior has been labeled deviant, the continuation of that behavior often seems to flow naturally from the alteration of individual self-concept and opportunities that accompany its identification.[39] The perplexing dilemma is: how do we alter or eliminate some unwanted behavior without triggering the negative consequences for self-concept and opportunities that often accompany singling out some specific trait in order to deal with it?

While the initiator's focus on the partner's flaws can have unintended detrimental consequences, rule violation and decreased interaction inadvertently can bestow on the partner an unanticipated benefit. True, the partner responds by initiating a break-up he or she is personally opposed to. It is hard to imagine someone in this position agreeing that unintended benefits have resulted. But, as the saying goes, it's an ill wind that blows nobody good. One of the fundamental rules of interaction is that we cooperate to help the other person save face.[40] By violating rules or decreasing interaction until the partner takes charge and changes the relationship's course, the initiator gives the partner an opportunity to save face. Rather than experiencing the humiliation of unilateral rejection, partners can tell themselves and others that *they* were the ones who had enough, and who asked for separation. Partners can assert that they had control over the outcome, rather than being the passive recipient of someone else's decision.[41] Perhaps the ultimate irony of uncoupling is that we follow the rules of interaction, even when ending it.[42]

§

SEVEN

The Initiator's Advantage

*T*HE decision to separate may be the result of discussion and planning, or it may occur spontaneously. It may be mutually agreed on, but more often it is not. Whether the decision is made in an angry shouting match under a street light, in a cool and controlled exchange from opposite sides of a living room, or silently by one who lets absence inform the other, the scene is so important to the participants that even years later they can recall the details. Other scenes from a relationship may grow hazy and confused, but not this one, for this moment carries with it the potential for finality.

Many initially welcome the distance, since it offers some relief from the tensions that precede it.[1] Ultimately, however, separation is experienced by both partners as a period of emotional and social disorder.[2] The other person is gone. The partner role is suspended, perhaps temporarily, perhaps permanently, threatening the newly separated with the loss of a major source of identity. Emotional reaction may range from euphoria to suicidal depression, from apathy to an all-consuming desire to do the other person in. The psychological dimensions of separation— feelings of sorrow, anger, rejection, fear, guilt, loneliness, and ambiguity—are well known.[3] Their familiarity does not diminish their importance. Less understood, however, are the social dimensions that intermingle with the psychological, affecting the individual experience.

Normal living patterns are disrupted. Without the other person, a major focal point around which both partners order their daily lives is gone. Economic status, friendship networks, personal habits, and sex life all need simultaneous reorganization.[4] This reorganization, however, is hindered by the ambiguity of the situation. For married couples, the off-again, on-again wearing of the wedding rings symbolizes the uncertainty characterizing this period. Whether married or cohabiting, at separation each of the partners searches for new roles, without yet being free of the old, and many couples continue interacting with each other. Disentangling a shared life into two separate ones is no easy trick. Few guidelines exist as to how to do it, and decisions must be made immediately. In some cases, initiators have little or no vested interest in the outcomes, and allow their partners to make the decisions. But for others, especially those with children, the rudimentary needs for redistribution of people, objects, and responsibilities result in near-constant negotiation. Ironically, some couples find that, though separated, they are interacting with even greater frequency and intensity than before, adding to the disruptiveness of this experience.

The disorder increases as the news of the separation becomes public. Some must be told of the separation—children, parents, close friends. Not only must the partners make the announcement, but, in an unpredicted and seemingly unjust turn of events, their lives become further confounded by the response to the news. Those among the first to know are intimates who care and are affected by it. As the word spreads, the two partners find themselves not only explaining the situation, but calming, consoling, and caring for these others. In need of comfort and consolation themselves, both can be overwhelmed by the increased (and frequently emotional) interaction.[5]

IDENTITY LOSS AND SOCIAL DISORDER

A lot is written about loss of the partner role and the disruption that follows. Inquiry has been restricted to heterosexual relationships, however.[6] Women, one argument goes, appear more vulnerable than men.[7] At an early age, girls learn to judge themselves in terms of their ability to care[8] and organize their identity around being able to make and maintain relationships.[9] Consequently, the partner role assumes a priority for women that it does not have for men. This difference is reinforced by men's economic independence and the dominance of the male occupational role, which provide men with alternative sources of identity absent from many women's lives. Moreover, many women depend on men not only for their economic well-being, but for their social life. They live vicariously for or through their husband or lover, and when he dies or leaves them, so does their sense of self.[10] If they do work outside the home, women are more likely to have jobs instead of careers.[11] Whatever the reason—differential opportunities for work, discrimination, socialization—women tend to engage in work that does not interfere with their relationships.[12] Consequently, many women, though working, still derive their identity primarily from their partner role.[13]

But the question of who is more vulnerable to its loss is not quite this easily settled. Though not as recognized, men, too, experience loss of identity when they lose their partners. Despite the importance of work in their lives, identity derived from the work role and the family role is, in many cases, interrelated.[14] At separation, both the motivation to work and an occupation's value as a source of identity and stability often diminish.[15] For men, the family and all its accumulated belongings symbolize to the community (and to themselves) who they are and what they have made of themselves.[16] When the relationship goes, the self-concept can be badly shaken. Moreover, this loss of identity is often compounded by a lack of social support.[17]

To complicate matters even further, the impact of separation does not always descend equally on members of the same sex.[18] The man who works an eight-to-five job, for example, and whose parent role is a priority, will probably be more vulnerable to the repercussions of separation than a corporate executive whose occupation is the center both of professional and personal life. A woman who works outside the home is likely to be less affected than a woman who does not.[19] A man at retirement age, or an older women with no recent work history and whose children are grown, tend to be more vulnerable than younger people, who have greater opportunities both for work and for new partners.[20] Potentially, then, the impact can fall harshly on members of either sex.

I find, however, that the role taken in the leavetaking is the primary determinant of how separation will be borne. In both homosexual and heterosexual relationships, the initiator is better prepared than the partner. Regardless of sex, age, occupation, or income—regardless of social class, duration of the relationship, social networks, or other factors known to be related to the disruptiveness of this experience[21]—the initiator has the advantage over the partner. Because alternatives offer identities other than the partner role, they mediate the importance of the relationship to the individual self-concept.[22] Although access to alternatives varies with sex, age, and the other factors mentioned, recall also that the initiator has had the advantage of time, having begun uncoupling earlier. And the time has been spent preparing for the physical break.

The Benefits of Time

Not only do initiators find some alternative to the relationship, but in the course of their transition they accumulate other resources—equally as important—that mitigate the impact of separation.[23] Not all of these resources are easily measurable or, indeed, even visible: an ideology of self and a negative chronology of the relationship, for example. Critical to managing the transition, they nonetheless can outweigh resources traditionally believed to affect how people manage this major turning point.

Consider, for example, social networks and income.[24] Given the supposed advantages of an extensive support network and an adequate income, how we can explain an initiator, unemployed and with few friends, who leaves a partner who not only earns a good living, but also has a busy and full social life? If we made a quick judgment about who would be harder hit by the loss of identity and disruptive consequences of separation, we might conclude that the initiator is in for a difficult time, and the partner obviously ahead. But we would be wrong to try to predict on the basis of a simple comparison of both people's social and economic assets.

Were we able to look beyond *quantity* and examine instead *quality* of the resources possessed by each, however, we might find indications of transition and redefinition of self. If we know, to elaborate on the previous comparison, that one partner has a $200 savings account and few close friends, and the other has $5000 and many close friends, we might attribute the comparative advantage to the person with more money and friends at the moment of separation. If, however, the $200 savings account is secret and separate, while the $5000 is in a joint account, and the few friends are single or divorced, while the many are coupled, we would make a different prediction.

Social and economic assets are important. So important are they to moving on that initiators do not separate without them. If they are not firmly secured, the initiator has at least developed confidence that they can be. But what is important is *not* their measurable aspects: how many friends, how prestigious the job, how much salary. Nor is it the abundance of the initiator's resources when compared to the partner's. The connection of these assets to identity is paramount. For the initiator they reinforce, not the coupled identity, but the initiator's own singularity.

Admittedly, securing the resources essential for uncoupling takes some longer than others. Married initiators must seek an ideology of self and negotiate social support for a choice that contradicts dominant values before they can make the break; homosexual initiators do not face this problem. The process of coming out is itself an illustration of uncoupling.[25] A homosexual lifestyle choice violates the strongest cultural criterion for partner selection after the incest taboo.[26] Prior to coming out, homosexuals develop an ideology of self and break with religious, social class, or ethnic traditions that endorse commitment to procreative heterosexual marriage.[27]

When they choose to live with a partner in a relationship they have publicly acknowledged as intimate, they negotiate further social support for a nontraditional lifestyle, distancing themselves from condemning friends and associates.[28] The situation for homosexual couples is the opposite of heterosexual marriage: gays are stigmatized for coupling, rewarded for uncoupling. Furthermore, in the gay community, endings are not seen as tragic, nor are they negatively sanctioned. They are taken as a matter of course. Hence, gay and lesbian initiators do not face the negative social consequences of ending a relationship to the same extent as married initiators do, who before they can uncouple must first minimize those consequences. The commonly held notion that homosexual relationships are short-lived because the partners are sexually permissive and promiscuous fails to take into account that, compared to heterosexual marriage, nontraditional relationships (both homosexual and heterosexual) have fewer social arrangements binding them together. Consequently, breaking up entails less negotiation in the social world.[29]

All initiators, regardless of sex, sexual preference, or marital status, need resources to uncouple, and these take varying amounts of time to acquire. Some initiators will have a greater need for the socialization necessary to the transition and also will have greater difficulty obtaining it.[30] Some will encounter more trouble creating alternative social situations for themselves. Some will experience hard times accumulating financial resources or social support.[31] Some will be more vulnerable to the potential loss of the parent role.[32] Others seem to be "fast uncouplers." Both in uncoupling and in other life experiences, they see themselves as people who quickly adjust to change. They not only perceive themselves as able to find the necessary resources, but also as capable of making the necessary psychological adjustment. As one person said, "I make quick transitions." For those who cannot, time itself becomes a critical resource. Initiators take whatever time they need to overcome the obstacles they face; when the break comes, they're prepared to try it without the partner.[33]

The Subtleties of Power

There are, of course, variations on this theme. The initiator's comparative advantage can diminish because of circumstances that change the balance of power in the relationship. Some initiators may find (as we will see later) that once on their own they are overwhelmed with uncertainty—their resources are insufficient for the realities of the break-up.[34] Initiators may then experience fully the trauma that accompanies separation, struggling to manage the basics of daily life with no more success than partners. Alternatively, sometimes the partner *is* prepared for the separation. The initiator's signals are forceful and consistent enough to overcome the barriers the partner constructs to receiving them and the partner concludes the relationship cannot go on. Whatever the mode of delivery, the message sent and finally received is "I don't love you." Acknowledging this has a powerful emotional effect on the partner. The social ramifications are equally significant. The partner begins seeking self-validation, stability, and identity elsewhere.[35]

I started saying I just can't live this way anymore. I mean, I had no physical relationship. He's going out with other people. We're living in the same house. He's sleeping in one space. I'm sleeping in another. If we're having any sort of sex, it's this love/hate thing going on. He was bringing people home to the apartment, which I had never done. I started having relationships out of the house. I was finding I needed other people. I was saying to myself, "Walt, you have to get rid of him because you've been doing real fine. You're still with him, but you're doing real fine without his help." [SOFTWARE SALESMAN, AGE 31, SEPARATED AFTER LIVING TOGETHER 3 YEARS]

Two days later he moved his bed downstairs, so he just slept downstairs, he wouldn't sleep with me, and disconnected himself totally. So I finally said "Look woman, you're banging your head against the wall with this guy." It was obvious that there was no investment. He felt guilty, maybe, came back, and it was crazy to try. So finally I just stopped. I stopped washing his clothes for him, I stopped cooking. I had a child that was tiny. We brought him home from the hospital at exactly five pounds. I had to take my energy and channel it into this child, you know, I mean you only have so much to give. So I totally closed down from Eddie and started emotional withdrawal. [SECRETARY, AGE 38, DIVORCED AFTER 10 YEARS]

I was singlehandedly keeping the relationship going, in spite of the obvious, which was that she really didn't care. I think I was unhappy for so long and disappointed so often, I mean how can a person live like that, that finally all my feelings just died. Being with her was like nothing, not pain, not happiness, it had been so long since there had been any happiness, just a sense of loss and then finally not even caring about that anymore, just needing to make some kind of life for myself. [PSYCHOLOGIST, AGE 36, SEPARATED AFTER LIVING TOGETHER 6 YEARS]

Under these circumstances the partner also keeps secrets, using time to advantage. Finding alternatives that decrease dependence on the relationship, the partner develops an identity independent of the initiator, adopts an ideology of self, and, when ready, confronts the initiator about terminating the relationship.[36] One consequence can be a congenial separation. The asymmetry that usually characterizes uncoupling is replaced by a more egalitarian situation. The partner confronts the initiator and both agree to separate. Each has alternatives, and both have been in transition for some time. Consequently the identity loss, emotional trauma, and social disorder are partially mitigated for each partner. Yet they are rarely avoided. Both people experience them throughout the transition, so that at the moment of physical separation, much of the trauma is over. In some cases, the two people are able to help each other over some of the remaining hurdles.

> Both his family and my family lived in the same city. Through all the years of our marriage we had all been very close. When we decided to separate, how to tell everybody was a big problem. Neither one of us wanted to do it. Somehow it seemed natural and better to do it together. So we took one week before we moved out and each night we drove to a different relative's home to sit in the living room and break the news. It was easier for both of us, but confused them, I think, because there we were, obviously friendly, sitting there together. But what they didn't know was that it was the first thing we'd really done together in years. [POLITICAL ORGANIZER/VOLUNTEER, AGE 58, DIVORCED AFTER 24 YEARS]

> We just remained very calm and for the first time talked about separating. We spent like a month and a half together after that, and then moved out simultaneously from the apartment to different places on the same day. We even said, look, you know, you're not going to leave me, I'm not going to leave you, we'll just move out on the same day. It was apparent that we were both ready to do this. When the time came I helped her move some of her things and she helped me move some of my things. The feeling between us was almost like lovers who for some reason had to leave each other. The night that we said goodbye—it was like 11 o'clock and the house was empty. Everything had been put into trucks and moved and so forth and we were in the house and there was no place else to go and so we sat down on the floor and laying down on the floor in our overcoats and I held her and we both cried and it was just heartrending and then we just separated and that was pretty much it. [SUPERVISOR, AGE 38, DIVORCED AFTER 19 YEARS]

But the balance of power between two people in an intimate relationship is often subject to sudden and subtle shifts. Even when both are prepared for separation, it does not always occur in egalitarian and harmonious ways. Whichever person expresses the wish to separate takes charge of the timing of the separation. One person, prepared to go, confronts the other about wanting to end it. The other, though perhaps also independent, suddenly loses charge of an important resource: the ability to control the outcome. The combination of the sudden loss of power plus the social embarrassment of being rejected can result in an unexpectedly devastating experience for even the most prepared.[37]

DISORDER DESCENDS

Although initiators and partners may vary in the extent to which they are prepared for separation, the typical situation is asymmetrical: the initiator is prepared and the partner is not. Partners find the stability of the relationship gone with nothing to emerge as a substitute.[38] They have not spent time preparing for individual existence. They have not planned for it—they do not want it.[39] Despite participation in work, family, or other roles, the partner role assumes a priority that gives meaning to all the others. With the loss of it, disorder descends.

> *Oh, the towel bar fell off and I just can't do this, and I need him to do it and we had just moved in and I couldn't find anything and I remember calling one night to ask him where the heck the drill was. I wanted him to come and do it. I wanted him to do what he always had done.* [FINANCIAL ANALYST, AGE 28, SEPARATED AFTER LIVING TOGETHER 2 YEARS]

The partner's vulnerability to the impact of separation increases when the physical break occurs at a time when the partner is particularly resource-poor. Whenever the partner's regular schedule is in abeyance—for example, during illness, unemployment, or vacation—sources of identity outside the relationship are diminished. The loss of the partner role, under these circumstances, can be extraordinarily difficult.

The partner who moves out has a particularly hard time. Whether leaving results from an angry, explosive exchange or from planning and negotiation between the two, whether it is the partner's idea or the initiator's, the effect is the same. The partner leaves behind some resources that could provide support during this period. When children remain in the home, partners are bereft not only of their role as partner, but as parent. Parenting becomes one more aspect of their life, formerly taken for granted, that now must be negotiated. Identification with a neighborhood, which sometimes contributes to self-concept, is also disrupted by the move. Not only do these partners leave their other roles, but also they leave the home and all vestiges of routine personal life. While these same conditions obviously are experienced by initiators who move out, their impact on partners is greater.

Symbolic Objects

We locate, invest, and store our feelings about ourselves in our material possessions. Thus, the objects we acquire are given meaning and become components of our "identity kit."[40] When our sense of self changes, some objects that fill our lives hold meanings that are incompatible with the person we are becoming. We feel uncomfortable with them, for they bind us to a past we are trying to leave behind. In order to move on, we sometimes deny the value of these objects and reject their importance in our lives.

The home and joint possessions represent the relationship and all that transpired between the partners.[41] For the initiator, objects that symbolize the partner and the relationship stand as all-too-ready reminders of an identity that has grown uncomfortable or perhaps was never fully assumed. Prior to the leavetaking, the initiator negatively redefines the objects that symbolize the coupled identity.[42]

> He used to walk through here and look around and say, "None of this is mine. I don't feel like I belong here. This isn't me" and I would say, "But you built this house, what do you mean, it isn't you?" [RETAILER, AGE 48, SEPARATED AFTER LIVING TOGETHER 14 YEARS]

Leavetaking is thus unaccompanied by nostalgic longings for the old home place. Furthermore, when initiators go, they travel light. They take none of the memorabilia of the relationship.[43] They bring their clothes and other personal belongings, and perhaps some items that are functional but neutral (a coffee pot), but the snapshots, gifts from the partner, souvenirs, and other objects symbolizing the other person get left behind, sold, or even destroyed.

> He started to tear off the covering of the wall, and began to break things, break china and stuff. It turned out to be a violent scene. I guess it was because, though he was the one who withdrew from the relationship, I was staying at the apartment we had worked so hard at. He didn't want the apartment, he just didn't want me to have it. He first withdrew from it, then ripped it up physically. [SERVICE CO-ORDINATOR/STUDENT, AGE 28, SEPARATED AFTER LIVING TOGETHER 1 YEAR]

> I took all of my art, but ending up destroying all of it that I created during that part of my life. [ARTIST, AGE 62, DIVORCED AFTER 10 YEARS]

I sold all my furniture. I carried a carload of clothes and things down here that I wanted and packed them in my aunt's attic. And from then on, I was free. I got rid of everything—11 years of accumulated stuff. I said forget it—I'm going to be me. [SECRETARY, AGE 35, DIVORCED AFTER 5 YEARS]

Initiators who remain in the home quickly make it theirs by divesting it of reminders of the partner.

Like I said, I'd been gone ten days and I got some plane tickets and Tommy and I flew back. I still had a key to the house. I let myself in. It was about four o'clock in the afternoon, and I went into Tommy's bedroom and his bedroom was totally empty. There was no furniture, no toys, just an empty room, and I went into the bedroom and looked in the dresser drawers because I had left most of my things behind and everything that belonged to me was missing. And apparently he had just stripped the house of everything that belonged to either Tommy or me. Tommy went into the backyard and came back in and said, "My swings are gone," so he had even dismantled the swings. [EXECUTIVE SECRETARY/SUPERVISOR, AGE 34, DIVORCED AFTER 9 YEARS]

By this negative redefinition, the initiator separates self from the bonds of the hearth before the physical separation. The partner often does the opposite. He or she not only covets the objects that symbolize the initiator and the relationship, but may devote increased time and energy to them. In the initiator's absence, the partner perpetuates and vicariously cultivates the relationship in the only way possible—through the objects that represent it.[44]

I spent as much time with the kids as I could. She had a lot of things she always wanted me to do around the house, so I thought I'd do those to surprise her when she came by to see them. A set had come out of her engagement ring and we'd never had it fixed. I thought, well, she would see how wrong she'd been if I did some things to show her I cared. [MECHANIC, AGE 33, DIVORCED AFTER 10 YEARS OF MARRIAGE]

Then I didn't think much about it, I just did it. I started wearing some of the things he left behind, especially his bathrobe, some shirts too, but only in the house. I read his books, I am embarrassed at this. I also did some things to the place I knew he would like. He always complained about my plants, so I got rid of them. It seems strange to think about it now, but at the time I found some comfort in it. [ACCOUNTANT, AGE 38, SEPARATED AFTER LIVING TOGETHER 13 YEARS]

Initiators who succeed in redefining the relationship and all that goes with it in negative terms leave home free of ambiguity. When the time comes, the separation brings the initiator such a sense of relief that the decision to part is totally confirmed. Indeed, some report experiencing a euphoria in which every phase of their life acquires new meaning.

The first night he left it was like somebody took a thousand pounds off my back. I went to bed and I had the best night's sleep that I had had in I don't know when. And I even changed sides of the bed because I wanted his side all along. It was just like a big load lifted off me. [COMPUTER SALESMAN, AGE 35, SEPARATED AFTER LIVING TOGETHER 10 YEARS]

Mourning the Loss

Not all initiators have the luxury of such confirmation and certainty, however. For those who grieve for their children, the adventure has a dark and painful underside. Nonetheless, the partner seldom sees the initiator's uncertainty.[45] What the partner sees is a person who is moving on with apparent confidence and peace of mind. Seemingly absent are the grief and despair that fill the partner's life, making even simple daily tasks a hardship. Not understanding that the initiator's ability to cope with the immediate effects of separation is the product of a transition long underway, the partner feels a heightened sense of rejection and loss.[46]

He seems so happy. And why shouldn't he be? He sits over there in that house and goes to work every day, like usual. And when he comes home at night, there she is. He has someone to cook for him, clean for him, and screw. He never thinks of me. He never thinks of Ken. And what do I have? I have the kid. This place is always a mess. Do I have someone to cook and clean for me? No. And there's no one to screw. [SOCIAL WORKER, AGE 44, SEPARATED AFTER 20 YEARS OF MARRIAGE]

What I don't understand is how she can just leave her home and family like this. I mean, I can understand how she might have some disagreement with me, but how she can just cooly deal with this I don't know. Her sister told me she's living in a trailer with this guy from work. She's forgotten all about us. How can she not miss us? I mean, I can hardly work, I feel like something's stuck in my gut, you know? [TYPESETTER, AGE 38, DIVORCED AFTER 14 YEARS.]

Initiators, like partners, do grieve and mourn the loss of the relationship. But they do it earlier, when they first admit to themselves that the relationship may not be saveable.[47] Then they begin confiding in others, working through their loss and grief. Yet the partner's willingness to admit to this and discuss the relationship frequently comes only when separation seems sure or after it happens. The partner is especially vulnerable to the possible negative reactions of others. Subscribing to an ideology that reinforces commitment to the other person, the partner views separation as nothing less than failure in a chosen and valued role. Negative reactions of others—whether real or imagined—compound the embarrassment. Seeking both consolation and support, the partner nevertheless turns to others, beginning to mourn. He or she is preoccupied with retrospective analysis, sorting through the relationship's history, examining past conversations, mentally reliving life with the other person. No longer having easy access to the initiator, the partner searches for explanations alone and with whomever will listen.

> *I tried to see what was wrong and pull out what this thing was all about but the question mark is where is she staying and where is she keeping the kids. I got evil thoughts, whether it's a boyfriend's house, boyfriend's apartment. I spent most of my nights without sleep. I just drove around.* [PROCESS INSPECTOR, AGE 47, DIVORCED AFTER 19 YEARS]

For some, the mourning and searching for explanation are still mingled with hope. Partners now have their turn at obsessive review.[48] Contrary to initiators, however, partners accentuate the positive characteristics of the initiator and their life together.[49]

> *I kept remembering this good time, that good time. All the friends and things we did with them. And the trips, all the trips.* [INTERIOR DESIGNER, AGE 32, SEPARATED AFTER LIVING TOGETHER 10 YEARS]

> *Our sex life was wonderful. Always he was passionate, tender, and always wanting me. No matter whatever else of whatever sort was going on between us, making love was a good connection, a special kind of communication. It is impossible for me to understand or believe that it could be like that for me and not for him. How could he walk away?* [STUDENT, AGE 21, SEPARATED AFTER LIVING TOGETHER 2 YEARS]

Because partners abstract and emphasize the positive, they find the present situation incomprehensible. Even in the initiator's absence, they won't define the relationship as unsaveable—separation is viewed as a temporary aberration. They do not yet give up, continuing to devote themselves to resurrecting the relationship.

> *When it was his turn to take the children, I would make sure the house was clean and that I looked pretty when he came by. I tried not to ask anything, you know, put any pressures on that would make*

him angry. [HOUSEWIFE, AGE 25, SEPARATED AFTER 5 YEARS OF MAR-RIAGE]

I continued to talk to his mother and his sister and see them so they would try to talk some sense into him. I met one of his friends for lunch and asked him please to tell Paul what a mistake he was making. I really did almost nothing for a whole year but try to get him back. My work suffered tremendously. I did nothing but try to fix things—that and see my therapist. [ECONOMIST, AGE 34, DIVORCED AFTER 6 YEARS]

The partner's preoccupation with and idealization of the initiator and their times together are not contingent on the quality of the partner's experience in the relationship. The partner may or may not have been happy. In focusing on the relationship now, the partner is simply entering a natural and necessary phase of the transition. Resistance to change is a fact of life. When a familiar pattern is threatened or disrupted, people will try to avoid reorganizing their environment[50] and their immediate impulse is to restore the past. The will to adapt has to overcome this nearly universal impulse.[51] Recall that in the earliest phase of uncoupling, initiators first respond to their own unhappiness by trying to fix things: to change partner and relationship so that the relationship could continue. Partners respond to the post-separation disruption in the same manner: they try to hang on to what they have.

Initiators sometimes acknowledge that the partner is starting down a painful road they've already traveled.

I remember saying this to my husband when he was suffering so after I'd decided to get a divorce. He was suffering terribly and telling me, you know, "How can you do this to me?" And I said, "Well, what you're feeling now, I felt seven years ago. I know what you're feeling. I felt abandoned seven years ago. It just took me this long to decide I wanted a divorce, and now you're feeling bad." I could really tell that what was happening to him was just what I had been through. [LEARNING DISABILITIES TEACHER, AGE 49, DIVORCED AFTER 23 YEARS]

In some respects I felt guilty because I know what Verna went through and I didn't have any of the trauma associated with, I mean I had some, it's unavoidable, but the whole transition period was not difficult at all. I was mentally divorced before I left, I think is a fair way of putting it. I went through a lot of trauma early on—it wasn't that I avoided that experience while she got it full blast, it was that I had that experience at a different time. [PSYCHOLOGIST, AGE 44, DIVORCED AFTER 12 YEARS]

The partner's response, however, is fueled by an element not present in the initiator's early attempt at restoration—the initiator does not want the partner. The partner is being involuntarily deprived of a role under circumstances that reflect unfavorably on the partner's capacity for it.[52] Even when partners initiate the separation, publicly assuming responsibility for the break-up, in their hearts they may know or suspect they were driven to it by the initiator. Public humiliation may be reduced by their action, yet private loss of face can still be great.[53] The quality of the relationship is outweighed by the alternatives: confusion and change that the partner did not (and would not) choose. The negative aspects of the relationship seem inconsequential, the positive aspects more valuable. As they try to figure ways to restore and understand it, partners intensify their involvement with it. Unknowingly, they participate in what appears to be a near-ritualistic response to involuntary loss and unwanted transition.[54]

The situation is loaded with irony. On the one hand, the separation increases the initiator's distance from the partner by adding physical distance to the existing social separation. On the other, despite this physical distance, the partner maintains and perhaps even increases the centrality of the relationship in his or her life.[55] Nonetheless, social forces are at work that interfere with the partner's hopes for reconciliation. Despite the continued importance of the relationship in the partner's life, the separation has social consequences that add impetus to the initiator's transition out of the relationship, initiate the partner's own transition, and widen the gap between the two.

§ ——————————————————————————

EIGHT

Going Public

A*LTHOUGH* our relationships "take place" in public, outsiders know little about the intimate environment we create with another person. Couples divide their time between many settings. They may appear together before multiple audiences, but no one group has continuous access to the relationship, not even friends, relatives, or children sharing the same dwelling.[1] What's more, partners actively generate privacy by giving their various publics only selected bits and pieces of information. We work to sustain a public impression of the relationship in keeping with the image we want to convey.[2] When we think other people might intervene, we work hard to cover up disagreements and difficulties.

Because our families are likely to do just that, we are most careful about how we present the relationship to them. As we become adults, our families no longer witness our lives unfolding on a daily basis, so they must rely on whatever news we pass on.[3] We change. They continue to regard us according to past definitions and the parts of our present that we grant them access to. Again, repressing information is a collaborative process, for families are as talented as anybody else at warding off facts that don't fit their world view.[4] Sometimes we tell them, but they don't want to know. The gap between who we are and who they think we are grows as time passes. These contradictions are sometimes painfully and deeply felt at family gatherings. Later, we complain, "They don't know me anymore."

When we separate, we display our discontent to a wide audience. Two distinct households demand public identification of the couple as two separate entities. New telephone listings, address changes, separate bank accounts and charge accounts all proclaim the new arrangement to intimates, acquaintances, and strangers alike. Going public has a powerful effect on a relationship, causing others to acknowledge that it is in trouble.[5] As others learn of the separation, they change their behavior. Their responses confirm the new situation, not the coupled identity, thus reinforcing the separation and creating obstacles to reconciliation.

REORDERING THE COUPLED WORLD

Alignments form, some along predictable lines. Both partners have longstanding ties with friends who quickly rally to support them;[6] parents, when pressed to choose, publicly support their own. Support does not always come through as expected, however. The partners are often surprised that someone they thought was aligned with them is in the other person's corner. A son, for example, finds his parents vow never to speak to him again—they declare for their daughter-in-law, who has acted as mediator between her husband and his family for years. Or an aggrieved partner, expecting the sympathetic support of a child, is dismayed when the separation reveals a longstanding alignment between the child and the other parent.[7]

More problematic are those who have strong bonds with both partners. Parents, children, siblings, and close mutual friends are "friends of the relationship" in a true sense, and they have a vested interest in the relationship's continuing. Their situation resembles the partner's in many ways. They are faced with involuntary change and threatened with some loss—reputation, relatives, friends, or perhaps their own relationship—and so are likely to oppose the separation. These people are important to both partners; their viewpoints and loyalties matter. Consequently, telling them about the separation becomes more than just reporting the news.[8] Faced with potential opposition, both partners want to retain their friendship and support—neither of which can be taken for granted.

The initiator, possibly for the first time, faces a tough audience. Displaying discontent all along, the initiator has disclosed this unhappiness to people who could be counted on to be supportive and has avoided those who might oppose the relationship's termination. At separation, however, the initiator must tell people who are likely to challenge, contradict, and condemn. And this time the partner has a voice. To maintain alignments they already have, to recover those previously lost, and to secure those as yet undeclared, both partners tell their side of the story. They no longer collaborate to portray a united front. Publicly, each begins to unravel the joint biography that together they have constructed for others.[9]

The initiator, in redefining partner and relationship to justify termination,[10] creates an account with the potential to withstand the scrutiny
of others. He or she has evolved socially acceptable reasons for the
break.[11] There's nothing wrong with relationships in general—it's just
that something is the matter with this one.[12] The initiator may publicly
legitimate the separation by redefining the partner as bad, or, if not bad,
at least "bad for me." The initiator may categorize the partner as sick,
focusing on the partner's abusiveness or alcoholism (for example), to
the exclusion of positive traits. The demise may be attributed to some
external event or person, which changed the partner in irrevocable ways
or possibly "there never was much of a relationship," and the initiator
can chronicle a stunning array of incidents testifying to this fact.[13] This
account will emphasize events that support the initiator's chosen course.[14]
From the history of the relationship, the initiator selects the information
to disclose, breaking the news in ways that will generate the desired
response from each audience she or he wants to woo and win.[15]

> And I did a lot of lying. I never, never to this day, have been able to
> tell them that I wanted that divorce all along, that I wanted it because
> I no longer loved Herb, and I wanted it because my work was more
> important and was something deeper and more meaningful. I have
> never been able to put it exactly that way. I told them that Herb and
> I had been working for a nontraditional relationship, and that Herb
> seemed unable or unwilling to work at that any longer—that my mother
> could understand. And I tried to say things like, "I don't think Herb
> loves me anymore." That was an out-and-out lie. But it was some-
> thing I thought that could justify this to them. [GRADUATE STUDENT,
> AGE 26, DIVORCED AFTER 2 YEARS]

The separation forces the partner to acknowledge that the relationship
is deeply troubled and, simultaneously, to explain to self and others why
this is so. Still picking through the relationship's history, the partner is
trying to understand what went wrong.[16] However indefinite and changing the partner's explanation, it differs from the initiator's. Like the
initiator, the partner wants to save face.[17] Like the initiator, the partner
seeks social support. Like the initiator, the partner needs to discuss,
work through, and, thus, make real this major life change.[18] Unlike the
initiator, the partner sees the relationship's positive attributes and wants
to keep the way clear for reconciliation. Both attempt to neutralize or
discredit the other's attempt to define the situation.[19] Both tailor their
definitions of self, other, and relationship to best convince the audiences
they address.[20]

Dividing Common Property: Intimates

Thus begins a competition for the first of the common property the two people have accumulated during the course of the relationship: intimates whom they both share.[21] They compete not only for the social support and positive self-image these others confer, but also to keep from losing still other relationships.[22] Friends of the relationship are seldom able to support both partners equally and eventually will be forced to choose. Losing these ties is equivalent to giving up yet other portions of self. Thus, the competition is likely to be keen, for substitutes are not easily found. Who could replace a mother-in-law who gently and uncritically befriended and advised a young wife through her transition into motherhood? Or the sister one never had, but who came miraculously by virtue of the partnership? Some are disadvantaged in the competition, for willingness to disclose information about one's personal life varies.[23] In general, however, the more valued the relationship, the more strongly both partners will try to defend their claim.[24] Severing ties with one's children is hard to contemplate, regardless of their ages. Children still in the home are a target of intense competition.[25] To save themselves, the older ones may disappear into peer groups, books, hobbies, part-time jobs, or their own relationships, emerging only after the dust settles. Some may even leave home. Younger children do not have as many alternatives,[26] but all children, as long as they are economically dependent on their parents, are a captive audience.

Threatened with the possibility of so significant a loss, the partners sometimes violate the rules of fair competition.[27] In an attempt to formalize the alignment, they fight to be legally awarded the children in a child custody case.[28] Professionals are brought in: lawyers, mediators, social workers, counselors. Both partners air their definition of relationship and partner in public forum, trying to influence these professionals to align with them, reinforcing the legitimacy of their argument, and shoring up their own resources for the competition.[29] Some people who would not consider it before now yield to the threat of permanent loss by intentionally distorting negative definitions of the other person and the relationship, or by publicly revealing secrets, once granted trustingly in the bond of intimacy. They reinforce the negative definitions of their competitor, increasing antagonism by their actions and the content of the accounts they present.

The good will and support of parents are as coveted as the loyalty of children. The situation of gays in relation to their parents differs from that of heterosexual couples because gays who uncouple do not usually risk the loss of support from family members—since that typically disappeared when the individual came out. Families may be unaware of their gay members' couplings and, if they are aware, they seldom qualify as "friends of the relationship." They tend to see the break up as a return to traditional values and therefore applaud it. But for heterosexual couples, the confirmation and approval of parents are not similarly guaranteed.

> *First I told my parents. The only thing I can say is that their approval and their support is the most significant. I remember telling a friend right after I told them I'd never again believe or even think that what my parents thought wasn't important to me. I had defined it as unimportant in other counsel decisions, I think because I could have taken their approval and their support for granted. This was the first real decision, the first real thing that I had ever done where I couldn't be sure that they would be supportive. And I couldn't be sure that they would approve. And then it became crucial for me to get that approval.* [COMPUTER PROGRAMMER, AGE 27, SEPARATED AFTER LIVING TOGETHER 4 YEARS]

Telling them about the separation results in both parties giving and receiving information about each other. Often for the first time in a long while, adult child and parent each glimpse who the other person has become. The outcome is unpredictable, for, as we have seen, the revelation of secrets can create bonds or terminate them. So people approach telling their parents with great trepidation.

> *What I wanted to do was to go down one weekend and tell them, my mom and dad, take them out to dinner or something, do something special, and say, hey, this is horrible but this is what's happening. As it turns out, they found out through a friend. I waited too long before I called them. I guess I really didn't want to enough. So my mom called me. I thought she would have a heart attack on the spot but she was remarkable. I mean, my mom and dad have grown so much and they love me so much. Coming from that Fundamentalist, narrow-minded orientation, they are in such a tough position because they catch hell if they, not catch hell, but like the people that they have to live with every day and go to church with, think I'm going to hell, because I'm divorced and because I've left the faith and all. My mom and dad somehow continue to be compatible with that orientation and yet they love me and they understand. What she said to me was, "This really hurts me and breaks my heart but, you know I love you, you're my son, I'll be praying for you." I was really surprised you know.* [SUPERVISOR, AGE 38, DIVORCED AFTER 19 YEARS

GAINS, LOSSES, AND NEGATIVE DEFINITIONS

Many report that ties with their parents and other family members, normally somewhat weakened when two people couple, are renewed as a result of disclosures at separation. One disclosure is often met by another, deepening each other's understanding. One man, married 30 years, flew to a distant city to inform his 80-year-old mother that he'd left his wife. He described the preliminary conversation, his mother's casual participation, his growing anxiety. His mother sent him on an errand, and he recalled thinking in desperation that maybe, in his absence, she would die and he wouldn't have to go through with telling her. But she didn't. He was surprised by her support and offer of love and sympathy. As he confided the troubles in his marriage, he was even more surprised when she correspondingly dropped the veil of privacy from the parental relationship. "Well, you probably didn't know," she confided, "but your father and I had affairs over the years—lots of them, but we didn't let it interfere with the marriage."

Often, the response from family members is mixed.

Oh, it wasn't just going to be heavy with mother. It was going to be heavy with the other 800 relatives. I was the first person to ever (a) get divorced, and (b) leave the church. You know, all those things, nobody had ever done this. Turned out I had all kinds of covert support. Then they all did it. And now the half of the family that's still Catholic hates me and the other half thinks I'm the best thing since sliced bread. [PSYCHOLOGIST, AGE 44, DIVORCED AFTER 12 YEARS[30]]

Presenting family members with the news can reveal ideological incompatibilities previously hidden, or, if recognized, glossed over. Some people will object to the separation on the grounds that a commitment is a commitment, no matter what. Others argue out of loyalty to the person being left behind or to the children. In the interest of other people's well-being, the relationship must continue. Surely differences can be resolved. Unable either to win over the opposition or cope with these people's objections and condemnation, partners who bear the brunt of it may eventually abandon the unconvinced, pushed away by their negative response. Or the unconvinced, similarly failing to convert, abandon them.

Mutual friends can react similarly. The sorry result of this competition is stunningly portrayed in Joyce Carol Oates' play, *Spoils*.[31] A couple preparing to separate are in their apartment, dividing possessions. A mutual friend from out of town comes for dinner. As the evening progresses, the couple shift attention from the division of inanimate objects to a struggle to retain the loyalty of this friend. The visitor, scarred by the competition, walks away from both.

Significant relationships are lost to both partners, as friends hear the conflicting accounts, and either align with one or the other or simply drop out of sight because they are unable to choose between the two and find it difficult to support both. They retreat, isolating the newly separated.[32] Disclosure can also terminate bonds, not because of the explanation's content but because it is presented in a socially unacceptable style.[33] People expect sorrow and remorse to accompany separation. Exhibiting euphoria, well-being, or peace of mind is considered bad form, which cuts short both conversations and relationships. As one initiator remarked,

> *If anything, during that period, what I felt uptight about was that people were responding with sympathy and pity, as if I had been the one on whom pain had been inflicted. I found myself responding as they expected me to, with a long face and saying how tough it was. But what I wanted was for people not to define it as a painful situation. Some of your close friends you do want sympathy from, just because you can also tell them the full situation. And I experienced this. But what I wanted was for someone to just say, "Well, congratulations. Get on with your life. It's not the end of the world. It's not a bad thing. It's something that happens. It has not been bad in my eyes."* [LAWYER, AGE 35, SEPARATED AFTER LIVING TOGETHER 10 YEARS]

A person who openly slanders the partner, rather than criticizing indirectly and allowing the listener to infer the rest, risks alienating others, as does someone who reveals how he or she deceived the partner (and, obviously, those who are now listening to the tale).[34] In addition to what is said, what's left unsaid can contribute to alignments. One partner may remain silent with certain audiences, sure that the other will behave so abominably that she or he will create good will and support for the silent partner who effortlessly reaps these benefits.

While some relationships may be lost through telling, others are lost through *not* telling. Sometimes the expectation of a negative reaction will cause one of the partners to let the other do the informing.

> *I sat and talked to her for about three hours, and told her everything. And I was very careful not to blame Don, or anything, about the whole situation. But I said, I'm tired of being the scapegoat in all this situation, and I'm tired of lying to you, and I've given Don opportunity to talk to you, and obviously he isn't going to, so I'm going to tell you, and I don't care if he gets pissed or not. This is the*

situation. He's living with this woman, he's got a telephone, he's been lying to you for years. And I'm tired of it. I went through the whole thing. [BLOOD DRAWER, AGE 38, SEPARATED AFTER 4 YEARS OF MARRIAGE]

The person who breaks the news has an advantage. By shaping the opinion of the listener, he or she often secures an alignment. Those who hesitate to tell others because they anticipate a negative response may be mistaken in their forecast of others' reactions. In walking away from the possibility of undiscovered animosity, they also walk away from the chance for undiscovered support.[35]

Sometimes, no one is willing to inform a concerned party about the change in the relationship. This often involves older relatives who are considered frail by family members. Aunt Emma is not told, for fear the shock would upset or kill her (they were, after all, "the perfect couple"). If the couple reconcile, no harm is done. But if they do not, another relationship is lost. The initial secret generates others. Aunt Emma is not informed of subsequent changes in their lives, for that would necessitate telling her about the break-up. Neither partner can send a letter or make a phone call without either contributing to the cover-up or exposing the secret. Maintaining distance is easier than maintaining lies. The shock may or may not have killed her, but Aunt Emma, in effect, dies anyway. Excluded from the future life of both partners, she dies a social death.[36]

Beyond the circle of intimates that both partners covet, each relationship has an audience of associates and acquaintances who know the partners more casually. Though more peripheral, they, too, get an explanation. The bowling partner, the co-worker, or the neighbor may inquire. Some people will be told for pragmatic reasons. The secretary at the office is informed of a changed phone number; the carpool members are given the child's new address. As the partners announce their separation to people farther on the periphery of their social world, the amount of explanation offered diminishes. Each account will have a smaller, tighter and less variable shape.[37] A perfunctory explanation now replaces extensive revelation.

The time-consuming and laborious problem of going public is sometimes reduced by intentionally telling a key person in a social network who, either from instinct or specific instruction, can be counted on to disseminate the news. Both partners are further relieved as those who are told tell others, spreading the news in circles increasingly distant from the two people involved. While some advantage comes from these more efficient methods of announcing the separation, a competing disadvantage also exists. Controlling others' definitions of the situation becomes impossible.

> *I did not want the responsibility for the failure. And there was a period during which I felt the need to run around and put out little fires. It was very important that people accepted it as a mutual decision that was better for both of us, because I did not want to be defined as the bad guy. Like starting most importantly with those closest to me—my children, my parents, and friends who had known us for years. But then there were these other people, who didn't know any of the details; who didn't know us either very well, but who were spreading rumors. And I went through a period of maybe three or four days of being angry at not being able to deal with that. And then finally resolving it by saying, I can't. But a feeling of almost being involved in public relations, you know, that they have got to get the straight goods.* [TEACHER, AGE 35, DIVORCED AFTER 11 YEARS]

Information gets distorted and the probability of breakdowns in other interactions is increased.[38] Moreover, without hearing from the participants, onlookers will create their own explanations. One or both partners are likely to be defined negatively, receiving social condemnation they cannot avert.

As the problems in the relationship become public knowledge, the couple's separate accounts uncover and reinforce ideological compatibilities that draw to each partner—and draw each partner to—people who hold similar values. Simultaneously, each partner leaves behind—or is left behind by—others with different world views. Both experience multiple leavetakings.[39]

> *It's important for me to talk about it because it's one of the most difficult things. It deals with a lot of separations. I lost my best friends. Our kids lost their best friends that they'd grown up with for years and years. I almost lost my childhood best friends. The only people I wasn't losing were my mother and my brother. It seemed like I was losing everybody else. I felt so disconnected.* [LEARNING DISABILITIES TEACHER, AGE 49, DIVORCED AFTER 23 YEARS]

The myth of "the ideal couple" quickly dissipates, as each partner discloses details of the relationship. In exchange, intimates begin revealing things about the absent member they did not air (or very carefully aired) while the couple was together. Intimates often hesitate to divulge information detrimental to one partner that they believe will be useful or of interest to the other. Uncertain as to how their contribution will be received, they may withhold it to protect their own connection with the partners or to protect one or both partners. At separation, they no longer feel bound by silence. Both partners are suddenly the recipients of previously untold information, observations, and opinions, as others reveal their secrets.[40]

My mother said, "Any man making $40,000 a year who would let his wife do the kind of work you do has probably been stashing it away for years. Let him go." [HOUSEWIFE, AGE 50, SEPARATED AFTER 28 YEARS]

My daughter said, "Right on, mother. You should have done it years ago. You should have done that when I was 13." [ASSISTANT PROFESSOR, AGE 37, DIVORCED AFTER 19 YEARS]

One of the things that happened was a lot of people who had wanted to say things to me about him finally did. I found out he had been going with my best friend. She used to ask me to babysit for her so she could go out, and they would go out together. I found out a lot of really rotten things he had done to me that I didn't know about. I mean he was just like a real running dog. [SECRETARY, AGE 30, SEPARATED AFTER LIVING TOGETHER 3 YEARS]

My friends all hated her. Only one of them ever said anything to me about her—one, a very close woman friend, who said to me flat out, many times, "Why don't you get rid of that creep?" When we split up, everybody had something to say. [SECRETARY, AGE 26, SEPARATED AFTER LIVING TOGETHER 5 YEARS]

The friend I ended up moving in with said, "I knew it was going to come to this because I could see from the day I met you that you didn't belong together." [ACCOUNTANT, AGE 29, SEPARATED AFTER LIVING TOGETHER 3 YEARS]

My parents said they thought that she had always been emotional and hard to get to know. They said they thought she was disturbed. [SALESMAN, AGE 30, DIVORCED AFTER 3 YEARS]

He told me he was seeing somebody. I had no idea. Well, as I talked it over later with the kids, the kids would say, "Mom, remember when he'd go on the motorcycle and take two helmets?" And I said, "Well, I never noticed that he brought two helmets. I don't know when he could have been seeing her. You know, he was a real family man." Except then my son said, "Ma, he used to leave the Little League games. He'd take me, stay a while, then come back at the end." [TEACHER, AGE 48, DIVORCED AFTER 22 YEARS]

There is something staggering about discovering that people who witness our relationships from a distance, exposed neither to our private thoughts nor intimate conversations, have knowledge we ourselves do not possess.[41] After separation, a man went to disclose the problems in the marriage to his wife's mother. When he arrived, it was he who was shocked, not she. His mother-in-law showed him a pack of letters dating back four years, in which her daughter had consistently written about wanting to end the marriage. More staggering than the simple fact that other people have secrets about our relationships is the *content* of what they know and reveal. One woman was outraged to learn her husband had been trying for years to seduce her sister. Her sister and mother, both practicing Catholics, had discussed it and decided not to tell her, for fear the knowledge would damage the marriage. They told her after he left. This outpouring of bad news affects initiator and partner differently. The initiator's thoughts and decisions about the relationship are confirmed. The partner, on the other hand, is stunned. These revelations result in social embarrassment and loss of face—the partner not only must adjust to the content of the lie, the hidden life, but the fact of the lie itself and the betrayal.[42] The partner contemplates not only the loss of the future, but of the past, for the past was not what it seemed. While many similarities exist between losing a partner who dies and losing one who no longer wants to be with you, here is one of the differences. When a relationship ends because one participant decides it should, people don't sit around with the survivor afterwards and reminisce about what a great person the departed was.

One wonders at the ability of others to disclose such painful information to a person already obviously in pain. Intimates frequently claim that they share their negative observations in order to diminish the partner's injury and help soothe the loss.[43] If the partner could only realize that the initiator is not a good person, then perhaps the partner will feel better about uncoupling. Moreover, intimates believe that by pointing out the flaws in the initiator and relationship, the partner will be discouraged from accepting responsibility for the failure, which she or he tends to readily assume, at least in the early stages of separation. But intimates who make disclosures about the initiator and the relationship must also overcome their own feelings of loss. In forming an alignment with one partner, friends of the relationship usually relinquish their bond with the other. The physical distance diminishes contact, which often is interpreted as rejection, especially by children.[44] By focusing on the absent member's negative characteristics, intimates work through their own rejection and loss and engage in their own social mourning process. By sharing their secrets with the partner, intimates contribute not only to the partner's ability to go on without the initiator, but also to their own.[45]

BARRIERS TO RECONCILIATION

After such disclosures, both partners' definitions of the relationship and the other person grow more negative, creating additional barriers to reconciliation. The partners are held to the path they have begun by what other people know.[46] It is almost as if, in the absence of a formal uncoupling ritual, those who uncouple devise one of their own. Each person assembles a supportive community, whose witnesses view with interest the subsequent unfolding of events. Each person feels pressure to behave in a matter consistent with what these witnesses now expect.

After we have described how the other person has done us in, explained how the match was a bad idea from the beginning, and carefully chronicled the partner's flaws, to behave in any way contradicting the negative impression we've created causes us to lose face. We can be assured that those sympathetic to our cause will not watch in silence. Either we were wrong then, or we are wrong now. Once grievances have been made public, anticipation of social response can curtail every exchange between the separated couple—from simple conversation, should they pass on the street, to the negotiation of a reconciliation. As one person said, "How could I ever have taken her back after I told everyone what a turkey she was?"

Going public interferes not only with possible negotiation for reconciliation, but with something even more basic: staying in touch. Two separate locations make getting together a matter of planning. When together, many partners find they have less to talk about; there are fewer common experiences, and some, when shared, are divisive, enhancing the sense of separateness. Conversation gets restricted to what they formerly shared ("How is your mother?"), the relationship ("I thought you had a good time on our last vacation. Did you?"), or matters related to the separation ("Can you take the kids on the weekend?"). In the absence of the partner, each discusses feelings and experiences with other people, thereby decreasing the need to share daily events.[47]

Approaching each other becomes harder and harder. Emotional tensions surface, and lifestyle differences are accentuated. Even when animosity is absent or at a minimum, encounters tend to have an aura of strangeness rather than familiarity. Alignments, too, inhibit access. When one partner resides with family or friends, for example, sympathetic and protective others witness and react to every phone call and visit between the two. Each partner can be pushed away by gossip believed to be circulating.[48] Should one of the partners live with a new lover, approach is made even more difficult.

The same problems of alignments and access can intervene in other relationships. The husband who leaves his wife for another woman finds that the children align with their mother. Determined to maintain his relationships with them, he visits home several times a week. The children, feeling abandoned, respond to his arrival with indifference, hostility, and verbal abuse. The pain of these visits causes him to come less frequently, adding to the children's sense of abandonment. The destructive cycle continues, and parent and children are forced farther and farther apart.[49] Relinquishing territory is easier than trying to hold onto it. Feeling more and more like outsiders, both partners tend to drift away from those who are aligned with the other person. Their absence allows the ties to weaken, perpetuating and strengthening the alignment that has begun.[50]

Also—separation is a lot of work. Informing others of the break-up then caring for those affected is draining. Changing established living patterns demands energy and constant negotiation. Once an apartment has been found, everybody has been told, clothing and money have been reorganized, the utility bills are in one name only, a household has been created, and a separate social life underway, getting back together becomes more and more difficult. As the news spreads from the intimate environment to family and friends, to acquaintances, and, finally, into the realm of public knowledge, a fragile situation becomes more and more stable. As separation makes the change in the relationship more and more public, the barriers to getting back together grow.[51]

Perhaps the effect of going public can be better understood by considering the tenuous character of an extramarital affair. The very nature of the relationship is private, a secret seldom shared. Without others to confirm it in conversation and interaction, its maintenance rests solely with the two participants. Terminating it does not require negotiation with multiple others. What Mother and Dad think is not a factor. Contrast this with a relationship in which one or both people are public figures. Separation is a media event, causing reactions among countless others who consider it their prerogative to comment, probe, and generally take actions that may affect not only the two people, but others close to them. The greater the audience, the greater the social pressures to stay together once together—or to stay apart, once apart.[52]

Some benefits may befall those couples who have a more obscure life—gays who keep their relationship a secret; couples who live in cities distant from their extended family; couples who have recently changed location, or move frequently, never integrating into the social life of

each new location;[53] couples who are childless. They have greater freedom to negotiate their relationship with each other without immediately
negotiating with others. Their isolation reduces the social disruption at
separation: fewer people to tell; fewer competing common ties; fewer
barriers to recoupling.[54]

While having a smaller public may reduce the disruption of separation, the benefits should not be considered without weighing possible
costs. The fact that others know and acknowledge the relationship creates pressure to try to work things out when people become unhappy.
Without that public confirmation, a relationship is less stable, more precarious.[55] Should the couple separate, each person will have less support. Who can partners turn to, for example, when their homosexual or
married lovers leave them, if no one knows that the relationship exists?

Couples who regularly commute or live together but are kept apart
for weeks or months by their work appear to have the best of both
worlds.[56] In their time apart, they each may develop their own social
life in addition to the one they share at the home base. These shared
friends at home lend stability to their relationship. If they separate, the
availability of individual support in their separate locations may reduce
the need to compete for support from friends and relatives who are common property.[57] Moreover, their frequent separations are taken for granted
by all who know them, who consequently raise no eyebrows at this
parting. The couple can negotiate with each other without interference,
or go their separate ways unchallenged. Because the separation does not
immediately become public, one or the other (or both) may continue to
parade under the guise of coupledom.

While remaining publicly coupled and privately separate may have
certain benefits (for example, optimizing tax deductions, keeping the
news from others until the right moment, restoring personal mental health,
preserving public reputation, retaining the freedom to negotiate), the
absence of public redefinition keeps both people from moving on. Initiators cannot fully endorse their chosen lifestyle; partners, still bound
to the past and present, can seek no future of their own. For, in addition
to validating their separate identities and presenting barriers to getting
back together, going public stimulates the processes that are central to
the transition: redefinition of self, other, and relationship. For initiators,
the covert simply becomes overt. Separation elaborates and confirms the
transition that has been going on for some time. For partners, however,
going public *precipitates* these processes, and thus their own uncoupling—wanted or not.

NINE

The Partner's Transition

*T*HE partner, now alone, sorts through memories, re-living conversations, arguments, and critical moments, searching through the history of the relationship for explanations.[1] Now it is the partner who begins to mourn, venting despair, questions, disappointment, sorrow, confusion, and anger to self and others.[2] In conversation and writing, the partner tries to create order out of the chaos.[3] Intermingled with the hurt and other emotions are positive reflections and longings. The partner mourns the loss of the happy moments and the other person's admirable qualities. Focusing on personal inadequacies, the partner takes the blame.

You know, I'd come home late from the Y and she was always a good housewife and that means she'd have to leave supper on the stove and that always bugged her—the fact that she'd have to come out afterwards when I got home. I always sat down and had a drink, you know. And she'd say, "You ready to eat yet?" And I'd say, "No, not quite." I'd say, "Well, I'm ready to eat now," and then she'd come out and fix my dinner. I think this bugged her. She complained several times about having to do dishes so late in the evening and things like that. This is my fault. I took advantage of her, I guess, and took her for granted. I did. [PRODUCTION MANAGER, AGE 52, DIVORCED AFTER 25 YEARS]

It's not fair to just say the man is a shit and he did this because he is a rotten human being, which would be nice to think but I don't know. It does take 2 people to destroy something, it really does. You have to do something in order to make somebody want to leave you,

153

even if it's just being yourself. [DANCE INSTRUCTOR, AGE 28, SEPARATED
AFTER LIVING TOGETHER 4 YEARS]

The partner begins to redefine the relationship's history to fit the present situation, painfully extracting the negative. The good has not been forgotten—the emphasis is merely shifting. The partner comes to suspect that the relationship has been in trouble for some time. In retrospect, the initiator's signals and attempts to communicate unhappiness become vivid and significant. The partner starts to see the other person's actions in a different light.[4]

The other day in the car I heard the song. He was very much into country-western, and we had lots of records. He would play the same song over and over and I used to think he just likes it. So when you hear a song over and over again you don't even listen to the words. The other day I heard the words. The man is singing about how important this other person is to him, that she is his whole life, that she is his this and that, but he can't get to her because he's caught in this other situation. I mean, how obvious is that. [TEACHER, AGE 35, DIVORCED AFTER 11 YEARS]

He was growing apart from me and I didn't notice. We once had a conversation that had to do with material things, that I realized had to do with emotions. I realized it later. What it was was that instead of being a couple, or being a unit, he wanted to have personal possessions, and personal interests, and personal emotions. [STUDENT/ SERVICE COORDINATOR, AGE 28, SEPARATED AFTER LIVING TOGETHER 1 YEAR]

The relationship assumes a less gilded, more somber hue. Though partners now redefine it as seriously troubled, many continue to hope for reconciliation.[5] They persist in seeing the initiator's good qualities and the relationship's positive aspects. Believing the relationship to be saveable, they still want to try and will not move on until they redefine it as unsaveable. What is true for initiators is also true for partners: they really cannot leave someone they like. To make their own transition out of the relationship, partners must redefine initiator and relationship negatively, legitimating the dissolution. Like initiators before them, they must work through their grief, not by abandoning the relationship, but by transforming its meaning in their life.[6]

TERMINATION STRATEGIES

But we do not construct our realities alone.[7] We do it with others, who deny, confirm, and shape how we see the world and ourselves. Those who have aligned with the partner help out by contributing to the partner's reordering of events. Yet it is the initiator's behavior that plays the critical role in altering the partner's view. Now separated, the initiator must convince the partner that the relationship is unsaveable. Some initiators try to ease out; they use kindness and concern, expressing affection and offering support to help the partner gradually adjust to the idea of going on alone.

> *I could not really tell him that I didn't love him because I thought it would kill him. So I told him, "I love you, but I can't live with you." I kept telling him that when he wanted an explanation. It was only partly true, but I kept telling him because I didn't know how else to do it.* [STUDENT, AGE 21, SEPARATED AFTER LIVING TOGETHER 1 YEAR]

> *I did wait to take the ring off until he had. I noticed at one point that he had stopped wearing his ring. I think he stopped doing that to hurt me. And then I didn't even really stop wearing mine completely until I had announced to him, talked to him about the dissolution. I wouldn't wear it the rest of the time, only when I knew I was going to see him, or friends of ours.* [DAY CARE CENTER ASSISTANT, AGE 24, DIVORCED AFTER 4 YEARS]

Even now, the partner gets mixed signals. In attempting to be kind and gentle, the initiator reinforces the partner's belief that reconciliation is possible. The partner may hear "I love you," or see the ring still on the finger, and, despite the separation, interpret these as signals that the relationship may be restored.

Some initiators continue to do little things for the partner: take care of the laundry, cut the grass, visit relatives, run errands, prepare casseroles, handle financial matters, or repair the car. These actions may arise from a sense of responsibility, guilt, caring, or simply politeness. Some originate out of a fear that the partner is going to withhold resources: money, the children, the stereo. Or perhaps initiators are able to give up the other person but not the partner role, so they continue to follow the patterns of the past out of habit. The partner views the continued caretaking as a positive sign.

Sometimes the initiator does some single act that confuses the partner.

> *He never called, he never came by. Whenever he had something to say to me, he wrote a letter. He kept a key and at times when he knew I would be gone, he would come by, you know, in and out, just picking up things that were his. Sometimes I'd come home and find something was gone or that he'd fixed something around the house. On Christmas eve, when we came home from church, he had been to*

the house and he'd left a present for me. He made a coffee table. He had started it last year, but finished it. There it was, finished. Honestly, I didn't know whether to cry or be angry. How can this man not want to live with me and do something like that? [SALESPERSON, AGE 35, SEPARATED AFTER 15 YEARS OF MARRIAGE]

The confusing act need not be such a grand gesture. It may be as simple as a heartfelt and genuinely warm greeting exchanged in an unexpected meeting on the street. For the person wanting the relationship to continue, the encounter implies a continued positive connection, generating hope that the other person will be back.

Often, partners cling to the belief that the relationship will be restored because of the behavior of initiators who conceal their true feelings about the course the relationship is taking. They are happy to be living separately. Released from the tensions of the relationship, initiators are also freed from the strain of living in two different worlds. Now (or soon) they will engage in the lifestyle they've been moving toward and will no longer have to continue the false life constructed for others.[8] But, not wanting to hurt the partner, some initiators mask their contentment. They convey, instead, an impression of loneliness, uncertainty, and introspective personal struggle.

Again, the partner receives mixed signals. Now separated, the initiator does not appear to be managing well alone. Maybe things can be worked out. Sometimes the initiator's introspective personal struggle may be genuine. Once away from the partner, the initiator may wonder if the decision to separate was correct and confess that uncertainty to the partner or, in fact, go home, then leave again. The partner who, on separation, concluded that the relationship was in serious trouble, now revives the belief that all will be well. Should coming and going become routine, the power of separation as a signal is obliterated by what follows, as in the following relationship:

He said, "I'm seeing someone." I said, "Do you love her?" And he said, "I don't know." "Do you love me?" And he said, "Yes." After a period of strain he announces, "It's all over. I'm not seeing her anymore." And I believed him. I thought everything was fine. We canned that summer together and did all kinds of things, you know. And then in November I came home one day and there was a note there and it said, "I've left. Don't look for me." And I started crying. The next day the car pulls in the drive and he was back. "I'm sorry. I'll never do that again." And he was crying.

One day, about 6 months later, I was cooking eggplant in the kitchen. I was so happy cause he was working at a regular job and every-

thing. Everybody was home from school. He used to come in every night around 6:00 and the doorbell rang so the kids answered the door and I was browning the veal and they're saying, "Mom, come to the door. Somebody wants ya." And I said, "But I can't. You tell 'em," you know. They said, "No, mom, they said they have to see you." I went to the door and the sheriff handed me a subpoena for a divorce. And the kids are saying, "Mom, what is it?" And they're all standing around me. Here I am with the kids standing around me. "Daddy wants a divorce?" And I started to cry. So, I mean everything is burned and we all sat in here. He's walking in the door at 6:00—"Hi, everybody." I said, "How can you say that? Look at this." He said, "Ah, Mary, you know, I been thinking about that for awhile." He had told me about the affair, but then he told me that it was over. So I said, "Is it her?" And he said, "No, I just want to be free and independent." He stayed here, and things got very strained, and he said, "Well, I don't know if I really want it or not." And I think when his 30 days was up he dropped it or something. [TEACHER, AGE 48, DIVORCED AFTER 22 YEARS]

The partner also receives mixed signals when a decision is made to separate, but for various reasons the two people continue living together. Whatever the logic behind it, the decision perpetuates the partner's hope that the relationship may yet be mended. The situation further disintegrates when, in response, the initiator vigorously displays discontent to convince the partner that this is not the case.

She seemed to have a need to keep discussing our problems so I could see it from her perspective. One night she was at it from 11 to 2:00 AM. She aired every past grievance. She seemed to be taking all the complaints she had never aired before and laying them out, making me a villain. It was punishing, it was devastating. [STUDENT, AGE 24, SEPARATED AFTER LIVING TOGETHER 4 YEARS]

He was not talking to me during this time. There was a big silent period there where he refused to say too many things to me. Not so much a silent period, but he did not explain anything to me. We shared meals. We talked casual conversation. Watched TV, you know. Everything. Go to a movie. But if I asked him a serious question, he refused to answer. I don't know why. He sure kept his distance. [CARPENTER, AGE 23, SEPARATED AFTER LIVING TOGETHER 1 YEAR]

No, the whole five months we lived in the same house but like I said he refused to allow me to do anything for him. Many nights he didn't come home and I had no idea where he was. A lot of times he would

*just come home at 7:00 in the morning and take a shower and change
clothes and go to work.* [WAITRESS, AGE 28, DIVORCED AFTER 7 YEARS]

Some initiators leave no room for doubts. After the physical separation, they realize the partner will not give up hope until all possibility
of reconciliation is eliminated. To terminate the relationship, initiators
who previously have withheld the full extent of their private feelings
now drop the bomb, revealing a secret guaranteed to end the relationship.[9]

*He said he hadn't loved me for seven years. Not at all. And I said,
"What about the time we went to Cleveland?" and he said that was
hard for him because he hadn't loved me. And I said "But I thought
you had a good time" and he said, 'I was acting." He finally said
to me, "Look, I never loved you. I married you because we went
together for six years and it was kind of an expected thing for us to
do and when I think about it I never did love you."* [EXECUTIVE SEC-
RETARY/SUPERVISOR, AGE 34, DIVORCED AFTER 9 YEARS]

*She would tell me about her big experiences with her new lover and
I would tell her she was hurting me. I don't think she was trying to
hurt me, I think she was thinking of me as a friend. She just said she
was happy to be free and I think she wanted me to share in her
happiness, as someone who was close to her, but obviously I couldn't,
it was just too devastating. I told her I just couldn't take it, that I
didn't know why we had broken up in the first place and I certainly
didn't want to hear about this woman. What she really wanted to
impress upon me was that she didn't love me. She loved somebody
else.* [GRADUATE STUDENT, AGE 35, SEPARATED AFTER LIVING TOGETHER 2
YEARS]

*He kept saying all along that there was nothing I could fix. I was the
perfect wife, the perfect mother. He just didn't love me anymore. He
drove me crazy because he couldn't give me a reason. I accused him
of cheating on me. If there had been a woman, I could have understood, or accepted it better. While at the time he denied it, after we
separated he told me he had been cheating on me. He—how can I
say this—had been experimenting with his sexuality.* [MEDICAL TECH-
NOLOGIST, AGE 30, DIVORCED AFTER 9 YEARS]

Others try to convince the partner that the relationship is unsaveable
by using the indirect methods that have been part of the display of discontent since beginning their transition. They decrease interaction to the
point that it is nonexistent.[10] They may leave town, giving the partner

no mixed signals, simply one clear one: they are gone. Some stay but convey the same message by refusing to interact. Some interact unpleasantly. They violate the rules of the relationship, demonstrating their lack of concern and caring in ways that offend the partner's dignity.

> *He never comes for the children when he's supposed to. He forgets, or is late, and sometimes they see him later at the shopping center or in the car with some woman. Am I supposed to tell the kids he's a good guy?* [CLERK, AGE 28, SEPARATED AFTER 6 YEARS OF MARRIAGE]

> *She was trying to get as much money as she could. Her lawyer came up with this unbelievable proposal, and she did know how much I made and what we had, yet this proposal was really calculated to strip me of everything. I would be poverty level. I mean, she was merciless. She showed no sign of human compassion, no sign at all.* [LAWYER, AGE 38, DIVORCED AFTER 12 YEARS]

> *The only time that I had any contact with this woman he was seeing was Thanksgiving Day. He had not been home for a couple of days and I was just feeling sorry for myself. I picked up the phone and called her because I knew her last name and had looked up her phone number, and I said to her, "Are you planning on seeing Ronnie today?" She said, "He'll probably stop by," and I said, "Well, wish him a happy Thanksgiving for me," and that was the whole conversation. Then he showed up in mid-afternoon and the son of a bitch came to borrow the electric knife to bring over to her house! He was having Thanksgiving dinner there!* [EXECUTIVE SECRETARY/SUPERVISOR, AGE 34, DIVORCED AFTER 9 YEARS]

The initiator feeds into the partner's negative reassessment of the relationship. Negative redefinition is important to the partner's transition for the same reasons it was important to the initiator's. By emphasizing the bad points, the partner begins to leave the initiator behind. But in order to uncouple, the partner also must find alternatives that yield the stability and identity the relationship provided. Finding alternatives is not simple however, and, as we have already noted, some people have more alternatives than others.[11] Unfortunately, partners face some immediate disadvantages that initiators didn't. First, partners do not have the luxury of time to weigh and choose among whatever alternatives they do have.[12] Requirements for money, housing, childcare, emotional support, and other basics of daily life cannot wait. Second, urgency notwithstanding, partners have trouble mobilizing resources in their own behalf.

BARRIERS TO MOVING ON

They have lost the sense of self necessary to rebuild a social world. Not only do partners suffer loss of identity, but they must also contend with the idea that they've failed a major test of adulthood: the ability to succeed in a relationship.[13] Some abandon the notion of their own self-worth to the extent that they come to believe they deserve to be left.[14] Often their sense of failure prevents them from initiating contacts from which they might gain support or important information about managing their changing life. They prefer the safety of solitude to the danger of social encounters.[15] By choosing isolation, they deprive themselves of the positive feedback so essential to rebuilding their self-confidence and their ability to use whatever resources they have.

In addition, partners have little motivation to get life going again, suffering not only a loss of identity, but the sense of having a societal niche. Expectations no longer have any meaning; partners have lost their future. They have little control over the changes in their life and feel forced to consider and choose among alternatives, none of which are preferable. Often, partners are not only unable but unwilling to see themselves in new roles and will not begin to actively pursue life on their own until it is clear that the relationship is unsaveable.[16]

Some react to the loss by temporarily abandoning the resources they do have. They drop out of their accustomed social setting, relinquishing other roles that have provided structure to their life in the past, giving themselves over to what observers may view as a chaotic existence. They terminate relationships with friends, parents, or children, quit their jobs or take a leave of absence, or move to a different location.[17] But many who appear to be succumbing to a life of total disorder are, in fact, creating an order that makes sense to them. Apparently random travelers may be renewing ties that contribute to a positive self-image: connecting with old friends, visiting places where things have gone well for them. They may find order simply in being free from the frequent crisis negotiation that besets the newly separated.

I left my job about the second week. I had to get away from all the hassle. I drove, then I would stop someplace and take any job I could find—even did yard work. One place I stayed two months, that was the longest. I'd find a room, stay there, go out, but mainly I needed the quiet to think. I had got so I couldn't think at home. I'd never done anything like that before—I'm really a responsible person with the kids and all. I'm a responsible parent. But I couldn't cope anymore. I needed the space. [MACHINIST, AGE 29, DIVORCED AFTER 6 YEARS]

Our notions about drop-outs as people whose lives are aimless and haphazard are mistaken, for survival itself demands organization. Partners who turn to drink or drugs may, in fact, organize a social life around their habits. Bag ladies, homeless men, mental patients, and hobos all have daily lives characterized by routine.[18] One partner, who lost his job just prior to separation and his house at separation, took a job driving a cab. Though all traces of his former routine were missing, he created a new one that gave him temporary solace. Gregarious, he worked through the history of the relationship with his passengers "thousands and thousands of times." When his shift was finished, he spent his evenings drinking alone. "I needed something to do," he said. Even promiscuity, random by definition, can add stability and order to the life of one willing to seek it, for securing multiple partners requires time, diligence, and organization.

Others increase their investment in resources that have given structure to their lives in the past. For many, the main source of stability comes from their personal space and the support they find from their neighborhood and friends. They may devote extended and concentrated time to their children. They may rely more on the comfort and company of those who have aligned with them. They may return to their parent's home, or have a grown child move in with them. They may spend more time with friends. They may find comfort in the routine of work and associations with co-workers. They may convert a friend to a lover.

Partners who quickly form a new intimate relationship are likely to choose someone with whom they feel safe and who presents little risk of a permanent connection. Still hurting and perhaps with many major life issues still unsettled, partners cannot bear the thought of another uncoupling. Safe people are, in some way, unavailable. They may be in town only temporarily, or be so different in age, occupation, or religion as to be inappropriate for a long-term relationship. The new lover may also just be out of an intimate relationship and thus similarly wary. Or perhaps the partner opts for a fantasy relationship—one that is more imagined than real. The new love may live far away, be coupled, or emotionally distant, and not reciprocate the partner's feelings of love. The partner derives identity from the other person, enhancing a fragile self-concept while at the same time protecting it by choosing a person who appears to be permanently elusive.

Some partners find solace in religion. Interestingly, I found no initiators who turned to religion as an alternative to the relationship. Indeed, many initiators mentioned turning away from it at some point during their transition. This difference is not surprising. Both initiator and partner strive for consistency, seeking alternatives that harmonize with their sense of self and their place in the world. Initiators do not find consistency in adherence to religious ideology that supports commitment to relationships, while partners frequently do, at least in the early stages of separation.

Some partners, unable to create stability in the absence of the initiator, withdraw from routine interaction, mentally breaking down or falling ill.[19] While this, too, may appear to outsiders as a complete disintegration, some partners find both comfort and identity in the role of victim—their lives become organized around the rejection. Because of their obvious vulnerabilty, resources come to them. They can focus their disordered life around their loss and the routine of professional care, either incorporated into their regular daily activities or administered within an institutional setting.

Partners tend to seek immediate comfort wherever they can find it, taking temporary refuge while they work through their experience. But this is not the equivalent of moving on. They continue to organize their lives around the relationship—they think about it; they talk about it; they write about it. They try to communicate with the initiator. They get the engagement ring fixed, repaint the house, talk to a counselor, slash the initiator's tires, dedicate themselves to self-improvement, trash the initiator's apartment, or abduct the children. They may pursue some favorite activity of the initiator's: following a particular athletic team, going out for Mexican food, reading mystery stories, working for some pet cause of the initiator's, or cultivating the initiator's friends.

And they wait. They wait for the phone to ring, for the letter to be answered, for the visit with the children, for the check to arrive. They plan for the next encounter: what they will say, what they will wear. They continue to invest themselves in the past and the other person. These activities testify to the strength of the connection. Perhaps they have managed, in the wake of the disorganization that accompanies separation, to find some stability. But they have not yet reorganized their identity.[20]

Sometimes that first refuge becomes a permanent lifestyle, but it happens by default. One choice precludes the possibility of others.[21] The partner who finds solace in a fantasy relationship, deriving stability from a romantic connection with an elusive partner, reduces both the need and the time available to pursue someone who might be a true companion. While in the beginning, this is, of course, the goal, the fantasy itself inhibits setting a different course, for naturally the real world will appear uninteresting in comparison. Another example of a supposed temporary alternative that becomes permanent is the partner who, unable to afford a place to live, moves in with parents. While the support and help at a time of crisis are invaluable, the partner again assumes, to some extent, the rights and obligations of a family member, decreasing the time available to pursue other alternatives. The choice confirms not some developing autonomy, but an old identity: dependent child.

Partners who remain in the dwelling the couple shared similarly limit their options. They prolong the sense of belonging to that other person and perpetuate the coupled identity. Living in the same neighborhood where (perhaps) everyone is coupled, or where everyone treats them as coupled, inhibits partners from creating new lives distinct from the past. Not all who are left behind, however, are comfortable with the idea of moving out, nor do they really have that option. For economic reasons or for raising and educating a family, some partners remain in the same setting.[22] They may gain support by drawing on these familiar resources, yet their transition to a separate identity becomes more difficult. If the partner rather than the initiator moves to a new location, this move will contribute to redefinition of self, speeding the partner's transition. The necessity of surviving in a new environment, making a new set of friends, and creating a nest without that other person all contribute to the establishment of a separate identity.

A variation of this temporary alternative-becomes-permanent theme involves the partner who seeks and acquires state aid. Transfering economic dependency from the initiator to the state reduces other options and may make working unprofitable. Having found a solution to financial problems, the partner is deprived of a work role that could confer a positive identity and lead to still other alternatives. Instead of a new positive identity, the partner assumes a discredited one, which has its own effect on alternatives.[23] Partners who make the parent role a primary source of identity sometimes invest themselves in their children to the extent that they deprive themselves of the possibility of any social life of their own. Moreover, they face still another transition when the last child leaves home.

Some partners forever wear the badge of rejection: they permanently assume the role of victim. While they initially attract attention and support from family, friends, and perhaps even the initiator, prolonged withdrawal from routine interaction eventually reduces potential alternative roles. They may give up access to or lose a job, or withdraw from other positions of responsibility that contribute to a positive self image. As these alternative roles atrophy, these partners, by default, invest increased energy in the victim role, intensifying their focus on the relationship and their loss. They dwell on and recant the episodes of their perceived victimization by the initiator and become so engulfed by a sense of social and personal failure that they are no longer able to project their usual image. Other people at first respond to their plight by giving them attention and support, thus rewarding them for their loss, and confirming and perpetuating the victim role.[24]

Eventually, however, the partner alienates these well-meaning others, who tire of the seemingly endless introspection, anger, and negativism. The situation that often occurs between partner and initiator is repeated: the partner is unable to be attractive when attractiveness is most needed.[25] Friends withdraw. With the gradual elimination of other possible roles, the partner tends to fall back on the only alternative remaining. Clinging to the victim role, partners continue to relate to the world on the basis of their loss.[26] I might speculate that partners who commit suicide may be those who no longer find confirmation of the victim role from any source. No longer deriving identity from the only role they have left, they take a step that brings self into consistency with social reality: they destroy the self altogether.

What reverses this downward spiral? Sometimes, with no apparent change in external circumstances, despairing partners seem to reach inward, at last finding an internal resource that causes them to re-engage in the social world. One person described spending an evening at home, reading a good book. "I forgot that I could have a good time all by myself. I had a lot of fun by myself before we started living together. Remembering that, I knew that I could make it alone." Another chronicled a history of depression that went on so long that she thought of taking her life. She recounted "Then one day, I noticed everyone was having fun but me. I decided if I didn't start having fun now, I never would. So I started having fun." A second way the downward spiral is reversed is that life suddenly bestows some unexpected gift to restore self-confidence and stimulate a re-engagement with life. A job applied for six months earlier comes through. A perceptive someone dispels the despair with a brief but marvelous love affair. Regardless of whether the job or the lover become permanent, the partner takes these events as symbols of another life that awaits, and begins anew.

REDEFINITION OF SELF

For most partners, however, the social impact of separation changes their lives so that the first refuge is not a permanent one, but a way station—a safe niche from which they eventually begin to move on. Partners, of necessity, have to negotiate other social settings on their own. They are pushed out of old paths to meet the normal demands of continued existence. And they are pulled toward the new.

In carving out a daily life, partners are brought into social settings where they observe and consider other lifestyles. They begin closely monitoring the world around them, weighing and gathering information that prepares them for life without the other person. A woman who has never before worked now spends her days in an office, observing the conversations, habits, and values of her co-workers. A man moves into a singles apartment complex, or temporarily shares a room with a partnerless friend, receiving a crash course on the social life of the unattached.

Some partners are better prepared to go on than others. Their life experiences have given them the skills necessary for survival. A man spoke of the importance of his military experience in teaching him how to fend for himself. A woman, raised as an "army brat," mentioned how the many travels of her family contributed to her ability to quickly adjust to change. Others described cultural differences and family expectations that made them experienced resource finders. One woman believed that more than anything else her marriage prepared her to live on her own.[27]

Some expect to draw some advantage from the fact that they have been through a similar loss before. As one said, "I know what happens next." They enter their unwanted singledom as a proven survivor. But they are often surprised. Regardless of the varieties of life experience that partners bring to the separation, this event is, to all, a unique loss. Previous experience may have left a residue of information about the pragmatic aspects of ending a relationship, of living independently, of finding resources. But it did not prepare them for the loss. If they have experienced rejection in the past, a new rejection may immobilize them, rendering the past experience utterly useless.

Consequently, partners try to understand their present experience and prepare for their new life. They may read books on parenting, sexual techniques, the art of communication, relationships, and self-improvement to learn what went wrong and do better in the future—if not with the initiator, then with the next person. They also begin to seek out information about separation, living singly, loss, transitions, and divorce. Some may resist for awhile, even as they resist accepting the seriousness of their own situation. But others are drawn to information about uncoupling. They devour whatever expertise exists on the subject. They may talk to a lawyer. They become fascinated with other people's relationship difficulties, hoping, perhaps, to gain some understanding of their own problems. They listen attentively to popular music with lyrics that characterize their plight. Some do not so much seek information as have it imposed on them. The sheriff serves them papers; they begin to learn about divorce.

The information may come through intimate conversations, as partners find confidants with whom they feel safe revealing their innermost thoughts and feelings. Some have trouble exchanging the details of their personal life with others. Others, not by choice but by lifestyle, have few resources on which to draw.

We lived together. We owned a business together. We worked together. When he left I was kind of isolated. At that time no one in my family knew I was gay. I really didn't have any close male friends, either. He had eliminated them very easily from my life. It was OK to have women friends, cause they weren't threats, but to have male friends, he felt it was some sort of threat to him indirectly. So I lived with that, that jealousy. I had two women friends—they were gay themselves, but I couldn't confide in them. I just couldn't talk to them. [FLORAL DESIGNER, AGE 29, SEPARATED AFTER LIVING TOGETHER 7 YEARS]

I was in town with my husband as the only person I knew. I think a lot of things happened to me because of the physical distance between all those people and Bill being the only one I know, I think I became very invested in the marriage at that time. What was for sure was that when we separated I was away from all of my family and friends. The people who were right on the scene were all his people—his sister, his parents, his business associates. I had no one. [SECRETARY, AGE 27, DIVORCED AFTER 5 YEARS]

My whole life had been work and the family, work and the family. I really had no good friends—she was my best friend. She arranged our social life, none of those people were people I had brought to the relationship. It's funny, but I never realized how little outside work and family I had till she was gone and I had, first of all, nothing to do in my spare time, but then the scary part was there was no one who cared about me, how I was doing. Even my family. She was the one who had gotten close to them. I had no one to talk to. I ended up, for the lack of anything better to do, spending all my evenings and weekends in bars, talking to whoever would listen. [RESEARCH ADMINISTRATOR, AGE 38, DIVORCED AFTER 16 YEARS]

Personal reservations and lack of potential confidants notwithstanding, at separation even the most hesitant find someone to listen to them.[28] They may turn to one trusted friend or relative, or may instead resist all who know them well, preferring to discuss their experience only with people outside their usual daily activities. Some do "talk to whoever will listen". the person on the barstool, or the one on the bus.

The partner may consult a minister, social worker, lawyer, or counselor. The more gregarious may join a singles club, group therapy, or a

women's consciousness-raising group. While the partner may seek out confidants to gain solace, advice, or help in pasting the relationship back together, these contacts have additional effects to aid the partner's transition. In regular contact with these experts (so-called either by profession or experience), the partner learns the new languages, habits, and lifestyle changes that accompany separation and rejection and observes how others have negotiated the transition.[29]

From those drawn to the partner and those whom the partner seeks out, from ties that are renewed from the past and those begun as a result of the separation, the partner finds a transitional person. People perhaps more peripheral to the partner in the past may suddenly become important because the partner perceives their relevant expertise: they live alone, or are separated or divorced. But the transitional person may be even more narrowly specialized. The partner is more likely to be drawn to other partners—those who've shared a similar experience. Initiators, by the way, seem to gravitate to other initiators. As was true for the initiator, the partner may find more than one transitional person since the partner also is modifying her or his life in ways that lead to the addition, subtraction, or modification of other roles. So perhaps the partner will rely on either a co-worker, a lover, an old friend, a lawyer, or a therapist—or perhaps expand and diversify, relying on a co-worker, a lover, an old friend, a lawyer, *and* a therapist.

Gradually, the partner's friendship groups change. The interplay of pushes and pulls, the social dynamic inherent in uncoupling, gives momentum to the partner's transition. Partners begin to drift away from the former social world[30] and seek people more like them.[31] They are bonded to their new life by what they have in common with those who share it and separated from the old life by growing differences in lifestyle and experience.[32] Having less in common, partners may continue to relate to old friends and acquaintances on the basis of past bonds, disguising the differences. They survive by creating secrets of their own. Some, on the other hand, may try to bring the others along by sharing the details of their changing life. The partner eventually may feel that friends from the coupled life "don't know me anymore." The bonds weaken, in spite of good intentions, due to the gradual withdrawal of partner, friends, or both.[33]

Symbolic Objects

As the partner's social world shifts to conform to a changing self-concept, so also does the physical world. Signs of the partner's transition become visible to others, as the partner takes an increasingly active role

in redefining self. Physical change often anticipates or accompanies a change in lifestyle. As the partner enters the work world or drops out of it, goes to school or tries the singles scene, takes up jogging or joins the welfare rolls, the transformation of identity may be reflected in weight loss or gain, change of hairstyle, clothing preference, or, similarly symbolic, change of name.

At some point in the transition, partners reorganize the residence they shared to suit the needs of one adult, rather than two. Furniture is rearranged or thrown out. Closets and drawers are reordered.

You know what happened? I went away on my birthday. I took my dog and went up camping. So I woke up—that was kinda sad. You know, the first birthday I'd ever spent alone. But it wasn't bad. I came back. I came in and I was kinda depressed, threw a few things around the house, got pissed off at things—but that day I decided I was either going to sink or swim on my own. And I was responsible for myself. And that's the day I changed. I remember I stayed up that night real late rearranging the house. And I did what I wanted to do. I moved things. I took the curtains off the walls and burned them cause I'd always hated the pattern and then I took all the crap off the walls that I didn't like. Drawings or paintings or things I didn't like. Mine. Hers. Just stuff. Mutual things. But basically what I did was I moved furniture around and I just did things in a manner that I wanted to do them. I set the place up the way I wanted it to be set up. And from that time on I did what I wanted to do and I felt good. [ART TEACHER, AGE 31, SEPARATED AFTER 6 YEARS OF MARRIAGE]

The partner's transition is reflected in the ability to get rid of objects that symbolize the relationship: pictures of the other person are put away—or slashed; the business card is torn up; the ring is removed.[34] One woman took a plastic bag and went through the house, eliminating everything her lover gave her. One man engaged in a near-ritual replacement of old with new by inviting his new lover over for the weekend. They spent the time dusting, sweeping, and polishing, as the man swore he'd get every last trace of his former partner's long hair out of the house. Another man gave away all the wedding presents he and his partner had received, the baby furniture they had been collecting in anticipation of starting a family, and all the matched sets of dishes, towels, silverware, and furniture. He started over with a living room empty of all save his proud possession, a new racing bike. Women tend to begin with the bedroom.

Over the Fourth of July weekend, a friend had mentioned new sheets. Everytime I changed the bed it made me angry, because those were Doug and my sheets. So I went shopping and bought new sheets, spread, shams, and redid the bedroom. I painted the walls and everything. I got rid of the marriage bedroom and made it mine. I always think of it as my Independence Day. [MEDICAL TECHNOLOGIST, AGE 30, DIVORCED AFTER 9 YEARS]

The initiator's belongings are returned or destroyed. Mutual property is divided. As the two now have "your friends" and "my friends," they also now have "your records" and "my records," "your furniture" and "my furniture."

Certain places and experiences also symbolize the initiator and the relationship to the partner: a favorite haunt, a vacation spot, a shared activity. While some avoid places and events that connect them to the past, others acknowledge that they try to reclaim this sentimental territory for their own separate biography.

One of the things I remember was how my feelings about the ball games changed. Helen always loved the ball games. For a time there I followed the games on TV and in the paper, but they made me so lonely. But it was important to keep up because I thought, you know, if I saw her, we could talk about the team. We'd have fun doing that. Then there was a period when I couldn't stand watching or reading about the team, and then I stopped noticing. Didn't know what the schedule was. In town, out of town, what. Later, I started seeing this woman, this Betty, and one night I heard myself ask her if she wanted to go. We did go. I want you to know, I wasn't sure how I was going to be, I mean she didn't have any idea what I was feeling. You know, it was fine. I mean I thought about Helen some, but mainly I had fun with Betty. I felt like I'd crossed some kind of hurdle, being able to go back with someone else. [ELECTRICIAN, AGE 62, DIVORCED AFTER 39 YEARS]

Occasionally, partners reclaim dates symbolic of the bond: New Year's Eve or Valentines Day, for example. Several initiators pointed out that their partners had made a public commitment to a new partner on a day that was special in the old relationship—the partner married, remarried, or began cohabiting on the couple's anniversary.

The partner continues to reorder personal space, meaningful symbols, friends, economic status, sex life, and habits to reflect and confirm a life and identity separate from the initiator. Now in mid-transition, the partner is caught up in two different worlds.

I still had a lot to get over. I was finding that I couldn't even keep relationships because my relationship with him still wasn't resolved. That people were saying like—well what's wrong—I was pushing people that wanted to have relationships with me—I was pushing them out of my life. They couldn't understand what was wrong with me. It was because the last relationship wasn't resolved. I was still in love with someone who I knew that it was over with and I could never live with again and could never have that same relationship with again. [LAB TECHNICIAN, AGE 26, SEPARATED AFTER LIVING TOGETHER 3 YEARS]

TEN

§ ———————————————————

Uncoupling

*U*NCOUPLING *is a railroader's term. When a relationship ends, it's like when a locomotive uncouples from a car or a car uncouples from another car. They're hooked together with knuckle couplers. They interlock, like your knuckles do when you clasp your hands together. When a locomotive uncouples, you pull a coupling pin on one side and one lets go, or you pull a coupling pin on the other side and the other lets go, or you pull both pins and they both let go. I know. I was a brakeman. I used to do that. Get the mechanical aspect of it? It's like a relationship. One can let go, the other can let go, or they can let go at the same time. But it's also a mechanical letting go because they no longer live together. They live separately. They do different things. They're no longer hooked up in mechanical ways.*
[MECHANIC, AGE 39, DIVORCED AFTER 12 YEARS]

Although now apart, each partner witnesses the other person's transition. Formerly participants in each other's life, they are now observers. They see the home transformed, or with new occupants. They see physical changes. They see the other person master new skills and demonstrate unexpected ones. They see the other person with someone else. For both initiator and partner, what they see brings with it some sense of exclusion and loss. Equally as important is what they don't see. Being physically excluded from the routine of life with the partner does not diminish one's awareness of it.[1] Knowing it's the other person's birthday and not being present, hearing they are having a personal crisis and not giving a hand, realizing it's Sunday and they are at the ballgame— all contribute to each partner's redefining self and other as separate.

171

Both people also witness changes in themselves, which feed into this redefinition process. As they negotiate life on their own, they begin learning who they are without the other person. They gain insight about the relationship as they remove themselves from the patterns developed with the former partner. People describe this experience as one of discovery:

I lived all my life with 18th century antiques. I went out to buy furniture and discovered that I liked Swedish modern. [LAWYER, AGE 50, SEPARATED AFTER 26 YEARS OF MARRIAGE]

Alex left, he said, because I didn't give him good enough sex. He said there wouldn't be anyone who would want me, as soon as they found out. Well, what I discovered was that Alex was a lousy lover. [OFFICE MANAGER, AGE 27, SEPARATED AFTER LIVING TOGETHER 5 YEARS]

I doubted that anyone would really come to visit just me. I discovered that they would. [HOUSEWIFE, AGE 60, SEPARATED AFTER 39 YEARS OF MARRIAGE]

She used to always want me to come watch TV with her after supper. I always had work to do. After we separated, I discovered myself watching TV in the evenings. I seldom worked. It must have just been my way of avoiding being with her. [POTTER, AGE 32, SEPARATED AFTER LIVING TOGETHER 9 YEARS]

Some of the discoveries are pleasant; some are not. In the other person's absence, we have no ready scapegoat for the ills that befall us. When the same things keep happening over and over, but under different circumstances, we eventually have to confront the painful fact that we must be contributing to them.

I always thought Jamie was holding me back in my career. I discovered after she was gone that it wasn't her. [LAWYER, AGE 32, DIVORCED AFTER 9 YEARS]

I always complained about the house. When I left, I moved in with a friend and discovered piles of newspapers, books, pencils, scraps of paper everywhere. I went home to visit and it was neat and clean. I was shocked to discover it was me all that time. [TEACHER, TECHNICAL SCHOOL WRITER, AGE 39, DIVORCED AFTER 18 YEARS]

I never had fun when we went out with other people. I thought it was because of who I was with. Since I've been seeing other people, I discovered I'm just not very good in groups. I get feeling inadequate, and that depresses me. [LEATHER CRAFTSMAN, AGE 42, SEPARATED AFTER LIVING TOGETHER 12 YEARS]

For those married, the decision to seek a lawyer and initiate legal proceedings adds formal confirmation to the relationship's demise. Institutional legitimacy may grant stability to an ongoing relationship, yet legal ties hinder the dissolution of a relationship in trouble. In order to uncouple, the married not only must redefine themselves as separate entities for relatives, friends, and acquaintances, but must also do so in official records. While those living together may feel the absence of legal ritual is to their advantage, formal proceedings facilitate the redefinition process that is essential to the transition. By taking legal action, the two people announce the change in the relationship to a broad audience. Partners display their discontent in a formal setting. The adversary proceedings sharpen and reinforce the separation of the joint biography, as each partner, seeking separate ends, attempts to manipulate public definitions.[2] The formal division of property, custody decisions, final removal of the rings, and the legal termination all convey the message that the relationship is over, not only to outsiders, but to the two main participants.

> *I had really wanted out of the relationship for ten years. It was all I had thought about. When he left, I did not once regret it or miss him. Yet when I read the separation agreement and saw his name and my name, the date and place of our marriage, the names and birthdates of our children, I was overwhelmed. Twenty years of a life were ending and reduced to a few pieces of paper. We were really doing this to ourselves.* [HOUSEWIFE, AGE 41, DIVORCED AFTER 20 YEARS]

> *I felt like an anvil had been lifted off me that day, so that it was over at last, because it was over two times before and two times back and I just wanted peace. The rest was a formality and the courthouse was that final scene, the curtain had dropped, you know, these are legalities that made it all real. It was scary. It was like it was this staged thing. It was a necessity that you had to go through. So much had happened. It was a final scene that I needed. I felt a great sense of loss, a great sense of failure. And this doom had set in.* [SECRETARY, AGE 38, DIVORCED AFTER 10 YEARS]

As the change in the relationship has become increasingly public, the result is a continuing decline in the precariousness of the new arrangement. Yet this is not synonymous with uncoupling, which is complete when the participants define themselves and are defined by others as separate and independent of each other—when being partners is no longer a major source of their identity. Instead, that identity comes from other sources. Arriving at this point depends on a complex intermingling of redefinition of self, other, and relationship. And this takes an unpredictable amount of time—separation or divorce are seldom the final stage.[3] People can live apart or be divorced and still not be uncoupled.[4]

The divorce didn't end it. When it took place, that day, you know, we weren't sure what had happened. Really, I mean we went to dinner and so on. She gives a kiss, I give a kiss. We went away on a vacation together. And when we visited her sister's house, we share the same bed, and her sister says, "Are you people divorced for real?" We went out. For six months we were very close. But she didn't want the marriage. I wanted it, but she didn't. [SOCIAL SERVICES WORKER, AGE 44, DIVORCED AFTER 19 YEARS]

I knew that I was in better shape than she was because I was the one who pushed for the split. Still, even a year later I was still very vulnerable to her actions. If I saw her at the supermarket, or someone brought her name up, or if she called about something, which she seemed to do pretty often—like she was trying to find stuff to talk to me about, did I see the exhibit, so-and-so called, the dog got sick, you know—I was always upset by it, by talking to her, being reminded of her. I just wanted it to be over and it just took a long time for that to happen, for that connection to be broken. [DENTAL ASSISTANT, AGE 27, SEPARATED AFTER LIVING TOGETHER 3 YEARS]

Uncoupling does not occur at the same moment for each participant. Both, to uncouple, make the same transition, but begin and end at different times. Initiators, as we have seen, have a head start. But ultimately, aided by the initiator's behavior, by comparison with alternatives, and with a little help from their friends, partners begin to put the relationship behind them. They acknowledge that the relationship is unsaveable. Through the social process of mourning they, too, eventually arrive at an account that explains this unexpected denouement.[5] "Getting over" a relationship does not mean relinquishing the part of our life that we shared with another, but rather coming to some conclusion that allows us to accept and understand its altered significance.[6] Once we develop such an account, we can incorporate it into our lives and go on.

Over time, partners' accounts change from the self-blame that characterizes first attempts to understand this experience. When partners believe they are at fault, they assume the relationship can be saved—for what they have ruined, they also can fix. As they come to the conclusion that it is unsaveable, their accounts will correspondingly justify the relationship's demise on the basis of something beyond their ability to correct.[7] Like initiators before them, partners conclude that the failure was the result of an unavoidable external circumstance, or some fatal flaw in the relationship—or perhaps the seeds of destruction were in their beginnings.

I really didn't feel like she left me. I felt like she was the victim of people who pulled her away from me. I think that if she had left me for another man because she didn't love me or whatever, that I could have handled that. But it was almost like those old Shirley Temple movies. Someone kidnaps her. I felt like it just wasn't fair, that she had been taken away—that somebody took her away from me and that was terrible and I was just overwhelmed with this feeling of there's no chance to get her back. [STUDENT, AGE 24, SEPARATED AFTER LIVING TOGETHER 4 YEARS]

She was the most emotionally demanding person that I've ever met because of the fact that she was emotionally starved her whole life. I blame everything that happened to us on her parents because they were just awful, miserable. They hated each other and they took it out on her. [PSYCHOLOGIST, AGE 36, SEPARATED AFTER LIVING TOGETHER 6 YEARS]

I think basically I blame the fact that I became divorced on the early age that I was married. I was married at 19 and he was 21 and I think our value systems weren't formed at that time and later we just grew apart. [EXECUTIVE SECRETARY/SUPERVISOR, AGE 34, DIVORCED AFTER 9 YEARS]

Why he started this behavior is all tied up with the fact that all of a sudden he found himself a father of teenage girls and he wasn't a father of little kids anymore. He was feeling old and going through a crisis of middle life. In his case he had an illness already, so it hit him worse than normal people. He just started acting crazier than usual. It just brought me to my senses. I thought he's never going to get better, in fact he's getting more nutty as he gets older. I think once I saw that, which was about six months or whatever after we separated, I was definitely sure that I didn't want him anymore. [HOUSEWIFE/HANDCRAFT GOODS SUPPLIER, AGE 35, SEPARATED AFTER 15 YEARS OF MARRIAGE]

The partner will define the relationship as unsaveable in ways that reduce both the personal sense of failure and the possibility of social stigma. When the partner develops an account that seems to be complete and makes sense, the time spent in reflective thought and conversation about the relationship diminishes. Partners, too, arrive at a point when the other person seems to be someone they no longer know.[8]

He's changed. He's gotten a permanent, and it's kind of frosted on top. The curls seem strange for him. He's changed his appearance so much that he doesn't seem like the same man I lived with. At this point he has changed drastically personally. I'm quite sure he is on drugs. He was the three-piece business suit, responsible man who went to gold chains, tight dungarees, open necked shirts overnight and his eyes were all glassy and pupils dilated. [TEACHER, AGE 35, DIVORCED AFTER 11 YEARS]

I see his face and I remember him as a person. But I've totally erased even what I thought at that point was an exorbitant amount of pain that I went through for all those years. I have no animosity toward him. I don't have any bad feelings at all. It's like looking at a stranger. Basically I must have dealt with him in a sound way because I came out on top. I can talk with him in a rational way. I can laugh with him, I can joke with him, and its like talking to somebody that I knew a long time ago and just had not seen for a long time. [ACCOUNTANT, AGE 38, SEPARATED AFTER LIVING TOGETHER 13 YEARS]

I didn't feel divorced when we separated. I guess you could say that something clicked inside of me in terms of feeling divorced when I realized that this woman who I supposedly loved so much responded to what I perceived at that particular time to be putting my life on the line to save her—when she responded to this with trying to send me to jail, something clicked inside of me and the rest was just over a period of time I felt more and more divorced and I began to live my life independently, not tied by emotional responses to her. [MACHINIST, AGE 29, DIVORCED AFTER 6 YEARS]

We came from the same kind of family background, and shared a lot of similar values. Manners and politeness were important to both of us, you know, respect for the other person. And then he abandoned that toward the end, and became wild and reckless and crazy. Rude and loud and disrespectful of others. He almost became a different person. [STUDENT/SERVICE COORDINATOR, AGE 28, SEPARATED AFTER LIVING TOGETHER 1 YEAR]

Many partners do not totally accept the idea that the relationship is over until the initiator becomes coupled with someone new. With that step, the tentativeness is gone. When the initiator recouples soon after parting from the partner, the news often shocks the partner and others close to the relationship. How could the initiator have found someone else so quickly? What others perceive to be a sudden incomprehensible change is, of course, not sudden at all, but a consequence of a transition that has prepared the initiator for this step. The shock is accompanied by a sense of loss, even when the partners have ceased being in touch in any regular way. When the other person forms a new partnership, it changes and limits interaction. For those who hope for reconciliation, it seals off the possibility. Children, friends, and family who have held on to a similar hope must also finally lay it aside.[9] For the initiator, the partner's recoupling is also a significant event, which often generates an unexpected emotional response.

When people have truly uncoupled—established a life confirming their independent identity—they will again be free to see both the positive and negative qualities of the former partner and the relationship. Negative definitions are essential to transition, but they are often temporary. When people achieve a valid self-identity, they no longer have to work at dissociating by focusing on negative attributes and displaying discontent. They are then able to reconstruct the history of the relationship to again include the good memories of the times shared.[10] Instead of discontent, they may display apathy. ("I don't hate him. I don't love him. I don't want anything awful to happen to him. I don't care if anything good happens to him either. I just feel neutral.") They may speak kindly and sincerely of the partner to others. ("He's a good father." "She's a hard worker.") They may even demonstrate good will and affection to the partner.

The initiator may be able to acknowledge the good in partner and relationship before the separation. When the partner is still dependent on the relationship, however, the initiator feels less free to reveal positive sentiments for fear of reinforcing the partner's hope that the relationship will continue. If, on the other hand, *both* partners are well along in their transitions prior to the physical break, vivid differences appear at separation. Each is free to take care of the other, appreciate the other, mourn the loss with the other, and, as in the case of the couple who held each other tenderly on the floor of their empty house, they may literally and figuratively help each other out of the door.[11]

Not only do the former partners tend to concede that the other has positive characteristics, but their generous reassessment can extend to other relationships left behind in the wake of uncoupling. Once they have achieved an independent identity, partners no longer need to dissociate from their former lifestyle. They are free to acknowledge the good qualities of former friends and family and perhaps incorporate them in their life once again. Sometimes these ties are renewed many years later, as when a lawyer at age 29 saw his father for the first time since his parents separated; the last time they were together, the son was 3.

Ties with family and friends are often renewed when one or the other recouples. Having made a public commitment to a new relationship, initiator or partner may return to the previous social circle, picking up the threads of the former lifestyle with the new person—naturally with some alterations and embellishments to account for the changed cast of characters.

Each partner's account of the relationship's demise makes still another shift, as each arrives at a stable explanation that either removes them both from blame or joins them in the responsibility.[12] As independence frees the partners to see both positive and negative aspects of the other, so eventually they are able to look back and assess their own contribution to the fall. They're aided by their discovery of who they are without the other person, for chances are they've learned some things about themselves that alter their view of the past.

> *I wasn't even looking at things and evaluating things like I should have been. You know, looking at me and saying, "What were you doing? How did you get hooked up with this other person?" I had to do all that in retrospect, after it was really over, after all the pain was gone, after all the problems were gone, after I could look him in the face and after my heart didn't skip a beat to see people walking down the street that looked like him. But that took time.* [STUDENT, AGE 21, SEPARATED AFTER LIVING TOGETHER 2 YEARS]

> *And when that dependence was broken on both our parts, that is when I said OK now, let me evaluate the whole situation in realistic ways. I'm not going to make excuses, I don't need to make excuses anymore. Then I began to think back—what did I say, what did I do—what did she put up with, what did I put up with—how did we stifle each other—and we paid a terrible price. Nineteen years of living a substandard existence. We have a lot to make up for. What she lost, what I lost.* [SOCIAL SERVICES WORKER, AGE 44, DIVORCED AFTER 19 YEARS]

For some, uncoupling can never be complete. One or both of the partners may not be able to develop a new life that becomes self-validating. When this is the case, the display of discontent signals their continued connection.[13]

> *I've spent a great deal of time talking about this, and thinking the whole thing through. And frankly, I've thought about it just as much as I think I want to. The thing is continuously a part of my life. No matter what I do, and no matter who I am with, those experiences and those memories are still going to be a part of my being. And a lot of them I don't want to get rid of. I know that I still have a lot of*

anger and hostility in relation to him that I have not expressed com-
pletely. I continuously think about those things but they're never any
different. And I find myself on certain occasions allowing all of the
anger and all of the hurt that I've suppressed to resurface at certain
times. And then, I guess I say to myself that . . . I'm sorry, appar-
ently I'm feeling some need to cry here, I'm feeling insecure here or
something or other . . . that I need to do this thing, to re-evaluate
the situation, or I get real angry, and hit this pillow, and say "God
damn you, I really resent what you've done to me." [GRADUATE STU-
DENT, AGE 30, SEPARATED AFTER 12 YEARS OF MARRIAGE]

CONTINUITIES

Even though people separate, move away, or divorce, visible indications of the bond between partners often remain.[14] Much as a vanished
glacier is traced by a terminal moraine, relationships leave behind social
reflections of the intimate connection. After formal termination, the bonds
between partners are visible both in continued interaction patterns and
in similarities of habit and lifestyle.

Former partners often continue to interact because they have in common something else that survives the demise of the relationship, drawing the two together. Most important and obvious of these are shared
loved ones—children, in-laws.[15] Though in-laws may, of necessity, be
excluded from the new life,[16] children rarely can be, and their very
existence is not only a reminder of the relationship, but often causes the
parents to keep in touch.[17] Former partners may also be thrown together
because of shared ownership of some property,[18] or because of some
event that grows out of their shared history. The partnership momentarily may be resurrected when, for example, a teenage child is arrested
for drunken driving; a former landlord demands reimbursement for a
damaged apartment; the IRS decides to conduct a tax audit of a joint
return. The former partners are sometimes rejoined at moments of great
sorrow or great joy. The relationship is temporarily renewed because
the time spent together has made each an expert on the other. When a
major life event occurs, sometimes only the former partner can thor-
oughly understand its significance. For both partners, the other is the
one they want by their side at such moments.

I didn't sleep with him when his father died, but I kind of acted like
his wife for the weekend. To make things easier, I did. You know, he
was very sad about this thing and I helped him. It's OK to still care
about somebody that you lived with all that time, you know. When

his father died, I had a history with him, a history that his present wife doesn't know. She only met his father once, so I think it's appropriate to comfort him when he called to tell me his father is dead, to comfort him and to say remember the times, remember this, that, and that he never really was happy since your mother died. [SECRETARY, AGE 38, DIVORCED AFTER 10 YEARS]

The promotion was something I had worked for for years, and I had to admit she had worked for it, too, in her own way. She had helped me in a lot of ways and I had recognized that it had cost both of us. When it was time to celebrate, there was no one who understood better than her what it meant to me, and she was the one I wanted to celebrate with. [LAWYER, AGE 36, SEPARATED AFTER LIVING TOGETHER 6 YEARS]

My lover of several years died unexpectedly at age 40. My ex-husband had been divorced a second time, and he suggested a trip together, so we went to Europe on a tour. The other couples on the trip commented that they were going to get divorced when they got home because, of all the couples on the trip, we seemed to get along best. [ANTIQUE JEWELRY DEALER, AGE 54, DIVORCED AFTER 18 YEARS]

Ironically, while divorce is usually taken as a sign of the end of a relationship, the divorce process itself can bind partners to each other, inhibiting them from going on. Two people are forced to continue to focus on the relationship and each other. The legal struggle consumes energies that would otherwise be spent in other directions. Suits and countersuits may take several years. The working and re-working of custody, visitation, and financial support can have people back in court long after what was thought to be the final judgment.[19]

In many cases, partners continue to interact not because of their previous role connections, but for reasons that seem to be actively created by one or both of the participants after or during the formal termination of the relationship. These "manufactured interactions" also reflect the bond between former partners. They illustrate the difficulty of severing the bond with the other person because, even when the continued contact is full of anger and conflict, the effect is to keep the relationship going.[20] Some examples from my interviews:

The initiator moves out. The partner spends the weekend helping with the relocation—hanging pictures, moving furniture.

The initiator moves out, leaving a set of tools behind. Several years later, even after the initiator's remarriage, the tools are still there. The initiator comes to borrow them one at a time. The partner is planning to move within the same city. The tools are boxed up, ready to be taken along.

The initiator moves out, but is slow to change the mailing address. Rather than marking a forwarding address on the envelopes and returning them by mail, the partner either delivers them once a week or the initiator picks them up.

The initiator moves out. The partner resists surrendering the initiator's grandmother's sewing machine. The conflict necessitates many phone calls and visits.

Sexual abuse was a constant part of the relationship. After separating, they each formed new partnerships. Nonetheless, the two kept a monthly rendezvous at a local motel, where they continued their abusive pattern.

The terms of the property settlement stated that a payment was to be made to the initiator every six months. Instead of mailing the check, the partner handed it over during an elegant semi-annual lunch.

The child support check was always late or missing, resulting in the partner making phone calls and writing letters, but getting no response. The partner got the check only by making a personal appearance.

Interaction between former partners tends to diminish, however.[21] As time passes, the partners become more engaged in their separate lives, thereby decreasing both their need and ability to interact with each other. For example, the creation of a new family often reduces the time and attention available for the old: visitation (and support checks) decrease; the elegant lunches no longer occur.[22] Some of the reasons to interact disappear. The children grow up, relatives move away, pets die, joint property is sold.[23]

As post-separation interaction decreases, the reality of their separate existences is sometimes again confirmed years later, surprising the former partners with a recurring sense of loss and a reminder of the finality of what they've done. Divorced for three years, two former partners decided to sell the family home that neither had lived in for some time. Instead, one of their grown daughters lived there, perpetuating the sense of family by reigning over the easy comings and goings of both parents, two younger children who lived with their mother, four other children, who, now single adults, lived nearby, plus miscellaneous friends of the family and assorted roomers. The week the new owners were to take possession of the house, the family organized a combined yard sale and party, billed in invitations as "A Celebration of New Beginnings." But, as one of the parents said, the effect of the divorce was nothing compared to the effect on everybody of the dismantling and sale of the family home. With the loss of the past and future locus of activity came the realization that for the nine of them, family life would never be the same.

Even though contact between former partners lessens, the bonds between them are reflected in similarities of habit and lifestyle that seem to persist after separation or divorce. Some people tend to take on certain traits characteristic of their partners after parting. Some examples: During a ten-year relationship, one person reported that his partner could not fall asleep at night with the bedroom closet doors open. He frequently left them open, which resulted in her getting up and closing them. (The impact of this near-nightly scenario on their bedroom intimacy is easily imagined.) After they separated, he found that *he* could not sleep with the closet doors open, and three years later was still compulsively getting up and closing them if a sleeping partner left them open. A woman, whose former husband complained during their marriage that she never was dressed appropriately when they went out, found that she spent her first vacation alone shopping for clothes. In the six years since the divorce, she has taken great pride in maintaining a fashionable wardrobe. Another person constantly fought with the partner during the relationship over the condition of their apartment.

> *I hated being chased by the vacuum cleaner and the washing machine was going all the time and she would empty ashtrays before the ashes got in the ashtray. I mean, I went out of my mind! We had fights like you wouldn't believe, and here I find myself today, obsessive-compulsive behavior about my apartment. It has to be neat and clean! I never figured out why I ended up being the same way she is. The very one thing I dislike a lot.* [ADVERTISING SALESMAN, AGE 38, DIVORCED AFTER 8 YEARS]

These examples involve small habits or values that could be explained simply by our unerring ability to locate the other's vulnerable points and "thrust home," as Cyrano said.[24] Equally possible as an explanation, however, is that in dissociating from the other person, we dissociate from that part of ourselves that is like them. When we uncouple, behaviors previously undemonstrated are expressed because they then become a reflection of our own identity, not our former partner's.

Sometimes, however, the similarities between the former partners are more encompassing. Instead of a similarity of habit, one takes on the lifestyle of the other. A married minister fell in love with someone else. The minister divorced his wife and moved away with his new partner. The former wife began working in the counseling center of the church he used to head, went back to school, earned a Ph.D. in counseling, and became a full-time staff member. A man who was an English professor found that soon after he and his partner separated, the partner enrolled as a graduate student in his department. He remarked with dismay that he had moved out of her bedroom and she had moved into his work space. Lifestyle similarities like these may occur, in part, because of shifting interdependence. No longer can either rely on the other person to carry out former tasks connected to the relationship. While ways exist to get around this problem (find someone else to do it; forget it), often each partner has to take on the duties of the other, in addition to his or her own. The classic example is a marriage with children, where divorce requires that the husband become more domestic and the wife be a wage-earner.[25] In the process, their lifestyles become more similar.

But lifestyle similarities also result because our merging is more than physical when we couple. Relationships develop an intangible complement consisting of tastes, opinions, attitudes, values, and ideas that we exchange and learn from each other. We create a common culture. While the physical aspects of our life are readily separable, the intangible ones are not. And so when we separate, we may take our bodies and our material belongings, but leave behind other signs that we were there.[26] In retrospect, we may think of our former partners as transitional people, for they play a major role in preparing us for whatever comes next. Both by what they teach us that we incorporate and what we reject, they change our course.

We may formally terminate our relationships and reconstruct a life without the other person. But our relationships continue to affect us, for past history affects the future and memory lies waiting to take us on unexpected journeys into the past. A friend wrote, "One never checks memory at the door. It is there to be evoked, even when unrecognized. It is perhaps because we come to accept it or can recognize and deal with it that we mature. But one is never free! Only free-er—or more/less chained."

Coupling changes us and so does uncoupling. But in most cases relationships don't end. They change, but they don't end. When both individuals develop an identity of their own, they're free to acknowledge the ties.[27] Some don't choose this option. But others transform their relationship with the former partner. Many evolve a new character, significantly different from the past and suited to present needs.[28] Former partners may become friends or confidants, turning to each other for occasional advice or support. They may become occasional lovers. They may develop a professional relationship that allows them to be included in each other's life in a regular way. It's almost as if we need to know that the period of our life we shared with another was not in vain.

I don't know that people ever lose that, that want, that wish, to be important to someone who's been, you know, such an important part of your life. And I think it has been good for me to have the feeling that he still feels the urge to come around and let off steam, or discuss something that was on his mind. [BANK TELLER, AGE 23, SEPARATED AFTER LIVING TOGETHER 3 YEARS]

I accept the fact that I'm angry with him but I'm also . . . there'll never be another man that I'll have children with. Just for the fact that we married and had children, he will always be special and because I understand his parents and his problems. I just can look at him and say, you know, the man is miserable, you know, but he is the children's father, so even though there is anger there, there's a certain amount of compassion I feel for him. [HOUSEWIFE/HANDCRAFT GOODS SUPPLIER, AGE 35, SEPARATED AFTER 15 YEARS OF MARRIAGE]

That's the mother of my kids, and I may not feel romantic about her, but I still have a sense of responsibility and she always will be somebody in my life. But there's still a sense of loss and of grieving. You know how, if someone you loved dies, you visit the grave because you want to remember. And maybe that's where you can feel the closest to them. I think that's it, there's a grief from that kind of profound loss, somebody you loved enough that you lived with for awhile, that they're gone, and it's almost, I think the emotional grief is almost as if someone died. But they're not really dead, so you want to hear them, see them and touch them once in a while. It's like going to the grave. It's like having a chance to have them come back from the dead and maybe something kind can pass between you. I don't want to possess her, I don't want to be her husband, I don't even want to have a necessarily on-going relationship, but there is that something—I want to know that she's OK and just every once in a while I want to touch base. [ADMINISTRATOR, AGE 44, SEPARATED AFTER 23 YEARS OF MARRIAGE]

And so we keep in touch, or we take something the other person gave us, incorporate it in our lives, and go on.

RECONCILIATION

Uncoupling is not a compelling journey that, once embarked on, allows no turning back. Granted, as the problems in the relationship become more and more public, resurrecting the relationship becomes more and more difficult.[29] Each phase closes yet another door. Yet the process may be interrupted at any point. Even after separation or divorce, a couple may reconcile.

Reconciliation can and does occur, but it is both a delicate and diffi-cult enterprise. To achieve a true reconciliation (as opposed to just mov-ing back in together), both partners must redefine the other person and relationship positively. In addition, they must change the definitions others hold. By deciding to reunite, both partners risk social embarrassment, for they have chosen to again create a life with the person whose flaws they have been announcing publicly for some time. They must, in other words, display their content, legitimating the reconciliation.

A further difficulty is that, for both partners, reconciliation will entail the same sifting and sorting of relatives, friends, and associates that accompany every coupling and uncoupling. Other relationships must be gained and lost, if the partners are to reconstruct a world they can share. Confidants and transitional people are often left behind—either because they're links to a lifestyle now to be forsaken, or because the secrets they know about the partners preclude their being included. By defini-tion, reconciliation entails a comparison of possible alternatives—both partners must redefine being in the relationship as superior to other pos-sibilities.

Reconciliation is not simply a return to what used to be. It is yet another transition, with its own costs. Both partners must be willing to endure the social, emotional, and financial disruption that accompanies the rearrangement of their physical and social worlds. Under what cir-cumstances do people consider it? Initiators may find that, once sepa-rated, the cost of terminating the relationship turns out to be higher than they thought.[30] They are overwhelmed by the ill will of family and friends, the loss of other relationships, missing the other person or the home environment, or the guilt associated with causing others pain. The lifestyle they have opted for may be disappointing: single life is harder than they thought; the lover proves difficult or unfaithful; work without someone to share life with is more drudgery than challenge; their in-come does not adequately meet their needs.

But if the initiator seeks reconciliation simply because going it alone is tough, but doesn't redefine self, other, and relationship, the contra-diction between the self-concept and the social niche will remain. The two may stay together, nonetheless, because the initiator hasn't suffi-cient alternatives to manage the transition, or because the initiator finds some alternative to make staying in the relationship possible. Sometimes the reunion turns out to be temporary.

We were married for 18 years and fought like cats and dogs. Finally we divorced. We were apart for three years and we both were so goddamned lonely that we decided to remarry. After three years, all the old problems finally got to us again, and we got divorced. My father said, "Alan, if you do that one more time, I'm going to have you committed." [INTERIOR DECORATOR, AGE 52]

Alternatively, the initiator may seek reconciliation after the requisite redefinitions. Separation changes the initiator, causing a reordering of priorities and commitments. The irony—rather, one of the many ironies—of uncoupling is that while separation imposes social barriers to reconciliation, living apart can itself bring about changes that leave both partners better prepared to interact: changes that, had they happened during the relationship, might have prevented all of this. Once the initiator is physically separate and has achieved some measure of autonomy, negative definitions are no longer required. Now free to compare the new life with the old on a more equitable basis, the initiator may conclude that more has been lost than won.

The initiator's ability to again redefine partner and relationship positively may occur not simply because the separation experience changes the initiator, but because it changes the partner.[31] An initiator who complained the partner was boring reconsidered on seeing the effects of a new job and regular aerobics classes six months after separation. One initiator who wanted to feel needed and care for the partner became resentful when the partner got an interesting and exciting job. As a result of the separation, the partner had a mental breakdown, and was unable to keep his job, becoming again needy and dependent. Another initiator complained about the partner's involvement with work. After divorce, the partner decided to cut back on the 60-hour-a-week job and attend to the more personal aspects of life. Another initiator felt that the partner never communicated feelings well, never spoke of love or demonstrated affection. Faced with the responsibility for the children after divorce, the partner sought therapy and began taking courses in communication. He learned to deal with his children in ways that might have made him a better partner if the problem had been rectified during the relationship.[32]

Post-separation changes in either or both people can precipitate a reconciliation, even though the partners have experienced many phases of the transition, as in the following case.

Ellen met Jack in college. They fell in love and married. Jack had been blind since birth. He had pursued a college career in education and was also a musician. Both admired the independence of the other. In the marriage, she subordinated her career to his and helped him pursue a master's degree, as well as his musical interests. Her time was consumed by his needs for transportation and the taping and transcribing of music for the musicians in his group. He was teaching at a school for the blind by day and performing as a musician at night. They had a son. Ellen's life, instead of turning outward, as the husband's, revolved around family responsibilities. She gained weight. Jack, after 12 years of marriage, left Ellen for his high school sweetheart. Ellen grieved for a while, then began patching up her life. She got a job, established her own credit, went back to college, and lost weight. She saw a lawyer, filed for divorce, joined Parents Without Partners, and began searching out singles groups. She dated. Throughout, Jack and Ellen saw each other occasionally and maintained a sexual relationship. The night before the divorce was final, they reconciled.

More often, however, post-separation changes reflect still another ironic twist in uncoupling. They happen too late.[33] Initiators may be unaware of changes in their partners. Or, if aware, initiators may have found their new social niche comfortable and confirming. So while they may note (and, in some cases, take pride in) the partner's accomplishments, they do not seek reconciliation. On the other hand, if the initiator does wish to get back together, it may be too late. The partner may have uncoupled. Often what makes the partner once again attractive to the initiator is that the partner has gone on. In creating a new life, the partner acquires the basic means of salvation. If reconciliation is what the partner desires, achieving it lies not in seeking it, but, perversely, in turning away. By giving up the past and building a future, the partner begins to create a different identity. In the process, the partner regains the sense of self that has been lost. Being once again "self-possessed," the partner interacts out of strength, not weakness.

To arrive at this point, the partner must have settled on an account of the break-up that has legitimated it. The partner has reordered the history of the relationship, concluding that it did not and could not meet his or her needs. Consequently, the partner may be unwilling to return to life as it was or to create a new one with the other person. The initiator wants to get back together. The partner says no. Now the initiator experiences rejection, and, focusing on the positive aspects of what has been lost, sinks into the morass from which the partner has so arduously climbed. Reconciliation, it turns out, is not only a matter of redefining self, other, and relationship, but of timing.

ELEVEN

Transition Rituals

U*NCOUPLING* is generally and correctly perceived by those who experience it as woefully chaotic and disorderly. Yet, despite the dubious gifts of confusion, anger, sorrow, and pain bestowed on both partners, there is an underlying order that appears across all experiences, regardless of sexual preference, regardless of the unique characteristics of the partners and their relationship.[1] Amidst diversity and disorder, patterns and natural sequences of behavior prevail.

In relinquishing the other person, both partners face loss and, consequently, change. Both, whether willingly or unwillingly, confront the same dilemma: in the absence of the other person, who am I? The search for the answer is characterized by patterns so strong and ingrained that uncoupling can be described as having ritualistic properties. Each partner redefines self, other, and relationship. Each participates in the social process of mourning, finding confidants and transitional people; each experiences the sifting and sorting of friendship groups; and so on. Language is crucial to this process. As the new definitions created by the two become public knowledge, their developing separateness is constantly confirmed in conversation. Eventually, self-realization comes from other sources rather than from the relationship. The outcome is identity transformation; the process is social transition.

In the course of life, we do move on. Ultimately, we all are bound to fall out of love, divorce, separate, lose loved ones through death, or die ourselves. We are constantly "uncoupling," from organizations as well as individuals. We leave behind jobs, parents, co-workers, churches, neighborhoods, hospitals, mentors, schools and universities, prisons, clubs, children, and friends. And they leave us behind. Though the circumstances of each leavetaking may be unique, they are held together by a common strand. They involve loss of role, and thus create the potential for redefinition of self. As a consequence, these other transitions exhibit many of the ritualistic properties we find in uncoupling.[2]

Consider, for example, the parallels between uncoupling and a transition so common that most of us experience it: changing jobs. Dissatisfied employees who voluntarily initiate the leavetaking behave similarly to initiators who become unhappy in their relationships and uncouple.[3] They sift through their experience with a company and express their dissatisfaction to people with whom they feel safe. They pursue information about alternatives. Perhaps they find a transitional person (maybe another disgruntled employee, a person who has already left the firm, or one employed by a firm they are considering). Once they have secured another position, they give notice that they are leaving. The immediate reaction of associates is often to focus on the person's positive contributions. Those threatening to depart are frequently courted with lunches, dinners, and promises of future promotions or other rewards. Should these attempts fail, however, co-workers tend to reconcile themselves to the rejection and loss by focusing on the failed moments of their former associate's performance in past and present, often displaying discontent in ways that reinforce the separation.

Suppose, instead, that the firm finds the employee unsatisfactory. Retrospectively, officials sift through the person's contributions and focus on the negative. They may fire the employee on the spot, or opt to terminate the employee by more indirect means: a temporary lay-off that turns out to be permanent, for example. Employees who are threatened with involuntary job loss seem to trace out a path similar to that of partners who are left behind.[4] They tend to emphasize the desirable qualities of the job, trying to save it, devoting energy to an improved performance, or perhaps initiating a legal battle. They thus limit their ability to investigate and pursue alternatives. Should they fail in their attempt to save the position, the entire experience causes them to focus on the firm's negative attributes. Alienated by the display of discontent, some co-workers will withdraw. Others withdraw because they are unable to take a stand. Some associates will lend comfort, however, aligning with the one who is leaving, and initiating the social process of mourning as the search for another job begins.

Whether one initiates a leavetaking or is involuntarily thrust into it seems to be fundamentally related to patterns that appear in many other transitions. Children growing to adulthood, for example, tend to become preoccupied with all the ways their parents fail.[5] Instead of working to perpetuate their parental connection, many seem to devote great energy to dissociating themselves publicly from the two people responsible for their birth until they've achieved some measure of independence—then they're free to acknowledge that their parents may have a few good qualities. In rock groups, lead guitarists, keyboardists, bass players and drummers are in greater demand than other members because of their virtuosity. Unable to satisfy their need for self-validation within the group, they are the most likely to move on.[6] People who undergo full conversion to a religious cult find a transitional person and develop bonds with one or more cult members prior to conversion, decreasing interaction with people who might try to intervene.[7]

In children's friendships, one child typically becomes disenchanted with the relationship sooner than the other. The one left behind struggles with rejection and loss, trying to puzzle out what went wrong.[8] Widowed partners tend to dwell on the positive characteristics of the departed, sanctifying objects that symbolize the relationship long after the other person's death.[9] When death is preceded by a long illness, partners tend to intensify their involvement with the other person, often giving up other activities and thus other sources of identity. After death, survivors sometimes perpetuate their link with the departed by continuing the other person's life work or crusading against the cause of their loved one's death. Retirees who leave their jobs because of age restrictions often continue to focus on the former job, both in conversation and in thought, deriving identity not from what they do in the present, but from the past.[10] For the aged, society gradually withdraws the alternative roles they might play, creating a tendency for the elderly to perpetuate the only role remaining—the sick role. Some ultimately relinquish it as well, by taking their own life.[11] If an old age subculture is available that provides an alternative identity, this downward spiral is not as likely to occur.[12]

The patterns found in uncoupling and these other transitions grow out of the observation of many lives—of many people dealing with loss of role and attempting to manage the consequences. Each experience defies absolute categorization, however. So fragile, so fluid, so idiosyncratic is the individual human situation that we can not foresee its course. Although we can identify patterns in uncoupling, we cannot conclude that all patterns will appear in every case. Many will occur, but not necessarily all. Neither can we conclude, on the basis of orderly patterns, that uncoupling is an irreversible transition. Such a conclusion wrongly denies the power of individual actors to overcome social barriers and to reconstruct the kind of personal world they want. Even though a given relationship has progressed through many phases of un-coupling, the process can be interrupted at any time.

Nor should the description of regularities obscure the complexity that exists. Patterns evolve out of myriad daily actions and reactions by the participants, with each other and with others, over an extended period. These patterns are so intertwined as to be virtually inseparable. Redefi-nition of self, other, and relationship, for example, are not separate phases of uncoupling, but occur simultaneously throughout the process. To write about them, I have disentangled them, giving them a clarity and simplicity of form they do not have in real life.

The discovery of ritualistic properties also should not obscure the confusion felt by the two people having this experience. An initiator, for example, is not someone who decides to end a relationship, creates a plan, then follows through. An initiator is a person who is unhappy. Sometimes, in the beginning, initiators do not even know why. They react to their situation by making a series of seemingly small choices. Unintentionally, they begin uncoupling. At some point the unintentional becomes intentional. Initiators decide they want out. But how they get out is seldom the result of a well-articulated plan devised during the first tinges of discomfort. The long-run effects of choice cannot be pre-dicted, because people do not recognize the implications their actions have on their identity, and consequently on their relationships.[13] They do not understand that their series of small choices are slowly initiating social change. An analogy would be a daddy longlegs sitting on a leaf being blown by the wind. To maintain balance, the insect carefully shifts one leg after another to a leaf nearby that seems more stable. Ulti-mately, the creature finds itself on a different leaf.

Reacting to their situation on a day-to-day basis, initiators evolve something I've seen across all cases—a termination strategy. What is an appropriate term for a pattern is an inappropriate description of what happens in the individual case. Behavior meets needs. The "strategy" is often a matter of short-run emotional response rather than long-range planning. The truth is, we don't know how to tell our partners we no longer want to be with them. There is no good way, no kind way, no easy way to do it without hurting the other person. Often, we are in such pain ourselves as we consider taking our leave that we act out of frustration rather than rationality, hurting others despite our wish to be humane.

Lacking any specialized techniques for painlessly delivering the bad news, initiators draw on life experiences. They fall back on the rituals for terminating interaction that they've used all their lives. Imagine, for example, two small girls sprawled on a rug, playing Monopoly. The game stretches on (as Monopoly tends to do) and one of them becomes unhappy. She is not having fun and wants to go home. She can immediately confront the partner about her unhappiness and her wish to go. Obviously, if she does, she runs the risk of an argument or some other emotional response—especially if her partner is losing. She may plan to confront the partner a little later, after inviting a friend to join the game or after playing so that the partner can accumulate some financial resources. Then the partner will not object so much to her departure. Should she be unable or unwilling to risk the social consequences of acting so directly, she can skip a confrontation altogether and simply walk off without a word. Or she may play on and on, wishing for the intervention of fate to relieve her of the responsibility for ending the game. Perhaps soon it will be dark and her mother will call her to come home.

But she can also opt for more indirect methods that shift the burden of ending the game to her partner. She may decrease interaction: she gives the appearance of continued participation because she remains at the board, but she withdraws from the game by burying herself in a comic book or becoming absorbed in television; or she repeatedly leaves the game for jaunts to the kitchen, bathroom, or outdoors; or she takes advantage of a planned break—she goes home for dinner and doesn't come back; or when the partner goes to the bathroom, the unhappy player leaves without saying goodbye. She has still other options. She may violate the rules of the game. She displays her discontent by complaining, becoming loud or silly, or destroying the order of the tokens and money on the board until the partner quits. Or she cheats. The partner catches her, calls her on it, and ends the game. Perhaps the partner makes a fatal mistake. The partner becomes angry at her absences from the board or her attention to the comic book. Our unhappy player seizes the opportunity and goes home, saying, "If you're going to get mad, I'm leaving."

The social consequences for terminating all kinds of interactions are always difficult to accept and to bear and we learn early in life how to avoid them. We routinely resort to indirect strategies to discontinue interaction rather than use direct confrontation. A dissatisfied employee takes advantage of the company's relocation and announces that he or she is unable to manage transportation to the new building and is not going to stay with the firm. After a first date that didn't quite click, the person departing promises "I'll call you," but with no intention of doing so. A disgruntled teenager, whose parents insist on his continuing his morning paper route, puts in such a poor performance that the route manager fires him. Students, bored with the lecture, repeatedly disrupt class until the teacher orders them out. A bus passenger pulls out a book or feigns sleep to avoid a chatting seatmate. A party guest, caught in the corner with a bore who never seems to pause for breath, goes to get a drink and never returns.

Although these methods have the potential to terminate other kinds of interaction with a minimum of effort, they do not guarantee an immediate exit from an intimate relationship. Such a relationship involves both a personal and public commitment, a shared residence and a shared history. Some are reinforced by legally binding contracts that can only be dissolved by the state. Consequently, intimate relationships cannot be ended as quickly as an encounter with a pesky salesperson. So many initiators, acting out of their own pain and needs, return to these rituals again and again, trying to convince their partners that the relationship is unsavable, displaying discontent, sometimes for years, perpetuating their own pain and the pain of their partners. The amazing fact is that there are moments of kindness and dignity at all.

Nonetheless, uncoupling is marked by a pattern as yet undiscussed: caring. Generally, uncoupling is thought of as a conflict-ridden experience that ends as a bitter battle between two adversaries intent on doing each other in. And this frequently is the case. Yet in the interviews for this research, the concern of each participant for the other revealed itself, even in the most combative uncouplings.[14] Apparently, the patterns of responsibility and caring that develop when people couple are not so easily dispelled. In many cases, they persist throughout the uncoupling process and afterwards.

Many people in the midst of uncoupling no doubt would deny vehemently that this concern is evident in what is happening in their lives. The need to dissociate by negative reinterpretation of people and events makes this necessarily so. Nonetheless, evidence of caring does exist and raises this question: is it possible for initiators to acknowledge this care and concern and harness it to effect a more humane way of dealing with partners? The question of what is humane must be considered by weighing a particular action's short- and long-run consequences. A direct confrontation has the initiator revealing secret feelings, thoughts, and acts with sufficient clarity to overcome the partner's ability to deny, minimize, ignore, or explain away the secrets. In the short run, direct confrontation appears to be cruel and inhumane. If the initiator holds back the secrets most likely to devastate the other person, or tries to deal with the partner with a kindness that allows the partner to hang on to dignity and self-respect, a still-loving partner will focus on the kindness, not the discontent, on the good news, not the bad. The partner will not acknowledge that the relationship is seriously troubled until confronted with a negative signal so clear it cannot be ignored. By definition, a direct confrontation is a painful revelation of secrets and a difficult moment for both people, for the disclosures are guaranteed not only to be an assault on the partner's dignity, but also to cause disruption of unpredictable effect and duration.

But consider the alternatives. Initiators who are unable to be painfully direct are usually painfully indirect. They react to being caught in an unhappy situation by becoming more and more upset by the partner's flaws, pointing them out repeatedly, perhaps resulting in the partner's erring in some fatal way, certainly destroying the other person's self-confidence in the process. Or by violating rules or decreasing interaction, they may eventually accomplish the same thing. While decreasing interaction may seem humane because partners sometimes gradually adjust to being on their own, eventually accepting or even initiating a separation, they are not spared the ebbing of self-respect and dignity that comes with the involuntary loss of a love.

Since there is no painless way of letting the other person know we no longer want to be with them, in the long run direct confrontation may be the kindest way of telling our partners we are unhappy. Direct confrontation lets the partner participate. It gives the partner opportunity to interject alternative interpretations of self, the relationship, and the other person. It allows the two people to negotiate with each other and try. It creates the possibility of transforming the relationship into one that may be better for both. And if trying does not work, the experience clarifies the situation. It enables the partner to come to grips with this turn of events as soon as possible. It frees the partner from the paralysis of hope and ignorance, opening the way for the construction of a new life.

The irony here is that care and concern for the other person—and for ourselves—keep us from direct confrontation in the early stages of our unhappiness. Relationships require constant negotiation, and that negotiation does not occur without direct confrontation. Yet our tendency is to avoid it altogether or to do it ineffectually. Only when we've found another niche for ourselves do we reveal our true feelings to the extent necessary to get the other person's attention. If only we could take charge of our transitions, breaking away from ritualistic patterns and routinely confronting our partners *before* we begin redefining the other person out of our lives and going on, we could create the possibility of transforming the relationship and thus take the other person along[15]—if that's what we want.

Consider the following example of early direct confrontation and its potential results. Relationships between couples who live together often come to a crisis over the question of having a child. The battle lines are usually drawn along the following positions. One wants to start a family. The other, perfectly content with the present arrangement, resists. Unable to resolve the dilemma, one or the other suggests separation. Still caring about each other, they separate. Neither is prepared to go on without the other person. Neither has developed an alternative to replace the stability and identity they derive from the relationship. And although both may be angry and hurt, they have not totally redefined the other person in negative terms. In the absence of the other person, they recall the positive qualities of the other person and the relationship. For both, the relationship remains central to their life and identity. They negotiate. Often, they work it out.

True, confrontations are risky. They change things. They can terminate bonds as well as generate them. Even if direct confrontation occurs in the early stages of unhappiness, the partner may respond so that the initiator's negative definitions are confirmed, speeding the initiator's transition. Another risk is that, in response to the initiator's discontent, the partner may begin to uncouple. But if both people could overcome the obstacles to telling and knowing and engage in direct confrontation when discontent is young, the possibility exists that both still will have a vested interest in the relationship's continuance. Never will the degree of investment and commitment be identical for both. But the relationship may be sufficiently central to the life and identity of each that neither may be prepared to go on. With early revelation of secrets, the asymmetry that characterizes most leavetakings is missing, creating the possibility that two people may try—and succeed.

On Telling Secrets to a Stranger

*A*N invitation to be interviewed was an invitation to make secrets public to a stranger. The interview itself promised a relationship—one made intimate by the revelation of private thoughts and acts. Although some people may refrain from disclosing the intimate details of their life to outsiders—and even to insiders—unless absolutely unavoidable, others are comfortable confiding in someone who is separate from their daily routine. For whatever reasons, those who agreed to be interviewed felt comfortable revealing secrets to me. Differences between those who were willing to disclose the secrets of their intimate relationships to a stranger and those who were not raise the possibility of bias in this work that deserves to be acknowledged and discussed. Therefore, it becomes important to examine how I included people in the study, conducted the interviews, and analyzed the data.

The pilot study I did as a graduate student consisted of interviews with people who were well educated, for that first inquiry was exploratory, and I began by interviewing people I knew, gathering additional names of people to be interviewed from them. From those interviews, I evolved a tentative model that I wanted to expand and develop. My hope was to enrich the original model by courting diversity absent in its evolution. I sought variation along certain dimensions, social class being only one. I also wanted to interview young and old, male and female, gay and straight, married and living together.

My first attempt to expand the research to include various social class backgrounds was a miserable failure. I sent 100 letters to individuals (not couples) systematically selected from newspaper divorce listings that appeared from one to five years prior to the selection date. Four responses trickled back. Follow-up phone calls revealed that many people had relocated. Some responded politely, some abruptly, but no one agreed to be interviewed. The meager response in exchange for the amount of time required to produce it caused me to seek more information before I proceeded. I gave copies of an article I had published on uncoupling to counselors who had special client populations: a priest whose parish was a working-class black neighborhood, a social worker who primarily counseled people in a Puerto Rican neighborhood with high mobility, a social worker who dealt with delinquents, many of whom were from broken homes, and a social worker whose clients were addicted to narcotics. I met with each of these specialists after they had read the article and asked them to compare it with what they knew about relationships among their own client group. Their responses were identical. Definitions of what a relationship was and expectations about them were so different as to make the experiences noncomparable. Negotiation and gradual transition were not an obvious part of relationships that ended.

While this was, in fact, exactly what I wanted to document, the counselors were uniformly pessimistic about my ability to get the details I was interested in from people like those in their client groups because they tend to view all outsiders as potentially threatening (e.g., as truant officers, probation officers, undercover officers, social workers, creditors, or others who sometimes intervene in their lives in unwished-for-ways). On the basis of the meager results of the newspaper announcement mailing and the pessimism of the counselors, I made a pragmatic decision. I limited the research (and consequently this book) to a description of how those in the vast middle of the class structure uncouple. Still, I sought variation in sex, age, legal status of the relationship, and sexual preference. I turned to a snowball sampling strategy reported to produce diversity and be unbiased by friendship networks.[1] The research requirement of disclosing secrets of intimate relationships to a stranger affected participation in the research. The people I interviewed were unwilling to give me the names of others unless they first got permission from them to do so. By definition, the referrals I got were close ties, not distant ones. To minimize the friendship network problem, I evolved my eventual strategy, which can best be described as snowballing from the multiple starts described in the Introduction to this book. Because I did not have easy access to some types of experiences, I purposely recruited to fill these gaps.

For those who chose to participate in the research, I became a confidante. As caretaker of their secrets, I felt a deep responsibility to minimize the extent to which I might intervene in their relationships or interfere with their personal well-being. I tried to create an interview environment in which they not only felt safe, but were safe. I suggested they choose a setting in which they were comfortable. Usually we ended up in my home or theirs, but occasionally in my office. Conscious of the potential effect on a person in a relationship in transition of being interviewed by someone interested in uncoupling, I was careful how I introduced the research. I said that while I was interested in how relationships end, the fact that I interviewed them did not necessarily mean that their relationship was ending. In truth, little is known about how people get back together after a crisis, and I was equally as interested in learning what I could about reconciliation, and I told them this. I discussed anonymity and confidentiality, explaining how I would blend their experience in with others, both in the analysis and in the writing. I told them I planned to highlight certain points by using anecdotes from individual interviews, and explained how I would identify the quotes. I offered them their interview tape or a copy of the typed transcript.

Then I asked them to tell me about their relationship, beginning with the moment when they first sensed something was wrong. They attempted to put their experience in chronological order, and I interjected questions along the way. People were often painfully candid, as evidenced by the quotes that appear throughout. I believe this frankness was, in part, a reflection of voluntary participation. Putting their experience in chronological order had an additional evocative effect. As each story unfolded, it seemed to develop a momentum all its own. The telling of it regenerated past emotions that carried the story along, often spawning a retelling of actions and reactions that were essential to explaining the sequence of events, regardless of how those actions and reactions reflected on the speaker's own character.

At the same time, they demonstrated concern with what I thought by apologizing for tears or anger, or asking me if something they felt or did or thought in the relationship was "normal." I was continually struck by how isolated individuals are from the experiences of others, and tried to respond in ways that put them in touch with that larger experience.[2] I would respond either from what I had learned doing the research (e.g., "People do sometimes cry when they talk to me. Separation is a traumatic experience, and in talking about it people sometimes feel it again very deeply'') or from my own life. Having been both initiator and partner, I always had a ready and heartfelt response. If asked for advice, I never offered it. I pointed out that I was not trained to counsel or give advice, but encouraged them to see a professional if they had questions or problems they wanted help resolving.

I did, however, take it as my responsibility to help them make a transition from the interview, with its focus on the past, into their present life. The chronology naturally eased them into the present, and I terminated the interview only when the person seemed to have said everything they wanted to say. Then I asked them questions about the interview, in order to bracket the interview as an experience and separate it from their experience in the relationship. Their reflections on the interview were important in their own right, because I wanted to know in what directions the content of the interview had been affected and to check their emotional well-being at its conclusion. I asked them if they had thought about it ahead of time, and, if so, what they had thought. I asked how they felt during the interview and at its conclusion. If they were upset by anything they had discussed, I listened until their emotions seemed to be discharged. Sometimes people made a comment as we were saying goodbye that indicated that, having just made me the repository of their secrets, they needed to know that I thought their life was OK. I could always respond positively and sincerely from the evidence they had given me, for I was touched by their ability to emerge in some way a victor from the experience.

In order to uncover the major patterns in the transition, I read each of the 103 typed interviews, examining each person's experience for what appeared to be major changes in the relationship. I re-examined the results of the pilot study I did as a graduate student, developing 26 turning points, or benchmarks, of the transition.[3] I used these as a guide, identifying particular statements in the interviews that seemed to indicate a particular phase. At this time, I made a decision about whether the interviewee was initiator or partner. Then I cut up the interview, taped each marked statement on a file card, and identified the card by the category I had marked in the margin. I identified the speaker by interview number, role, type of relationship, sex, and sexual preference. I filed the cards according to the categories I had established, arranging them in what I believed to be chronological order. For example, the first phase was "Secrets."

I created another card file of material from other sources: interviews with counselors, literature review, observations from visits to groups for the separated and divorced, conversations and other personal observations, autobiographies, magazines, newspapers, and so on. These, too, were organized using the original 26 turning points as a guide. Then I proceeded through each of these files, making finer distinctions, looking for negative instances, developing categories and subcategories based on the material that was there. When I developed a new category in the "interview file" I added it to the "other sources" file and vice versa. Working both within and between files, I identified 120 categories and subcategories in the transition.

I then returned to clean, intact copies of the interviews and analyzed them again on the basis of the expanded categories, extracting additional material and entering it under the appropriate file heading or making a new one. I continued distributing and redistributing cards between and within files, increasing within-category variations, until I had a sense of closure. When I finished, I had three file boxes of "interview" cards and three of "other sources" cards, arranged to reflect the chronology of the transition and, not coincidentally, the chapters of this book. I wrote the book category by category, working from the front of the boxes to the back, integrating material from both sets of files as I wrote.

The writing and analysis were emotionally turbulent work. In the interviews, I was often moved by what people said, but preoccupied with my role as interviewer. Any emotional response on my part was fleeting, because I had to analyze and reflect on each succeeding statement to guide the interview. I was surprised to discover that I reacted emotionally to these people's lives when I began analyzing their transcripts. Reading the interviews in the attempt to identify the patterns in the transition caused me to reflect on each experience in its entirety. As I worked refining the phases of the transition, certain statements struck me, making me laugh aloud, cry, or become angry. The writing process, too, which required not simply merging the files but dwelling on and integrating data from many sources, was an immersion not only in the life experience and human vulnerability of others, but my own.

Eventually, the repetition of working through these many life experiences again and again, along with the coding, assigning categories, and all the other trappings of social science research reduced the salience of the individual experience, desensitizing me emotionally and allowing me to concentrate on the patterns the combined experiences revealed. Throughout the data gathering, analysis, and writing, I relied on the procedures of systematic generalization as a precaution against the unwitting incorporation of bias into the ongoing work.[4] The individual experiences remain with me still, not only because the people, their histories, and their insights are remarkable and memorable in their own right, but because, whether taken singly or together, the interviews reflect the centrality of relationships in these people's lives.

METHODOLOGICAL ISSUES

Despite their willingness to reveal their secrets to a stranger, I believe that those interviewed were selective in what they revealed, both out of notions of privacy and the natural tendency to save face. In addition, they had to explain a very intricate situation to an outsider, uninformed of their history and their cast of characters, in an interview bounded by natural limits in time and energy. They were forced to be selective, even when they sought to explain in detail. So they did not tell me all their secrets, but then I did not need them all. The broad outlines of each experience, when combined with all the others, were sufficient to define the major patterns of the transition. Moreover, I wanted to know not only how they experienced their lives, but how, in addition, they explained, justified, and communicated those experiences.

Talk, after all, is behavior. Because the construction of an account is an integral part of the transition, the account itself is of interest.[5] Accounts varied in content (definition of self, other, and relationship), form (stability, conciseness, length, and coherence), and emotional tone in ways that allowed me to identify important differences in how an individual experienced the relationship at different points in its history. When I was able to interview the same person several times after the separation, I could see how the account changed over time. Moreover, because I interviewed many people in various stages of transition, I had the opportunity to learn about the various stages by comparing the accounts of those who were contemplating separation, were recently separated, and who had been separated for some time.[6]

The selectivity in the construction of individual accounts raises an important question regarding the roles of initiator and partner. Given that the people I interviewed constructed an account for me, how did I determine with certainty the role assumed in the leavetaking by a particular individual? I never asked people if they were initiator or partner. I never used these terms in an interview. Instead, I examined the entire chronology of events they described. Determining who is initiator and who is partner cannot be based on attitudes or actions that occur at physical separation or divorce. Sometimes both people want and are ready for that step. In response to my opening question, "Tell me about your relationship from the moment when you first began to sense that something was wrong," initiators began with an experience or feelings of unhappiness that were accompanied by thoughts of wanting distance from the other person. These thoughts were followed by a sequence of actions directed toward separating from the other person, first socially, then physically. Partners, on the other hand, began by describing some incident or feelings of unhappiness that led them to believe the other person wanted the relationship over. Their subsequent actions were directed toward resisting a break-up. The presence or absence of resistance to breaking up was the definitive criterion.

Because this book is based on the accounts of individuals, the characteristics of those who participated in the research deserve close scrutiny. Do their uncouplings differ from the experiences of others who did not participate? Because I have no information about those who did not participate, I can only speculate about how their uncouplings might differ from those who did.

Certainly, *Uncoupling* is limited in application by the social class of the people interviewed. Most of those I interviewed had a high school education or better, but neither the very wealthy nor the very poor were included in the research. How the people at the extremes of the class structure define relationships, what their expectations are about them, the connection between their participation in relationships and their identity, and the presence or absence of negotiation and gradual transition in relationships that end are all matters that are unknown to me. The resolution of these issues must await further research.

In addition to the social class issue, the requirement of disclosing secrets to a stranger may have biased this work in other ways. Consider, first, how differences in those who participated and those who did not may have affected the material in Chapter 8, "Going Public." That chapter describes how telling others affects the development of a personal account and the accumulation of social support. I argue that both are necessary to the transition for each partner. If, however, the research selectively attracted people who, in general, were more willing to confide personal experiences to others (they did, after all, confide in me), then Chapter 8 may misrepresent how uncoupling occurs because it is the experience of "talkers." Those who did not participate may confide in others, but differ in the extent to which they do so, or perhaps some people do not confide in others at all, developing their account and making their transition alone.

Because of the many resources I relied on in addition to the interviews, I am convinced that the description in Chapter 8 is valid. Both social support and an account that justifies the loss are essential, not only to uncoupling, but to all transitions.[7] Without them, people do not go on. These essentials can be attained by talking to few or to many, however. Perhaps those who participated, on average, tend to confide in more people about their personal lives, while those who did not participate were less willing, in general, to talk about private matters and therefore confide in fewer people. I reject this as a possible bias as well, because both initiators and partners whom I interviewed varied in the number of people they confided to about their relationships. Regardless of role in the transition, some reported that they went public in a massive way, talking to friends and relatives, therapists, participating in discussion groups, and talking to whomever would listen. Others said they had discussed their situation with only one or two people.

If those who participated in the research differ in the way they go public from others of the same social class who did not, I surmise that the difference is not in whether they do or whether they don't, or in the extent to which they do, but rather in their choice of confidants. I return to the issue of willingness to confide in a stranger, but with "stranger" defined both as a person who is unfamiliar and as a person about whom some fact is known that makes them strange by setting them apart in some way. Nonparticipants were of two kinds: those who were not asked to participate, and those who had the opportunity to volunteer and did not (i.e., groups I recruited from, people who received letters, interviewees who asked permission of others to give me their names, people whom I asked directly). To these people, I was not totally unfamiliar when they made their decision. Either they had spoken to me, heard of me and the research from someone else, or received a letter asking them to participate. Of those who had the opportunity to be interviewed, both those who agreed and those who did not no doubt were influenced by some characteristic of mine: profession, the way I presented the research, personality, age, race, or sex.

I do not believe that differences in choice of confidants in any way challenges the substance of "Going Public." Some people chose not to participate because I had previously interviewed their partner, however. Occasionally, I interviewed (separately) both partners in a relationship. While this strategy introduced some obvious biases, it allowed me to gain additional insight on communication between the two and the timing of the transition for each partner. The fact that some were unwilling to participate because of the participation of their partners raises the question of a second possible bias. Chapter 10, "Uncoupling," should be considered in light of the following. By the behavior of those who consented and those who refused, I concluded that my ability to interview both partners in a relationship was influenced by the connection between them.

When I first began interviewing, people's response to my request to interview their partners raised my concern that I might somehow affect their dealings with each other. Once sensitized to this possibility, I only made the request when the circumstances seemed stable (i.e., they had been apart for a long time). Nonetheless, I learned something from those first few attempts that gave me additional insights about willingness to disclose secrets to strangers and bias. When I asked people about the possibility of interviewing their partners, I made it clear that I was not trying to get at some "truth" by comparing accounts, for each person's experience was "true" for them. I was interested, however, in comparing the timing of the transition for both partners in a given relationship. Interviewing both people allowed me to do that. (In fact, with time and other interviews intervening between the first interview and the second, I could not recall the details of the first interview.)

When I did receive permission to interview the second person, the relationship differed from the relationships where I did not. The first person interviewed was able to negotiate my request with the other and allow the other person to present their own story. From this fact and from the content of their individual interviews, I concluded that the former partners were able to see each other in a positive light and had transformed the relationship. They each had evolved a stable lifestyle without the other. In response to one of the debriefing questions I routinely asked at the conclusion of each interview about the interview itself, they noted that prior to that day they had not thought about or talked about the relationship for a long time. (Recall that arriving at a stable account allows a person to go on—people no longer try to explain to self and others why the relationship ended.) Moreover, each had arrived at an account that justified the loss, either by sharing the responsibility with their former partner or by placing it outside the control of either of them ("Our values were too different." "We were too young." "He changed sexual preference."), as opposed to blaming themselves or the other person.

In relationships where I did not get permission to interview the second person, one or both appeared to be in mid-transition. Negative definitions of the other were salient for one or both of the partners. The first interview caused me to be regarded by both as aligned with that person. When the first interviewee expressed the wish that the partner not be interviewed, the response was often phrased in ways that reflected my perceived alignment. One person expressed concern that the other person's story would challenge what he or she had said and that as a consequence, I might like the other person better; another worried that the other partner might become angry about confiding in me, and that this would affect their negotiations. Even if they agreed that I might approach the other person, they preferred not to negotiate the contact for me. Under these circumstances, I sent a letter explaining the research and followed up with a phone call. The conversation would proceed cordially until I mentioned having interviewed the partner. The recipient of the call then quickly terminated it.

Extrapolating from these early "couple" interview attempts to other people who were asked to participate in the research, I conclude that their willingness to be interviewed also may have been affected by the nature of the connection to their former partner. People's willingness and ability to talk about their relationships peak when the relationships are most traumatic for them—when they most need to understand them, when they most need the support of others. The farther along they are in their own transition, the less the need to discuss the relationship. This raises the question of why people who have been out of their relationship a long time would agree to be interviewed.

Such people may have agreed *because* they have transformed their relationship and have established a positive and, to some extent, cooperative relationship with their former partners. People separated for some length of time who had the opportunity to participate and didn't may not have transformed their relationship in positive ways. They may have had no linkages with their former partners, and apathy, rather than caring, may better describe their sentiments. They may have made their transitions and gone on to such an extent that they had not thought or talked about it for quite some time. They may have seen the interview as reconnecting with a past they did not want to be reconnected with or reminded of.

True, many of the people separated many years who *did* talk to me fit this description. Nonetheless, the majority evidenced either caring, linkages, or both. On the basis of my interviews and other sources, I concluded in Chapter 10, "Coupling changes us and so does uncoupling. But in most cases relationships don't end. They change, but they don't end. When both individuals develop an identity of their own, they're free to acknowledge the ties." I do go on to note, however, that some don't choose this option. If people separated a long time who were willing to talk to me did so because they had a positive connection to their former partner and those who were not willing did not, then selective participation may have confounded my data. Perhaps more people uncouple and never look back than I would surmise on the basis of my interviews. But because they don't, they were unwilling to talk to me. Ultimately, of course, the behavior of nonparticipants must remain in the realm of speculation. Nonetheless, what is unknown is worthy of speculation because often it can suggest the boundaries of what is known.

NOTES

INTRODUCTION

1. Peter Berger and Hansfried Kellner, "The Social Construction of Marriage," *Diogenes* 46(1964): 1–25.

2. For discussions of the proliferation of survey research over studies of process and negotiations, see Ralph LaRossa and Jane H. Wolf, "On Qualitative Family Research," *Journal of Marriage and the Family* 47 (1985): 531–541, and Reuben Hill, "Whither Family Research in the 1980's: Continuities, Emergents, Constraints, and New Horizons," *Journal of Marriage and the Family* 43 (1981): 255–257.

3. See, for example, Eleanor D. Macklin, "Review of Research on Nonmarital Cohabitation in the United States," in Bernard I. Murstein, ed., *Exploring Intimate Lifestyles* (New York: Springer Publishing, 1978), pp. 197–243, and Michael D. Newcomb, "Relationship Qualities of Those Who Live Together," *Alternative Lifestyles* 6 (1983): 78–102; Eleanor D. Macklin, "Nontraditional Family Forms: A Decade of Research," *Journal of Marriage and the Family* 33 (1980): 905–922. Research on gay and lesbian relationships remained relatively ignored until the mid-1970s. See, for example, Alan Bell and Martin Weinberg, *Homosexualities* (New York: Simon and Schuster, 1978), Carol Warren, *Identity and Community in the Gay World* (New York: John Wiley, 1974), and Joseph Harry, *Gay Couples* (New York: Praeger, 1984). For additional references, see Chapter 7, note 25.

4. Jetse Sprey, "The Family as a System in Conflict," *Journal of Marriage and Family* 31 (1969): 699–706; Scanzoni, p. 62.

CHAPTER ONE

1. Erving Goffman, *The Presentation of Self in Everyday Life* (New York: Anchor, 1959), p. 64.

2. Kurt H. Wolff, ed. and tr., *The Sociology of Georg Simmel* (New York: Free Press, 1950), pp. 315–316, 326–239.

3. The comments of initiators and partners appear throughout the book. Despite di-

versity of backgrounds, those who share the same role in the leavetaking experience the transition similarly. Consequently, I have illustrated the points along the transition by selecting passages from the interviews of initiators and partners that are not only typical of the experience, but also demonstrate those points in the most compelling way. I have noted the age, occupation, type, and length of relationship of each speaker simply to supply a context. The only editing liberties I have taken with these passages are changing names mentioned in the quoted material and eliminating redundancy within a given comment. I have recorded the occupation exactly as the person described it to me.

4. George J. McCall and J. L. Simmons, *Identities and Interactions* (New York: Free Press, 1966), pp. 90–94.

5. Steve Duck, "A Topography of Relationship Disengagement and Dissolution," in Steve Duck, ed., *Personal Relationships. 4: Dissolving Personal Relationships* (London: Academic Press, 1982), p. 9.

6. Sissela Bok, *Secrets: On the Ethics of Concealment and Revelation* (New York: Pantheon, 1982), p. 19.

7. Bok, p. 23. Bok states further that secrets are essential to all exchange relations. "Control over secrecy provides a safety valve for individuals in the midst of communal life—some influence over transactions between the world of personal experience and the world shared with others. With no control over such exchanges, human beings would be unable to exercise choice about their lives. To restrain some secrets and to allow others freer play; to keep some hidden and to let others be known; to offer knowledge to some but not to all comers; to give and receive confidences and to guess at far more: these efforts at control permeate all human contact." Bok, p. 20.

8. Bok, p. 26; Wolff, p. 314, p. 337.

9. McCall and Simmons, pp. 67, 80–94.

10. George Eliot, *Middlemarch: A Study of Provincial Life* (Edinburgh and London: William Blackwood and Sons, 1871), Chapter 42.

11. See also Julia Brannen and Jean Collard, *Marriages in Trouble: The Process of Seeking Help* (London: Tavistock, 1982): pp. 47–71, 72–92, 140–167. They describe the behavior patterns of clients who seek help from medical practitioners and volunteers who staff voluntary agencies in Great Britain.

12. Simmel discusses the consequences of changing form by adding a third member to a dyad. See Wolff, pp. 118–169.

13. Simmel notes in his discussion of secrecy, "For even where one of the two does not notice the existence of a secret, the behavior of the concealer, and hence the whole relationship, is certainly modified by it." Wolff, p. 330. Simmel also cites an extreme example of one member changing a relationship without the consent of the other. A dyad, while dependent on both members for its life, can experience death by the action of only one. *Ibid,* p. 124.

14. Goffman, pp. 19–76.

15. From my interviews, couples who live together seem to do a better job of advanced planning than do those who marry. In marriages, most often a common understanding is simply assumed. Couples who live together, however, regardless of sexual preference, frequently report designing their relationships before they move in together. In particular, they tend to create rules about division of labor and sexual intimacy with other people. See also Carol Warren, *Identity and Community in the Gay World* (New York: John Wiley, 1974); Joseph Harry and William DeVall, *The Social Organization of Gay Males* (New York: Praeger, 1978), p. 92; Joseph Harry, *Gay Couples* (New York: Praeger, 1984), pp. 65–66; Ira L. Reiss, *Family Systems in America* (New York: Holt, Rinehart and Winston, 1980), p. 105.

16. See also Kristine M. Rosenthal and Harry F. Keshet, *Fathers Without Partners: A Study of Fathers and the Family after Marital Separation* (Totowa, N.J.: Rowman and Littlefield, 1981), p. 35; Dennis T. Jaffe and Rosabeth Moss Kanter, "Couple Strains in Communal Households: A Four-Factor Model of the Separation Process," *Journal of Social Issues* 32(1976): 181.

17. Norman K. Denzin, "Rules of Conduct and the Study of Deviant Behavior: Some Notes on the Social Relationship," in George J. McCall, Michal M. McCall, Norman K. Denzin, Gerald D. Suttles, and Suzanne B. Kurth, *Social Relationships* (Chicago: Aldine, 1970), pp. 66–70; Murray S. Davis, *Intimate Relations* (New York: Free Press, 1973), p. 329.

18. McCall and Simmons, pp. 81, 88–104, 104–124, 125–166.

19. See also Michael P. Johnson, "Social and Cognitive Features of the Dissolution of Commitment to Relationships," in Duck, p. 33.

20. McCall and Simmons, pp. 244, 249.

21. Lillian Breslow Rubin, *Worlds of Pain: Life in the Working Class Family* (New York: Basic Books, 1976), p. 82; Rosenthal and Keshet, pp. xviii–xix, 48.

22. Stanton Wheeler, "Double Lives" (Paper presented at American Sociological Association Annual Meetings, Washington, D.C., 26–30 August 1985).

23. Sam D. Sieber, "Toward a Theory of Role Accumulation," *American Sociological Review* 39 (1974): 567–578.

24. Stephen R. Marks, "Multiple Roles and Role Strain: Some Notes on Human Energy, Time, and Commitment," *American Sociological Review,* 42 (1977): 931; Jaffe and Kanter, p. 179; McCall and Simmons, pp. 188–189, 229–244.

25. I interviewed no initiator who reported a dependency on drugs or alcohol, both alternatives disvalued by the dominant culture. To explain this as a function of the research method (people are perhaps unwilling to admit socially disvalued behavior in an interview) is a possibility, but people nonetheless did discuss with great frankness many aspects of their lives, regardless of whether their behavior was socially approved or not. In addition, some *partners* reported turning to drugs and alcohol. Perhaps initiators who develop these dependencies do not continue as initiators. They may find that the physiological effects of these substances reduce the salient effects of the relationship. Hence, it is no longer the source of unhappiness that it was, and they are able to continue in it. Alternatively, they may still be unhappy in the relationship but find self-validation in the social world that accompanies their dependency: a drug subculture or lifestyle that they develop in connection with their drinking. A third possibility is that the dependency becomes so debilitating that other alternatives are unavailable to them and their dependence on the relationship increases, eliminating all possibility of ever leaving.

26. See also Brian Miller, "Adult Sexual Resocialization: Adjustments toward a Stigmatized Identity," *Alternative Lifestyles* (May 1978): 226.

27. Denzin, in McCall et al., pp. 62–94.

28. In some relationships, the freedom to form sexual liaisons with others is part of the agreed-on rules of the relationship. (See, for example, Naomi Gerstel, "Marital Alternatives and the Regulation of Sex: Commuter Couples as a Test Case," *Alternative Lifestyles* 2 (May 1979): 165; Joseph Harry, *Gay Couples,* pp. 65–66.) These affairs may be engaged in discreetly and not discussed, or the couple may deal with other liaisons openly and matter-of-factly. The agreed-on rules usually specify that casual sex is legitimate but meaningful relationships are not. A casual affair, even though not discussed, does not create a breach between the partners because it has been previously agreed on, in principal, by both partners. Hence, the existence of such relationships is

not secret, though the particulars usually are. Sexually open relationships usually are a source of contention between partners, because of the threat that a casual relationship will turn into a meaningful one, and then uncoupling will occur. Should one of the partners develop a meaningful relationship with another person, however, the rule is violated, creating a nonshareable secret with predictable consequences in terms of social separation.

29. Miller, p. 229. In interviews I talked only with people for whom the change was from a heterosexual relationship to a homosexual one. I would assume, however, that the need for secrecy also exists when the choice is the reverse, for one social group is being left behind for another. In both cases, initiators must ponder the assumption of a new sexual identity considered deviant according to the norms of the group they presently belong to. The change from gay to straight does have different social consequences than the change from straight to gay, however, which may create variations in the degree of secrecy in the two situations.

30. Erving Goffman, *Interaction Ritual* (New York: Anchor, 1967), p. 127.

31. Wolff, p. 345; Goffman, *Presentation of Self*, pp. 141–142.

32. Wolff, pp. 314, 330.

33. Johnson notes that the demise of a relationship is accompanied by a gradual loss of intimate conversation over time. Therefore, uncoupling generates a need to develop new lines of communication. The process could work both ways: finding new lines of communication decreases the need to rely on the relationship for intimate conversation, or the decrease in communication in the relationship increases the need to find intimate conversation elsewhere. Johnson, in Duck, p. 67. Milardo, in a longitudinal study of conversation patterns, found that individuals in deteriorating relationships significantly increased the frequency and duration of their interactions with network members as their relationships declined. P. Milardo, "The Social Context of Developing Relationships" (Ph.D. dissertation, Pennsylvania State University, 1980), in Johnson, in Duck p. 60.

34. Berger and Kellner, pp. 1–25.

CHAPTER TWO

1. See also Steve Duck, "A Topography of Relationship Disengagement and Dissolution," in Steve Duck, ed., *Personal Relationships. 4: Dissolving Personal Relationships* (London: Academic Press, 1982), p. 18.

2. Michael P. Johnson, "Social and Cognitive Features of the Dissolution of Commitment to Relationships," in Duck, pp. 70–72; Duck, in Duck, p. 13; pp. 17–21.

3. Murray S. Davis, *Intimate Relations* (New York: Free Press, 1973); Johnson, in Duck, pp. 70–72.

4. Duck, in Duck, pp. 21–24.

5. David R. Unruh, "Death and Personal History: Strategies of Identity Preservation," *Social Problems* 30, No. 5 (February 1983): 345; Peter L. Berger, *Invitation to Sociology* (New York: Anchor Books, 1963), pp. 54–65.

6. Unruh, p. 341.

7. Unruh, p. 342; Berger, p. 57.

8. Berger, p. 61.

9. Unruh, pp. 341, 345.

10. Waller, p. 122; Kurt H. Wolff, ed. and tr., *The Sociology of Georg Simmel* (New York: Free Press, 1950), p. 168.

11. See also Dennis T. Jaffe and Rosabeth Moss Kanter, "Couple Strains in Communal Households: A Four-Factor Model of the Separation Process," *Journal of Social*

Issues 32 (1973): 179; Brian Miller, "Adult Sexual Resocialization: Adjustments Toward a Stigmatized Identity," *Alternative Lifestyles* (May 1978): 207–234.

12. When we couple, the act of committing ourselves to live with another person restricts other choices we might make. We make one choice, and that one shapes succeeding choices, limiting and narrowing the future possibilities of each partner. (Peter Berger and Hansfried Kellner, "Marriage and the Construction of Reality," *Diogenes* 46 (1964): 15. In uncoupling, the reverse occurs. Choices are made that potentially *expand* the range of possible choices in the future.

13. J. W. Thibault and H. H. Kelley, *The Social Psychology of Groups* (New York: John Wiley, 1959).

14. Willard Waller, *The Old Love and the New* (New York: Liveright, 1930), p. 126; Peter M. Blau, *Exchange and Power in Social Life* (New York: John Wiley, 1964), pp. 115–142; Sam D. Sieber, "Toward a Theory of Role Accumulation," *American Sociological Review* 39 (1974): 567–578.

15. Jaffe and Kanter, p. 179.

16. Georg Simmel specifically notes the connection between writing and making secrets public. He states: "In being written down, the intellectual content receives an objective form, an existence which in principle, is timeless, a successively and simultaneously unlimited reproducibility in the consciousness of individuals. But its significance and validity are fixed, and thus do not depend upon the presence or absence of these psychological realizations. Writing, thus, possesses an objective existence which renounces all guarantees of remaining secret." Kurt H. Wolff, p. 352.

17. Berger and Kellner, pp. 5–11: George McCall, "Becoming Unrelated: The Management of Bond Dissolution," in Duck, p. 220.

18. Scanzoni describes the psychological roots of this behavior. Unresolved conflict results in negative displacement onto other areas. John Scanzoni, *Sexual Bargaining: Power Politics in the American Marriage* (Englewood Cliffs, N.J.: Prentice-Hall, 1972), p. 75.

19. Goffman, *The Presentation of Self*, pp. 190–191.

20. See also Weiss, p. 30.

21. Goffman, *Interaction Ritual*, p. 24.

22. Jaffe and Kanter, pp. 185–186.

23. Berger and Kellner, pp. 11–12.

24. McCall, in Duck, p. 221.

25. While I found this tendency to seek out "experts" as confidants to be a consistent pattern, I also can substantiate this tendency from personal experience. Not only do people confide in me as a person who has experienced divorce and thus has some personal expertise, but also my research in this area results in friends and strangers alike turning to me for information when their relationships get in trouble. Frequently, I am the stranger to whom they reveal secrets they are unwilling to reveal to others.

26. Julia Brannen and Jean Collard, *Marriages in Trouble: the Process of Seeking Help* (London: Tavistock, 1982), p. 185. Eli Coleman, "Developmental Stages of the Coming Out Process," *American Behavioral Scientist* 25 (1982): 473.

27. Ibid., p. 62.

28. Richard Schickel, *Singled Out* (New York: Viking, 1981), pp. 16–28; Kristine M. Rosenthal and Harry F. Keshet, "The Impact of Childcare Responsibilities on Part-Time or Single Fathers: Changing Patterns of Work and Intimacy," *Alternative Lifestyles* 4 (November, 1978): 465–491. One limitation of this approach is that defining a person as transitional hinges on their eventual departure. Thus, this role as traditionally described only can be identified in retrospect. That is, we can only think of a person as

transitional after they have left us—or we have left them. The timing of the departure creates further ambiguity. Can a lover who accompanies an initiator through an uncoupling and sticks around for six years before disappearing be thought of as transitional?

29. This shift does not go unnoticed by the partner. "Many spouses are deeply troubled to discover that with the addition of the therapist another important person has joined the marriage, a person the spouse may have never even met. Intimate thoughts that were once discussed with the spouse may now be reserved for the therapist. The result is that the relation between spouses may grow more distant and cold, and meaningful communication between them may reach an all-time low." "Demands of Intense Psychotherapy Take Their Toll on Patient's Spouse," New York Times, 28 December 1982.

30. John Lofland and Rodney Stark, "Becoming a World-Saver: A Theory of Conversion to a Deviant Perspective," in Howard Robboy, Sidney L. Greenblatt, and Candace Clark, Social Interaction: Introductory Readings in Sociology (New York: St. Martin's, 1979), p. 466. For a complete description of this transition, which in many ways seems to parallel uncoupling, see John Lofland and Rodney Stark, "Becoming a World-Saver: A Theory of Conversion to a Deviant Perspective," American Sociological Review 30 (1965): 862–875.

31. George J. McCall and J. L. Simmons, Identities and Interactions (New York: Free Press, 1966), pp. 76–81, 229–243; Barney G. Glaser and Anselm L. Strauss, Status Passage (London: Routledge and Kegan Paul, 1971), pp. 142–156.

32. Berger and Kellner, p. 17.

33. Brannen and Collard, pp. 50–61; Judith S. Wallerstein and Joan B. Kelly, Surviving the Breakup (New York: Basic Books, 1980), p. 21.

34. Albert K. Cohen, Deviance and Social Control (Englewood Cliffs, N.J.: Prentice-Hall, 1966), pp. 7–8.

35. Berger and Kellner, pp. 21–25.

36. Erving Goffman, The Presentation of Self in Everyday Life (New York: Anchor Books, 1959), pp. 77–105.

37. See also Robert S. Weiss, Marital Separation (New York: Basic Books, 1975), p. 30.

38. John J. La Gaipa, "Rules and Rituals in Disengaging from Relationships," in Duck, pp. 193–196.

39. See also DeMonteflores, p. 64; Miller, p. 227. Garfinkel, discussing the effects of public denunciation on identity, states: "The work of the denunciation affects the recasting of the objective character of the perceived other: the other person becomes, in the eyes of his condemners, literally a different and a new person. It is not that the new attributes are added to the old 'nucleus.' He is not changed, he is reconstituted." Harold Garfinkel, "Conditions of Successful Degradation Ceremonies," American Journal of Sociology 61 (March 1956), 421–422.

40. Marvin Scott and Stanford M. Lyman, "Accounts," American Sociological Review 33 (1968): 904–913. See also Gresham Sykes and David Matza, "Techniques of Neutralization: A Theory of Delinquency," American Sociological Review (22 December 1957): 664–669.

41. Wolff, pp. 328, 330. See also Laurel Walum Richardson, "Secrecy and the Construction of Intimacy: Relationships Between Single Women and Married Men" (Unpublished Manuscript, Department of Sociology, The Ohio State University, 1981).

42. Weiss, p. 30.

43. Goffman, Interaction Ritual, p. 106.

44. Coleman, pp. 473–475; Barry Dank, "Coming Out in the Gay World," Psy-

chiatry 34 (1971): 180–197; Carmen DeMonteflores and Stephen J. Schultz, "Coming Out: Similarities and Differences for Lesbians and Gay Men," *Journal of Social Issues* 34, No. 3(1978): 65. Blood and Wolfe state that the visibility of a relationship to others is an integrating force, preventing "transgressions," such as divorce. R. O. Blood and D. M. Wolfe, *Husbands and Wives: The Dynamics of Married Living* (New York: Free Press, 1960). Jaffe and Kanter's commune study, however, indicates that others' observations of a relationship can be *either* a separating or integrating influence *depending on the norms and belief systems of those in the situation* (p. 186).

45. Berger and Kellner, pp. 1–11.

46. Berger and Kellner; Unruh, p. 349; see also George McCall, "Becoming Unrelated: The Management of Bond Dissolution," in Duck, p. 220.

47. Goffman, *The Presentation of Self,* pp. 49, 137–140; Goffman notes that audience segregation is a device frequently used for protecting fostered impressions: "the performer segregates his audiences so that the individuals who witness him in one of his roles will not be the individuals who witness him in another of his roles," p. 138. Furthermore, "It should be clear that just as it is useful for the performance to exclude persons from the audience who see him in another and inconsistent presentation, so also is it useful for the performer to exclude from the audience those before whom he performed in the past a show inconsistent with the current one," pp. 138–139.

48. Berger and Kellner, pp. 12.

49. Robert K. Merton, "Socially Expected Durations: A Case Study of Concept Formation in Sociology," in Walter W. Powell and Richard Robbins, eds., *Conflict and Consensus: A Festschrift in Honor of Lewis A. Coser* (New York: Free Press, 1984), pp. 262–283.

50. Scott and Lyman, "Accounts." For the details of this extensive cognitive restructuring, see Johnson, in Duck, pp. 55, 69.

51. Willard Waller, *The Family: A Dynamic Interpretation* (New York: Cordon, 1938), cited in McCall, in Duck, p. 218. McCall suggests that the mourning process starts with the wish to terminate and, whether the relationship terminates or not, the wish to terminate spoils the relationship, triggering the process of social mourning in order to cope with the loss. Ibid., pp. 217–220.

52. Weiss (pp. 78–81) notes that obsessive review normally accompanies identity change whenever there is a major relationship loss. Thus, physical separation triggers obsessive review for *both* partners. I find, however, that the initiator's intensive preoccupation with the relationship and with the partner normally precedes the separation, while the partner engages in obsessive review later. The difference in the timing of obsessive review (and, thus, the mourning process) for initiator and partner varies because, for each, the transition begins at different times. For initiators, mourning begins long before separation. For partners, most often it is the physical separation that triggers their transition, and thus the onset of obsessive review and mourning. For details, see discussion in Chapter 7.

53. Scott and Lyman, "Accounts"; for styles of accounts and the process of mourning relationships, see McCall, in Duck, pp. 211–231.

54. Weiss notes, "Those who end a marriage because of their spouse's failings often suffer intense guilt and remorse. Only when the spouse's shortcomings are truly unbearable do they feel justified in leaving and even then they may continue to feel that they have done wrong in deserting their spouse." Weiss, pp. 19–20. See also Duck, in Duck, p. 13; and Weiss, "The Emotional Impact of Marital Separation," in Peter J. Stein, ed., *Single Life: Unmarried Adults in Social Context* (New York: St. Martin's, 1981), p. 75.

CHAPTER THREE

1. John Van Maanen and Edgar H. Schein, "Toward a Theory of Organizational Socialization," in Barry Staw and L. L. Cummings, eds., *Research in Organizational Behavior* (Greenwich, Conn.: JAI Press, 1979), pp. 214–215; Jeylan T. Mortimer and Roberta G. Simmons, "Adult Socialization," in *Annual Review of Sociology* 4(1978): 421–454; O. G. Brim Jr. and Stanton Wheeler, eds., *Socialization After Childhood* (New York: Wiley, 1966). Barney G. Glaser and Anselm L. Strauss, *Status Passage* (London: Routledge and Kegan Paul, 1971), pp. 60–73.

2. See also George McCall, "Becoming Unrelated: The Management of Bond Dissolution," in Steve Duck, *Personal Relationships. 4: Dissolving Personal Relationships* (London: Academic Press, 1982), p. 221.

3. Austin Sarat and William L. F. Felstiner, "The Ideology of Divorce: Law in the Lawyer's Office," Paper presented at the Workshop on the Study of the Interaction Between Lawyer and Client, Rijksuniversiteit, Groningen, The Netherlands, October 1984.

4. McCall, in Duck, p. 221.

5. Peter Berger and Hansfried Kellner, "Marriage and the Construction of Reality," *Diogenes* 46(1964): 5–7.

6. Dennis T. Jaffe and Rosabeth Moss Kanter, "Couple Strains in Communal Households: A Four-Factor Model of the Separation Process," *Journal of Social Issues* 32, No 1(1976): 182–183.

7. Michael P. Johnson, "Social and Cognitive Features of the Dissolution of Commitment to Relationships," in Duck, pp. 67–68.

8. Lucia H. Bequaert, *Single Women: Alone and Together* (Boston: Beacon, 1976), pp. 12–13. Ambert, based on her research on separated and divorced women's beliefs in the women's movement, concluded that gender role liberation *follows* divorce. I found that the timing of identification with the women's movement for a married woman who separated or divorced varied, depending on whether she initiated the break-up or was the partner who resisted it. In my research, of those women who were married and who also brought up the women's movement as significant in their transition, initiators noted its importance prior to the separation, partners noted its importance after. The difference in findings between Ambert's study and *Uncoupling* can be explained not only by the fact that Ambert did not take into account the role assumed in the breakup, but also by the differences in the way the information was obtained in the two studies. See Anne-Marie Ambert, "The Effect of Divorce on Women's Attitude Toward Feminism," *Sociological Focus* 18, No.3 (1985): 265–272.

9. Lynnette Triere with Richard Peacock, *Learning to Leave: A Woman's Guide* (New York: Contemporary Books, 1982), p. 75.

10. George J. McCall and J. L. Simmons, *Identities and Interactions* (New York: Free Press, 1966), pp. 80, 220. Erving Goffman, *The Presentation of Self in Everyday Life* (New York: Anchor, 1959), p. 81. For a thorough discussion of reference group theory, see Robert K. Merton, "Contributions to the Theory of Reference Group Behavior" (with Alice Rossi) in Robert K. Merton, *Social Theory and Social Structure* (New York: Free Press, 1968), pp. 279–334; Robert K. Merton, "Continuities in the Theory of Reference Groups and Social Structure," ibid., pp. 335–440.

11. Merton, "Contributions," p. 324; McCall and Simmons, pp. 105–124, 125–165.

12. McCall and Simmons, pp. 251–254.

13. McCall, in Duck, p. 221.

14. McCall and Simmons, p. 84.

15. Gerald R. Miller and Malcolm R. Parks, "Communication in Dissolving Relationships," in Duck, pp. 136–137.

16. See also Robert S. Weiss, *Marital Separation* (New York: Basic Books, 1975), p. 97.

17. Merton, "Contributions," p. 324. See also Carmen DeMonteflores and Stephen J. Schultz, "Coming Out: Similarities and Differences for Lesbians and Gay Men," *Journal of Social Issues* 34(1978): 62.

18. Murray S. Davis, *Intimate Relations* (New York: Free Press, 1973), p. 248; McCall and Simmons, pp. 188–189, 197–198.

19. Erving Goffman, *Interaction Ritual* (New York: Anchor, 1967), p. 126.

20. Merton, "Contributions," p. 324.

21. Ibid.

22. McCall and Simmons, pp. 190–191.

23. Ibid.

24. Kristine M. Rosenthal and Harry F. Keshet, *Fathers Without Partners: A Study of Fathers and the Family After Marital Separation* (Totowa, N. J.: Rowman and Littlefield, 1981), pp. 2–5.

25. Peter L. Berger and Hansfried Kellner, "Marriage and the Construction of Reality," *Diogenes* 46(1964): 12–13.

26. Blau notes, "If one party does not feel that the cost-reward ratio is satisfactory to him, he may cut back inputs, thereby reducing the satisfaction of the other, and thus increase the likelihood that the relationship will be terminated." Peter M. Blau, *Exchange and Power in Social Life* (New York: John Wiley, 1964), p. 84; Kanter, in her study of utopian communities notes how loyalties to outside relationships or to children weaken the system. As an individual's options for relationships elsewhere increase, willingness to make peace with the group decreases. Rosabeth Moss Kanter, *Commitment and Community: Communes and Utopia in Sociological Perspective* (Cambridge: Harvard University Press, 1972), p. 83. See also Davis, p. 232, and Weiss, pp. 26–27.

27. Kurt H. Wolff, ed. and tr., *The Sociology of Georg Simmel* (New York: Free Press, 1950), p. 146.

28. Miller and Parks, in Duck, pp. 136–137. The dissociation that appears in speech reflects, in part, an unwillingness to be publicly paired with the other person. It also reflects a distance that is real. The two don't talk as much, because of the initiator's unwillingness to disclose personal feelings, and also the two people are spending less time together, so they do not have as much in common.

29. Glaser and Strauss, pp. 60–73. Adult socialization precedes all role transitions. (See Mortimer and Simmons, pp. 421–454.) For a classic study that examines socialization of inmates both after entering and prior to leaving a prison, see Stanton Wheeler, "Socialization in Correctional Communities," *American Sociological Review* 26(1961): 697–712.

CHAPTER FOUR

1. My ideas about communication in intimate relationships are derived from Spence's explanation of organizational decision-making under conditions of product uncertainty. See Michael Spence, *Market Signaling* (Cambridge: Harvard University Press, 1974). For another application, see Diane Vaughan, *Controlling Unlawful Organizational Behavior: Social Structure and Corporate Misconduct* (Chicago: The University of Chicago Press, 1983), Chapter 4. But for the conceptual groundwork for both Spence's

work and mine, see Erving Goffman, *The Presentation of Self in Everyday Life* (New York: Anchor Books, 1959), p. 249. For an insightful (and discouraging) discussion about the natural decline of intimacy in relationships as habits developed between two people, see John J. Macionis, "Intimacy: Structure and Process in Interpersonal Relationships," *Alternative Lifestyles* 1(February 1978): 113–130.

2. See also, Steve Duck, "A Topography of Relationship Disengagement and Dissolution," in Duck, p. 19.

3. Stephen R. Marks, "Multiple Roles and Role Strain: Some Notes on Human Energy, Time, and Commitment," *American Sociological Review* 42 (December 1977): 927.

4. Ibid., pp. 921–935; See also Dennis T. Jaffe and Rosabeth Moss Kanter, "Couple Strains in Communal Households: A Four-Factor Model of the Separation Process," *Journal of Social Issues* 32(1976): 178–182.

5. Goffman describes how a given performance (or, as I am describing it, a given set of signals) "tends to become institutionalized in terms of the abstract stereotyped expectations to which it gives rise, and tends to take on a meaning and stability apart from the specific task which happen at the time to be performed in its name." *The Presentation of Self,* p. 27.

6. Marian R. Yarrow et al., "The Psychological Meaning of Mental Illness in the Family," *Journal of Social Issues* 11(1955): 12–24; Jerome K. Myers and Bertram H. Roberts, *Family and Class Dynamics* (New York: John Wiley, 1959), pp. 213–220.

7. Erving Goffman, *Interaction Ritual: Essays on Face-to-Face Behavior* (New York: Anchor Books, 1967), pp. 126–129.

8. Erving Goffman, *The Presentation of Self in Everyday Life* (New York: Anchor Books, 1959), pp. 17–76, 248–255.

9. Goffman, ibid., p. 43; Kurt H. Wolff, ed. and tr., *The Sociology of Georg Simmel* (New York: Free Press, 1950), p. 311.

10. Wolff, ibid., pp. 311–312.

11. Goffman, *The Presentation of Self,* p. 60; Spence, *Market Signaling.*

12. Goffman, *Interaction Ritual,* p. 127.

13. Goffman, *The Presentation of Self,* pp. 58, 251. For an application of these same ideas to the manipulation and falsification of signals between organizations, see Vaughan, pp. 78–81.

14. Goffman, *The Presentation of Self,* pp. 58, 249.

15. Peter Marris, *Loss and Change* (London: Routledge and Kegan Paul, 1974), pp. 5–22; Peter L. Berger and Thomas Luckmann, *The Social Construction of Reality* (New York: Doubleday, 1966).

16. Marris, pp. 9–11; Gerald Zaltman, "Knowledge Disavowal" (Paper presented at the Conference on Producing Useful Knowledge for Organizations, Graduate School of Business, University of Pittsburgh, October 1982).

17. Barney G. Glaser and Anselm L. Strauss, *Status Passage* (London: Routledge and Kegan Paul, 1971), pp. 33–56; Robert K. Merton, "Socially Expected Durations: A Case Study of Concept Formation in Sociology," in Walter W. Powell and Richard Robbins, eds. *Conflict and Consensus: A Festschrift in Honor of Lewis A. Coser* (New York: Free Press, 1984), pp. 262–283.

18. Gerald Zaltman, "Knowledge Disavowal."

19. See Kenneth Arrow, *The Limits of Organization* (New York: W. W. Norton, 1974), pp. 37–39, for a discussion of the limited capacity of individuals to acquire and use information.

20. Sissela Bok, *Secrets: On the Ethics of Concealment and Revelation* (New York: Pantheon, 1982), p. 60. For discussions of the individual's capacity to keep secrets from self, see Goffman, *The Presentation of Self*, p. 81; Paul Ekman, *Telling Lies: Clues to Deceit in the Marketplace, Politics, and Marriage* (New York: Norton, 1985); Daniel Goleman, *Vital Lies, Simple Truths: The Psychology of Self-Deception* (New York: Simon and Schuster, 1985).

21. If we accept Goffman's description of a performance as so delicate that the slightest discordant event can destroy the impression the performer is trying to create (*The Presentation of Self*, p. 56), we must wonder at the partner's ability to disregard cues that disrupt the impression being presented to them. The answer may, in part, lie in the interdependence between initiator and partner. If the performer and the audience (to use Goffman's terms) are not interdependent, the audience has no vested interest in the impression being presented, thus the interjection of a discrepant cue is duly observed and noted. If, on the other hand, performer and audience are interdependent, then the audience (in this case, the partner) has a vested interest in the continuing smoothness of the performance. A signal that the performance is taking a direction that would ultimately be costly consequently would be disregarded. (See also Marris, *Loss and Change*, pp. 5–22.)

22. Bok, p. 69; Marris, pp. 5–22. Zaltman; Julia Brannen and Jean Collard, *Marriages in Trouble: The Process of Seeking Help* (London: Tavistock, 1982, p. 70.

23. Bok, p. 71.

24. Joan Emerson, "Nothing Unusual is Happening," in Tomatsu Shibutani, *Human Nature and Collective Behavior* (Englewood Cliffs, N.J.: Prentice-Hall, 1970); Brannen and Collard, p. 70.

25. William H. Gram, "Breaking Up: A Study of Fifty-Nine Case Histories of Marital Collapse" (Ph.D. dissertation, Northwestern University, 1982), p. 176.

26. Goffman, *The Presentation of Self*, pp. 77–105.

27. In their research examining how people with marital difficulties come to seek help from agencies, Brannen and Collard found that people who had truncated friendship networks and who were highly dependent on their spouse were less likely to have defined the existence of a marital problem. See *Marriages in Trouble*, p. 89.

28. Lecture, Sargeant Harold ("Sonny") Weatherman, Columbus Police Department, March 1976, Department of Sociology, Ohio State University.

29. Ibid., p. 64.

30. Brannen and Collard, p. 70. Brannen and Collard studied this issue in great detail, noting (in marriages) men's relatively greater power at deflecting "the problem" onto the wife and correspondingly, women's greater tendency to accept the blame, pp. 58–61.

31. For an historical account of a similar response to perceived individual deviance by communities, see Kai T. Erikson, *Wayward Puritans* (New York: John Wiley, 1966).

32. Brannen and Collard, p. 64.

33. Ibid., p. 62.

34. Ibid., p. 163.

35. Brannen and Collard, pp. 50–61; Judith S. Wallerstein and Joan B. Kelly, *Surviving the Breakup* (New York: Basic Books (1980), p. 21.

36. Marris, pp. 5–22.

37. Goffman, *Interaction Ritual*, pp. 15–18, 31, 97–112.

38. Ibid., p. 17.

39. Ibid., pp. 18–19.

218 / NOTES

CHAPTER FIVE

1. For a discussion of the importance on studying action, reaction, and interaction between partners, see Gerald R. Miller and Malcolm R. Parks, "Communication in Dissolving Relationships," in Steve Duck, ed., *Personal Relationships. 4: Dissolving Personal Relationships* (London: Academic Press, 1982), p. 146.

2. Davis describes various conversation forms that can occur in a confrontation. See Murray A. Davis, *Intimate Relations* (New York: Free Press, 1973), pp. 217–235.

3. See John Lofland and Rodney Stark's discussion of "turning points" in "Becoming a World-Saver: A Theory of Conversion to a Deviant Perspective," in Howard Robboy, Sidney L. Greenblatt, and Candace Clark, *Social Interaction, Introductory Readings in Sociology* (New York: St. Martin's, 1979), p. 465.

4. J. W. Thibault and H. H. Kelley, *The Social Psychology of Groups* (New York: John Wiley, 1959).

5. Barney G. Glaser and Anselm L. Strauss, *Status Passage* (London: Routledge and Kegan Paul, 1971), pp. 83–84.

6. For a discussion of identity as a determinant of agendas, see George J. McCall and J. L. Simmons, *Identities and Interactions* (New York: Free Press, 1966), pp. 244–249. Goffman calls such plans "strategic secrets": intentions and capacities that are concealed to prevent others from adapting effectively to an intended goal. Erving Goffman, *The Presentation of Self in Everyday Life* (New York: Anchor, 1959), p. 142.

7. Lucia H. Bequaert, *Single Women: Alone and Together* (Boston: Beacon, 1976), p. 27.

8. Lofland and Stark, p. 465.

9. Glaser and Strauss, pp. 17, 21–24.

10. Gram, p. 151.

11. Nicky Hart, *When Marriage Ends: A Study in Status Passage* (London: Tavistock, 1976), pp. 94–95.

12. See also Judith S. Wallerstein and Joan Berlin Kelly, *Surviving the Breakup: How Children and Parents Cope with Divorce* (New York: Basic Books, 1980), p. 136. See also Carmen DeMonteflores and Stephen J. Schultz, "Coming Out: Similarities and Differences for Lesbians and Gay Men," *Journal of Social Issues* 34(1978): 62.

13. See also Robert S. Weiss, *Marital Separation* (New York: Basic Books, 1975), p. 22.

14. Peter M. Blau, *Power and Exchange in Social Life* (New York: John Wiley, 1964), p. 84.

15. Oscar Wilde, "The Picture of Dorian Gray," in Richard Aldington, *The Indispensable Oscar Wilde* (New York: The Book Society, 1950).

16. Rule violation is related to the distribution of power in a relationship. For a discussion, see Chapter 6, note 34. See also Norman K. Denzin, "Rules of Conduct and the Study of Deviant Behavior: Some Notes on the Social Relationship," in George J. McCall, Michal M. McCall, Norman K. Denzin, Gerald D. Suttles, and Susan B. Kurth, *Social Relationships* (Chicago: Aldine, 1970), pp. 62–94.

17. Davis, pp. 265–267.

18. Erving Goffman, *Interaction Ritual: Essays on Face-to-Face Behavior* (Garden City, N.Y.: Anchor Books, 1967), pp. 5–45, 97–112.

19. See also Weiss, p. 30. He notes that the extraordinary power of violation of the fidelity norm comes from its symbolic meaning. Such a violation not only questions the initiator's commitment, but suggests the partner's sexual inadequacy; thus it is potentially damaging to both the public esteem and the self-esteem of the partner.

20. See also Gram, p. 83.

21. Erving Goffman, *Frame Analysis: An Essay on the Organization of Experience,* (New York: Harper & Row, 1974), p. 463.

22. The tendency for initiators to prefer avoidance styles rather than confrontational ones is also noted in R. E. Kaplan, "Maintaining Interpersonal Relationships: A Bipolar Theory," *Interpersonal Development* 6 (1976): pp. 106–119, and Steve Duck, "The Personal Context: Intimate Relationships," in P. Feldman and J. Orford, eds., *Psychological Problems: The Social Context* (London: John Wiley, 1980), pp. 73–96.

23. Paul Ekman, *Telling Lies: Clues to Deceit in the Marketplace, Politics, and Marriage* (New York: Norton, 1985).

24. Steve Duck, "A Topography of Relationship Disengagement and Dissolution," in Duck, ed., p. 22.

25. Erving Goffman, *Interaction Ritual,* pp. 126–129.

26. Erving Goffman, *The Presentation of Self in Everyday Life,* p. 210.

CHAPTER SIX

1. See also William H. Gram, "Breaking Up: A Study of Fifty-Nine Case Histories of Marital Collapse" (Ph.D. dissertation, Northwestern University, 1982), pp. 174–175.

2. Ibid., p. 176.

3. Kanter notes a similar phenomenon in communes. An individual's potential for satisfaction within the group increases as his options for relationships elsewhere decrease, for "he must make his peace with the group because he has, in fact, no place else to turn." To lose the group, then, would leave the individual totally without resources. See Rosabeth Moss Kanter, *Commitment and Community: Communes and Utopias in Sociological Perspective* (Cambridge: Harvard University Press, 1972), p. 83.

4. Murray S. Davis, *Intimate Relations* (New York: Free Press, 1973), p. 217.

5. How reconciliation comes about is discussed in Chapter 10.

6. Peter M. Blau, *Exchange and Power in Social Life* (New York: John Wiley, 1964), pp. 118–122.

7. Lillian B. Rubin, *Women of a Certain Age: The Midlife Search For Self* (New York: Harper & Row, 1979) p. 73.

8. Schwartz notes the relationship between waiting and the distribution of power "to possess the power to make a person wait is, above all, to possess the capacity to modify his conduct in a manner congruent with one's own interests. To be delayed is to be dependent upon the disposition of the one whom one is waiting for." See Barry Schwartz, "Waiting, Exchange, and Power: The Distribution of Time in Social Systems," *American Journal of Sociology* 79 (1973): 841–870.

9. Blau calls this the "cost of alternatives foregone." A particular social association costs individuals the opportunity to devote time and other limited resources to other associations where they could have obtained rewards. See Blau, *Exchange and Power in Social Life,* p. 101.

10. For a discussion of how position in a particular structure can trap people in self-defeating cycles that bind them and limit them even further, see Rosabeth Moss Kanter, *Men and Women of the Corporation* (New York: Basic Books, 1977), pp. 250–253.

11. See also Davis, *Intimate Relations,* p. 272.

12. David Mechanic, "Sources of Power of Lower Participants in Complex Organizations," *Administrative Science Quarterly* 7(1962)3: 349–364.

13. See Blau, *Exchange and Power in Social Life,* p. 121.

14. See discussion in Chapter 1 at note 25.

15. Barney G. Glaser and Anselm L. Strauss, *Status Passage* (London: Routledge and Kegan Paul, 1971), p. 26.

16. Goffman (p. 457) notes one method of cooling the mark out is to give the person another chance to qualify for the role they have failed at. He points out that while second chances are often given, they seldom are taken, "because failure at a role removes a person from the company of those who have succeeded, but it does not bring him back—in spirit, anyway—to the society of those who have not tried or are in the process of trying. The person who has failed in a role is a constant source of embarrassment, for none of the standard patterns of treatment is quite applicable to him. Instead of taking a second chance he usually goes away to another place where his past does not bring confusion to his present," p. 457. Goffman's conclusion, I believe, depends on the degree to which the failure is public. Social expectations about one's inability to perform, plus the social stigma attached to failure can undermine both abilities and courage, thus causing the person to leave the setting rather than risk another failure. But when a second chance is offered before failure becomes public (even public to self, as with partners who believe they have not had a chance to try, or for employees, called into the boss's office, who believe they can rectify the mistake) the chance is perceived as an opportunity to succeed, and thus taken. It is when the second chance is perceived as an opportunity to fail, and to fail publicly, that the person will not accept it. See Erving Goffman, "On Cooling the Mark Out: Some Aspects of Adaptation to Failure," *Psychiatry* 15 (1952): 451–463.

17. Ibid, pp. 457–458; Gram, "Breaking Up," p. 125.

18. See also Julia Brannen and Jean Collard, *Marriages in Trouble: The Process of Seeking Help* (London: Tavistock, 1982), p. 81.

19. Goffman, "On Cooling the Mark Out," p. 454.

20. Erving Goffman, *Interaction Ritual* (New York: Anchor, 1967), p. 127.

21. Goffman, "On Cooling the Mark Out," p. 452; Davis, *Intimate Relations*, p. 263.

22. Goffman, "On Cooling the Mark Out," pp. 452, 457.

23. Ibid., p. 457.

24. Goffman (ibid., p. 458) notes that the business of psychotherapists is "to offer a relationship to those who have failed in a relationship to others."

25. In a study of partners seeking divorce, 30% saw no professional at all during the year preceding the first interview. William M. Holmes, Gay C. Kitson, and Marvin B. Sussman, "Social Supports and Adjustment to Divorce," Mimeographed (Case Western Reserve, 1981).

26. Brannen and Collard, pp. 47–71.

27. Goffman, "On Cooling the Mark Out," pp. 457–458.

28. For a general discussion of the ways in which the addition of a third party to a dyad can change the form of interaction, see Georg Simmel, who notes: "often the relation between two parties and a non-partisan emerges as a new relationship. The third element, before unequally connected with either, becomes involved and forms an interactional unit with one or the other that changes the power distance and thus the set." Kurt H. Wolff, ed. and tr., *The Sociology of Georg Simmel* (New York: Free Press, 1950), pp. 154–155. For application to the counseling situation specifically, see John P. Speigel, "The Resolution of Role Conflict within the Family," in N. W. Pell and E. F. Vogel, eds., *A Modern Introduction to the Family* (New York: Free Press, 1968), pp. 391–411, especially p. 409.

29. Harold Garfinkel, "Conditions of Successful Degradation Ceremonies," *American Journal of Sociology* 61 (1956): 420–424.

30. A similar outcome has been noted in educational counseling. Cicourel and Kitsuse describe how school guidance and counseling continue and confer the very class distinctions these services were intended to change. See Aaron V. Cicourel and John Kitsuse, *The Educational Decision-Makers* (Indianapolis, Bobbs-Merrill, 1963). For a theoretical explanation of how official processing perpetuates the phenomena it is intended to discourage by bestowing a label that affects individual self-concept and societal reaction, see Edwin Lemert, *Social Pathology* (New York: McGraw-Hill, 1951), and Edwin Lemert, *Human Deviance, Social Problems, and Social Control* (Englewood Cliffs, N.J.: Prentice-Hall, 1967).

31. Goffman, "On Cooling the Mark Out," p. 458. Gram notes that in 88% of the break-ups he researched, the rejector wanted to end the marriage when he or she first initiated the break-up. Not only did they want to end it permanently, but had wanted to do so for years. See Gram, "Breaking Up," p. 174.

32. R. E. Kaplan, "Maintaining Interpersonal Relationships: A Bipolar Theory," *Interpersonal Development* 6(1976): 106–119, and Steve Duck, "The Personal Context: Intimate Relationships," in P. Feldman and J. Orford, eds., *Psychological Problems: The Social Context* (London: Wiley, 1980), pp. 73–96.

33. Davis, p. 263.

34. Quantitative research on separation and divorce among heterosexual couples reveals that women are more likely to terminate relationships than are their male partners. See Charles T. Hill, Zick Rubin, and Letitia Anne Peplau, "Breakups Before Marriage: The End of 103 Affairs," *Journal of Social Issues* 32 (1976): 147–168; Zick Rubin, "Loving and Leaving: Sex Differences in Romantic Attachments," *Sex Roles* 7 (1981): 821–835; William J. Goode, *After Divorce* (Glencoe, Ill.: The Free Press, 1956); Maureen Baker, *Support Networks and Marriage Dissolution,* Final Report (Toronto: Connaught Foundation Project, University of Toronto, 1980). These data reflect the final decision, however (who asks for separation, who files for divorce), without examining the interaction leading up to the decision. Data from other research based on in-depth interviews give some details of the process of ending relationships that offer an explanation for these findings. Women are more likely than men to report they did not want a separation, but were driven to it by the spouse's rule violation (Gram, p. 165; Baker, p. 19; p. 49), or else they made a fatal mistake (as I have called it here) and suggested a separation or left in the hope that reconciliation would be the outcome, only to discover that the other person used that as an opportunity to end it (Gram, p. 165). To explain the statistical evidence, some researchers have pointed out the possible existence of a "Let Jane do it" chivalry factor in breakups (Goode, pp. 133–135; Hill et al.; Gram, pp. 95, 154). This would suggest that the fundamental rule of social interaction that Goffman describes (helping the other person to save face) is adhered to even more strongly by male initiators wanting to end heterosexual relationships than their female counterparts.

This line of argument ultimately reduces to one based on sex role socialization, which I believe is an oversimplification. It emphasizes altruism while ignoring social pressures to stay in relationships and initiators' tendencies to act in their own behalf by avoiding the negative social response that befalls those who dump their partners—regardless of sex. Women also receive social condemnation for terminating relationships (perhaps to an even great extent than men do, especially when families are involved.) Why would existing data not reflect women similarly resorting to strategies that shift the social responsibility to the other person?

While I do not have anything approximating a generalizable sample, my information on uncoupling in both homosexual and heterosexual relationships suggests that power has greater explanatory value than sex role expectations. In both homosexual and heterosexual relationships, direct confrontation (a direct strategy) and rule violation (an indirect strategy) tend to be used by the person who is perceived to be the most powerful in the relationship. Initiators (regardless of sex or sexual preference) who view their partners as more powerful than they, (either physically, financially, or in some other way that gives them control over initiators' outcomes) tend to rely on strategies that mitigate the other person's response. For example, of the direct strategies, initiators who are less powerful are more likely to leave than to directly confront the other person with their wish to terminate. Of the indirect strategies, the initiators who are less powerful are more likely to resort to decreased interaction or take advantage of the partner's fatal mistake, rather than rule violation. The common thread here is that if the initiators do not directly confront partners with their wish to terminate because the partner is perceived by them at some level to be more powerful, it makes sense that they would not resort to an indirect strategy (rule violation) with potential to precipitate the same repercussions as a direct confrontation: anger, retaliation, or the curtailment of some resource.

Thus, available statistical data that indicate women more often initiate the breakup in heterosexual relationships may be distorted by all of the following:

1. Women partners sometimes are likely to initiate break-ups because they have been manipulated into doing it by more powerful male initiators.
2. Women in this situation are likely to recognize it and report it to researchers as manipulation because men resort to rule violation, a strategy likely to cause partners to think perhaps they *have been* manipulated.
3. Men sometimes are likely to initiate break-ups because they have been manipulated to do so by their less powerful female initiators.
4. Men in this situation are *not* likely to recognize it and report it to researchers as manipulation because women initiators use the more subtle of the indirect strategies (decreased interaction, the fatal mistake) when they perceive their partners as more powerful.
5. If men do recognize that they have been manipulated, they may be unwilling to admit it.

35. Gram also uses the criterion of resistance to breaking up to distinguish initiator from partner. William H. Gram, "Breaking Up: A Study of Fifty-Nine Case Histories of Marital Collapse" (Ph.D. dissertation, Northwestern University, 1982), p. 141.

36. Glaser and Strauss, pp. 28–29. Hawkins, studying regulation of water pollution, notes how establishing deadlines can be used as a strategy to bring both parties to define a situation similarly. "A deadline that is met offers an index of progress, of making headway, while a polluter who fails to meet a deadline can be mutually recognized as having failed, even as being uncooperative." See Keith Hawkins, "Bargain and Bluff: Compliance Strategy and Deterrence in the Enforcement of Regulation," *Law and Policy Quarterly* 5, No. 1(1983): 55.

37. See also Davis, *Intimate Relations*, pp. 263, 265–266.

38. Gram, pp. 82, 105, 106; Judith S. Wallerstein and Joan B. Kelly, *Surviving the Breakup: How Children and Parents Cope with Divorce* (New York: Basic Books, 1980), p. 21.

39. For a thorough discussion of labeling deviance and the consequences for social control, see Stephen J. Pfohl, *Images of Deviance and Social Control: A Sociological History* (New York: McGraw-Hill, 1985), pp. 283–328.

40. Erving Goffman, *Interaction Ritual: Essays on Face-to-Face Behavior* (New York: Anchor, 1967), pp. 15–18, 31, 97–112.

41. Erving Goffman, "On Cooling the Mark Out," p. 458.

42. I thank Patricia M. Ewick for this observation.

CHAPTER SEVEN

1. Abigail Trafford, *Crazy Times: Predictable Stages of Divorce* (New York: Harper & Row, 1982), pp. 95–96; Maureen Baker, *Support Networks and Marriage Dissolution*, Final Report (Toronto: Connaught Foundation, University of Toronto, 1980), p. 41.

2. Robert S. Weiss, *Marital Separation* (New York: Basic Books, 1975), pp. 3–4, 36–68; Judith S. Wallerstein and Joan Berlin Kelly, *Surviving the Breakup: How Children and Parents Cope with Divorce* (New York: Basic Books, 1980), pp. 13–34, 108.

3. See, for example, Weiss, *Marital Separation*, pp. 36–68; Robert S. Weiss, *Loneliness: the Experience of Emotional and Social Isolation* (Cambridge: MIT Press, 1973); John Bowlby, *Attachment and Loss* (New York: Basic Books, 1969–1982); James J. Lynch, *The Broken Heart: The Medical Consequences of Loneliness* (New York: Basic Books, 1977); Abigail Trafford, *Crazy Times;* Paul Bohannon, *Divorce and After* (Garden City, N.Y.: Anchor Books, 1971); William J. Goode, *After Divorce* (New York: The Free Press, 1956); John Bowlby, "Processes of Mourning," *International Journal of Psychoanalysis* 44 (1961): 317–335; Robert S. Weiss, "The Emotional Impact of Marital Separation," in Peter J. Stein, ed., *Single Life* (New York: St. Martin's, 1981), pp. 69–78; Graham B. Spanier and Linda Thompson, "Relief and Distress After Marital Separation," *Journal of Divorce* 7(Fall 1983): 31–49; Bernard L. Bloom and Robert A. Caldwell, "Sex Differences in Adjustment During the Process of Marital Separation," *Journal of Marriage and the Family* (August 1981): 693–701; John F. Crosby, Bruce A. Gage, and Marsha Croy Raymond, "The Grief Resolution Process in Divorce," *Journal of Divorce* 7, No. 1(Fall 1983): 3–18.

4. See Willard Waller's classic, insightful description in *The Old Love and the New* (Carbondale: Southern Illinois University Press, 1930).

5. Ibid.; John J. LaGaipa, "Rules and Rituals in Disengaging from Relationships," in Steve Duck, ed., *Personal Relationships. 4: Dissolving Personal Relationships* (London: Academic Press, 1982), pp. 189–210.

6. See, for example, Naomi Gerstel, Catherine Kohler Riessman, and Sarah Rosenfield, "Explaining the Symptomatology of Separated and Divorced Women and Men: The Role of Material Conditions and Social Networks," *Social Forces* 64 (September 1985): 84–101; Weiss, *Marital Separation*, pp. 69–82; Nicky Hart, *When Marriage Ends: A Study of Status Passage* (London: Tavistock, 1976); Starr Roxanne Hiltz, "Widowhood: A Roleless Role," in Peter J. Stein, ed., *Single Life* (New York: St. Martin's, 1981), pp. 79–97; Helena Lopata, "On Widowhood: Grief Work and Identity Reconstruction," *Journal of Geriatric Psychiatry* 8(1975): 41–55; Bernard L. Bloom and Cheryl Clement, "Marital Sex Role Orientation and Adjustment to Separation and Divorce," *Journal of Divorce* 7 (1984): 87–98; Graham B. Spanier and Linda Thompson, "Relief and Distress after Marital Separation," *Journal of Divorce* 7 (1983): 31–49.

7. Nicky Hart, *When Marriage Ends: A Study of Status Passage* (London: Tavistock, 1976), p. 45. Some argue that women are pervasively more vulnerable to the emotional impact of undesirable life events than men. This notion is explored and repudiated in Ronald C. Kessler and Jane D. McLeod, "Sex Differences in Vulnerability to Undesirable Life Events," *American Sociological Review* 49 (1984): 620–631.

8. Carol Gilligan, *In a Different Voice: Psychological Theory and Women's Devel-*

opment (Cambridge: Harvard University Press, 1982), pp. 17, 27; Lillian B. Rubin, *Worlds of Pain: Life in the Working-Class Family* (New York: Basic Books, 1976), p. 119; McCall notes that "females appear to give greater weight than males to bonds of commitment at virtually all ages in all personal relationships." George J. McCall, "Becoming Unrelated: The Management of Bond Dissolution," in Duck, p. 215. For a thorough discussion of gender differences in socialization, see Laurel Walum Richardson, *The Dynamics of Sex and Gender: A Sociological Perspective* (Boston: Houghton Mifflin, 1981, 2nd ed.), pp. 1–97.

9. Jean Baker Miller, *Toward a New Psychology of Women* (Boston: Beacon Press, 1976), p. 83; Lillian B. Rubin, *Women of a Certain Age: The Midlife Search for Self* (New York: Harper & Row, 1979), p. 117.

10. Peter M. Blau, *Exchange and Power in Social Life* (New York: John Wiley & Sons, 1964), pp. 88–142. Blau (p. 104) notes the importance of social context in understanding exchange relationships. Exchange is affected by the "role set" of each partner; that is, by the role relations each has by virtue of occupying the social status relevant to the exchange. The role relations govern the alternatives of the two. Women who are economically dependent and in relationships based on traditional sex role expectations generally have fewer alternative roles than their male counterparts. Therefore, they depend more on their partner role for identity than their spouses do. Wallerstein and Kelly (p. 193) note that more women than men seemed affected by loneliness as a result of lack of opportunity to initiate social engagements. Opportunity clearly increases or decreases in relation to number of roles and degree of participation in those roles. See also Samuel Sieber, "Toward a Theory of Role Accumulation," *American Sociological Review* 39(1974): 567–578. For research verifying this relationship between women's well-being and multiple roles, see Grace Baruch, Rosalind Barnett, and Caryl Rivers, *Life Prints: New Patterns of Love and Work for Today's Women* (New York: McGraw-Hill, 1983). See also Weiss, *Marital Separation*, p. 74; Rubin, *Women of A Certain Age*, p. 121, 125; Hiltz, pp. 79–97; Helena Lopata, "Self Identity in Marriage and Widowhood," *Sociological Quarterly* 14(1973): 407–418; Lopata, pp. 41–55.

11. John Scanzoni, *Sexual Bargaining: Power Politics in the American Marriage* (Englewood Cliffs, N.J.: Prentice-Hall, 1972), p. 70.

12. Ibid., p. 70.

13. Rubin, *Women of a Certain Age*, pp. 42, 114, 121, 125. Weiss, *Marital Separation*, p. 74.

14. Hart, p. 47.

15. Historical evidence indicates that both sexes are treated by their partners as objects from which they derive identity. See Constantina Safilios-Rothschild, *Love, Sex, and Sex Roles* (Englewood Cliffs, N.J.: Prentice-Hall, 1977) for a description of how women, historically and to the present, have often been considered as objects to be traded, exchanged, and used (pp. 26–40), and how women, in turn, reduce men to objects, to be related to and dealt with in terms of their earning ability, prestige, and power (pp. 41–53).

16. Ibid., pp. 47–48; see also Weiss, *Marital Separation*, pp. 74–75.

17. Gerstel et al., pp. 84–101.

18. Hart, pp. 45–51.

19. Kanter notes, "the norms of other legitimate social roles may over-ride those associated with gender roles (of both sexes), thereby freeing the occupant of a given position to behave consistently with the demands of the position. In exchange-theory terms, this suggests that when females occupy social positions with acknowledged rights and privileges vis-à-vis persons in counter positions, their social exchange behavior will

be similar to that of males who occupy similar positions.'' Rosabeth Moss Kanter, "Some Effects of Proportions in Group Life: Skewed Sex Ratios and Responses to Token Women," *American Journal of Sociology* 82, No. 5 (1977): 965–990. Martin and Osmond also note the importance of social structural conditions for explaining similarities and differences in the behavior of men and women toward each other in social exchange relationships. See Patricia Yancey Martin and Marie Withers Osmond, "Gender and Exploitation: Resources, Structure, and Rewards in Cross-Sex Social Exchange," *Social Forces* 15, No. 4 (October 1982): 412–413.

20. See Hart, p. 50, on the relationship between age, the duration of a relationship, and opportunities. See also Johnson, in Duck, p. 55, and Kenneth Arrow, *The Limits of Organization* (New York: Norton, 1974), pp. 39–40, on "irreversible investments" and consequent decreases in alternatives. See also W. P. Cleveland and D. T. Giranturco, "Remarriage Probability After Widowhood: A Retrospective Method," *Journal of Gerontology* 31 (1976): 99–103, and "Plight of the Gray Divorcee," *New York Times Magazine,* 19 December 1982, pp. 89–95.

21. Hart, pp. 45–51, especially p. 50.

22. Sieber, pp. 567–578; Blau, p. 104, note 12; Stephen R. Marks, "Multiple Roles and Role Strain: Some Notes on Human Energy, Time and Commitment," *American Sociological Review* 42(1977): 921–936.

23. Glaser and Strauss note that scheduled events, or events that are predictable, are less likely to represent crises than unscheduled events. The initiator, who "schedules this event," has the benefit of preparation. The partner does not. Barney Glaser and Anselm Strauss, *Status Passage* (London: Routledge and Kegan Paul, 1971). See also McCall and Simmons, pp. 197–198, 248–251.

24. Hart, p. 50. For discussions of the relationship between gender and social networks and income, see Gerstel et al., pp. 84–101; Beth B. Hess, "Friendship and Gender Roles Over the Life Course," in Peter J. Stein, ed., *Single Life* (New York: St. Martin's, 1981), pp. 104–115; Elaine Cumming and William E. Henry, *Growing Old: The Process of Disengagement* (New York: Basic Books, 1961), p. 160; Lillian B. Rubin, *Intimate Strangers* (New York: Harper & Row, 1983); Baker, pp. 3–6; Wallerstein and Kelly, pp. 22–23; Scanzoni, p. 70; Hart, pp. 129–158; Daniel J. Levinson, *The Seasons of a Man's Life* (New York: Ballantine Books, 1978), p. 335; Peter Stein, "Men and Their Friendships," in Robert Lewis, ed., *Men in Troubled Times* (Englewood Cliffs, N.J.: Prentice-Hall, 1981); Kristine M. Rosenthal and Harry F. Keshet, "The Impact of Childcare Responsibilities on Part-Time or Single Fathers: Changing Patterns of Work and Intimacy," *Alternative Lifestyles,* No. 4 (1 November 1978): 465–491.

25. See, for example, Eli Coleman, "Developmental Stages of the Coming Out Process," *American Behavioral Scientist* 25 (1982): 469–482; Henry L. Minton and Gary L. McDonald, "Homosexuality: Identity Formation as a Developmental Process," *Journal of Homosexuality* 9 (Winter 1983/Spring 1984): 91–104; Carmen DeMonteflores and Stephen J. Schultz, "Coming Out: Similarities and Differences for Lesbians and Gay Men," *Journal of Social Issues* 34, No. 3 (1978): 59–72; Barry Dank, "Coming Out in the Gay World," *Psychiatry* 34 (1971): 180–197.

26. Joseph Harry, *Gay Couples* (New York: Praeger, 1984), p. 7.

27. Enrique Ruedo, *The Homosexual Network* (Old Greenwich, Ct.: The Devin Adair Co., 1982), pp. 75–145, 240–283; Marcel Saghir and Eli Robins, *Male and Female Homosexuality* (Baltimore: Williams and Wilkins, 1973), pp. 157–158; Letitia A. Peplau, K. Rook, and Cathy Padesky, "Loving Women: Attachment and Autonomy in Lesbian Relationships," *Journal of Social Issues* 34 (1978): 10; S. Abbott and B. Love,

226 / NOTES

Sappho Was a Right-On Woman: A Liberated View of Feminism (New York: Stein and Day, 1972); DeMonteflores and Schultz, p. 70; Deborah Goleman Wolf, *The Lesbian Community* (Berkeley: University of California Press, 1979), pp. 48–71. In their study of heterosexual cohabitation, Henze and Hudson note that cohabiters attend religious services less frequently, having attenuated ties with the church in their endorsement of a nontraditional lifestyle. Lura F. Henze and John W. Hudson, "Personal and Family Characteristics of Cohabiting and Noncohabiting College Students," *Journal of Marriage and Family* 36 (1974): 722–727.

28. Harry, p. 8; Michael P. Burk, "Coming Out: The Gay Identity Process," in Bernard I. Murstein, ed., *Exploring Intimate Lifestyles* (New York: Springer Publishing, 1978), pp. 257–272. See also Peter J. Stein, "Singlehood: An Alternative to Marriage," *The Family Coordinator* 24 (1975): 489–503.

29. See, for example, the discussion in Harry, pp. 14–21. For an exception, see Joseph Harry and Robert Lovely, "Gay Marriages and Communities of Sexual Orientation," *Alternative Lifestyles* 2(1979): 177–200.

30. McCall and Simmons, p. 236. Mortimer and Simmons argue that the need for adult socialization will vary with the life stage of the individual, the demographic characteristics of the individual's cohort and the individual's social location within that cohort, their sex, socioeconomic status, race, and religion. Jeylan T. Mortimer and Roberta G. Simmons, "Adult Socialization," *Annual Review of Sociology* 4 (1978): 421–454. See also the discussion on the "delayed exit" in Gunhild O. Hagestad and Michael A. Smyer, "Dissolving Long-Term Relationships: Patterns of Divorce in Middle Age," in Duck, pp. 178–182. See also Weiss, *Marital Separation*, p. 17.

31. McCall and Simmons, p. 236.

32. Lynette Triere with Richard Peacock, *Learning to Leave: A Woman's Guide* (New York: Contemporary Books, 1982), pp. 30–31. William H. Gram, "Breaking Up: A Study of Fifty-Nine Case Histories of Marital Collapse" (Ph.D. dissertation, Northwestern University, 1980), p. 171; Kristine M. Rosenthal and Harry F. Keshet, *Fathers Without Partners: A Study of Fathers and the Family After Marital Separation* (Totowa, N. J.: Rowman and Littlefield, 1981).

33. McCall and Simmons, pp. 80, 188–189, 197–198. Some initiators never find stability and identity in the partner role. They discover that when they commit themselves to live with the other person, they lose identity rather than assume it. (See, for example, the first quote in Chapter 1.) In this circumstance, the transition does not involve decreasing commitment to partnership and increasing commitment elsewhere. The loss of the partner role results in minor disruption because the initiator maintained other sources of identity *throughout* the relationship. See Karl E. Weick, "Educational Organizations as Loosely Coupled Systems," *Administrative Science Quarterly* 21 (1976): 1–19.

34. McCall and Simmons, pp. 235–244.

35. McCall and Simmons, pp. 198, 248–251. Baker, in her study of divorcing couples, found that in 57% of the relationships, both partners were having affairs at the time of the breakup (p. 19). While she does not present information that allows us to draw any conclusions about roles in the break-up or about initiator-partner interaction, we nevertheless can conclude that simultaneous affairs indicate that the partner has turned to alternative resources.

36. McCall and Simmons, p. 200. The deteriorating effect of decreased interaction on relationships has been noted elsewhere. A chain of separations gradually can accustom both partners to divorce, as has also been pointed out in Willard Waller and Reuben Hill, *The Family: A Dynamic Interpretation* (New York: Holt, Rinehart, and Winston, 1938) and Hart, p. 114. Davis notes that physical separation can have a similar effect

on loving intimates. See Davis, *Intimate Relations,* p. 251. Extended or frequent separation weakens the bond between the partners. With the decreased interaction is a decrease in touching and communication, a shrinking of the common world, a decrease in information and favors exchanged. As a result, both partners' dependence on the relationship decreases as they become accustomed to living alone. Of necessity, they begin to find alternative resources of their own. Yet another possibility is, of course, that the decreased interaction in troubled relationships results in the relationship continuing. Obviously, relationships that stay together are not the subject of this research. Nonetheless, some relationships (dual career couples, couples where one member is hospitalized or imprisoned, or other cases where one partner is away a good proportion of the time for some reason) can thrive under these circumstances. Ironically, should the situation alter so that the couple spend more time together, the relationship may undergo a period of stress and not survive the changed circumstance.

37. For elaboration of this situation, see Chapter 10.

38. Robert K. Merton, "Socially Expected Durations: A Case Study of Concept Formation in Sociology" in Walter W. Powell and Richard Robbins, eds., *Conflict and Consensus: Festschrift in Honor of Lewis A. Coser* (New York: Free Press, 1984), pp. 262–283.

39. Glaser and Strauss; Blau, *Old Age in a Changing Society,* notes 27 and 29.

40. Erving Goffman, *Asylums* (Garden City, N.Y.: Anchor Books, 1961): pp. 18–20.

41. Mihaly Csikszentmihaly and Eugene Rochberg-Halton, *The Meaning of Things: Domestic Symbols and Selves* (Cambridge: Cambridge University Press, 1981). David R. Unruh, "Death and Personal History: Strategies of Identity Preservation," *Social Problems* 30, No. 5 (February 1983): 340–351; Austin Sarat and William L. F. Felstiner, "The Ideology of Divorce: Law in the Lawyer's Office," Paper presented at the Workshop on the Study of the Interaction Between Lawyer and Client, Rijksuniversiteit, Groningen, The Netherlands, October 1984, p. 32.

42. If the dwelling belonged to the initiator in the first place and the partner moved in, or if for some other reason the initiator defines the home as his or her own—so that it confirms, not the relationship but the initiator's own identity—the initiator will experience a loss in leaving it.

43. Davis refers to these keepsakes as "intimacy trophies." Davis, however, credits the term to an unpublished lecture given by Erving Goffman at Brandeis University, in Spring 1967. See Davis, pp. 176, 318, note 19.

44. Unruh (p. 344) notes how objects also symbolize the identity of the deceased to survivors. Consequently, at death, they evoke memories and become more precious.

45. Goffman, *Interaction Ritual,* pp. 126–129.

46. The concept of relative deprivation and its effects was introduced in S. A. Stouffer et al., *The American Soldier: Combat and Its Aftermath* (Princeton: Princeton University Press, 1949). For a discussion and critique of relative deprivation, see Robert K. Merton, *Social Theory and Social Structure* (New York: Free Press, 1957), pp. 279–334.

47. See Chapter 2. Also, see George J. McCall, "The Dissolution of Commitment to Relationships," in Duck, pp. 217–219.

48. Weiss, *Marital Separation,* p. 247.

49. For a parallel, see Helena Z. Lopata, "Widowhood and Husband Sanctification," *Journal of Marriage and Family* (May 1981): 379–389.

50. Peter Marris, *Loss and Change* (London: Routledge and Kegan Paul, 1974), pp. 5–22.

51. Ibid., p. 5.

52. Erving Goffman, "On Cooling the Mark Out: Some Aspects of Adaptation to Failure," *Psychiatry* 15(1952): 454.

53. See Weiss, *Marital Separation*, p. 99; Wallerstein and Kelly, p. 191.

54. Peter Marris, *Loss and Change*.

55. Rosabeth Moss Kanter, *Commitment and Community: Communes and Utopias in Sociological Perspective* (Cambridge: Harvard University Press, 1972), p. 70.

CHAPTER EIGHT

1. Goffman notes that the temporal length of a performance is important to secret-keeping. If the audience is to see only a brief performance, the couple will be likely to get through it without giving away their secrets. As the length of the performance and the familiarity with the audience increases, the possibility of revealing the true situation increases. Erving Goffman, *The Presentation of Self in Everyday Life* (New York: Anchor Books, 1959), p. 221. Frequency of performance appears to be as important as length. Those who see the couple often, and for longer performances, are more likely to witness breakdowns than infrequent short-span observers. Nonetheless, for those who get the couple's performance in a relatively continuous run (e.g., children) the display of discontent occurs routinely and becomes accepted as a part of the relationship, not as a sign of deterioration.

2. Goffman, *The Presentation of Self*, pp. 77–140, 141.

3. Michael Spence, *Market Signaling* (Cambridge: Harvard University Press, 1974), pp. 6–11. See also Erving Goffman, *Stigma: Notes on the Management of Spoiled Identity* (Englewood Cliffs: Prentice-Hall, 1963), pp. 57–127 for a discussion of information control in the context of impression management and social interaction.

4. Marris, pp. 5–22.

5. Wallerstein and Kelly point out how parents' physical separation changes the children's definition of the relationship: "This is a step that children cannot fail to perceive, however much they may consciously or unconsciously deny the impending rupture. The actual physical separation forces the children to revise their perception of their parents as a unit and to confront the visible evidence of the splitting of their family" (p. 36). Despite witnessing quarrels and abuse between parents, children had little knowledge of the imminent dissolution of their parents' marriage. Some had only a brief awareness of the parents' unhappiness prior to the decision to separate. For others, divorce and threat of divorce had become a chronic but accepted part of family life, yet they found no evidence that this knowledge prepared them. Most parents made pronouncements, but with no attempt to prepare the children for the eventual break-up. Parents did not recognize that children needed a gradual process of understanding, brought about by information exchange that would prepare the child for the important transition to come. "In effect, they awoke one morning to find one parent gone." Different childcare patterns, for example, are arranged quickly at separation, without a transition period. Out of insecurity and frequently without resources outside the home, the emotional reaction is anger, upset and clinging to the remaining parent—a reaction not unlike that of the unprepared partner, who is suddenly left without the other person. Wallerstein and Kelly, pp. 38–39.

6. George McCall, "Becoming Unrelated: The Management of Bond Dissolution," in Steve Duck, ed., *Personal Relationships. 4: Dissolving Personal Relationships* (London: Academic Press, 1982), p. 224.

7. More often, it seems, it is partners who are surprised when a child aligns with the initiator. Their sense of loss is confounded by this revelation, and the partner responds

angrily to what they view as an unjust turn of events. Initiators do not "steal the child" from the other parent, however. The development of a confidant is not a unilateral process. Self-selection is involved, based on the pre-existence of some ideological compatibility. Children who become confidants of initiators bring to the alignment their own negative definition of the other parent, which has grown out of their own experience. Both initiator and child-as-confidant feed into each other's definitions, confirming them and enhancing them as the bond between them grows. See also Judith S. Wallerstein and Joan B. Kelly, *Surviving the Break-up: How Children and Parents Cope with Divorce* (New York: Basic Books, 1980), p. 88.

8. Steve Duck, "A Topography of Relationship Disengagement and Dissolution," in Duck, ed., *Personal Relationships. 4: Dissolving Personal Relationships*, p. 13.

9. Berger and Kellner, pp. 14–15.

10. McCall, in Duck, pp. 225, 227.

11. Marvin B. Scott and Stanford M. Lyman, "Accounts," *American Sociological Review* 33(1968): 46–62. For a typology of accounts used by both partners during marriage dissolution, see William H. Gram, "Breaking Up: A Study of Fifty-Nine Case Histories of Marital Collapse" (Ph.D. dissertation, Northwestern University, 1982). See also John J. LaGaipa, "Rules and Rituals in Disengaging from Relationships," in Duck, pp. 192–203, especially p. 193, and Erving Goffman, *Interaction Ritual: Essays on Face-to-Face Behavior* (New York: Anchor Books, 1967), pp. 97–112.

12. LaGaipa in Duck, p. 193.

13. Ibid., p. 196.

14. McCall, in Duck, pp. 225, 227.

15. LaGaipa in Duck, p. 207; Gram, pp. 173–183.

16. McCall, p. 227, states that a stable account is the result of the completion of the process of mourning. As partners are just entering this phase, their accounts will vary, both in form and content.

17. Goffman, "On Cooling the Mark Out: Some Aspects of Adaptation to Failure," *Psychiatry* 15(1952): 461.

18. Berger and Kellner, pp. 4–5; McCall, in Duck, p. 227.

19. LaGaipa, in Duck, p. 197. In interviews, I found two circumstances under which both initiator and partner gave the same account to others at the time of separation: (1) the relationship was heterosexual and one of the partners changed sexual preference, or (2) at separation, both partners had uncoupled, and agreed to the separation. In a heterosexual relationship that dissolves because one partner changes sexual identity, partners are likely to conspire and agree to a common account, which probably hides the truth. Because the failure of the relationship is attributed by each to something "out of their control," the power imbalance that usually develops when one rejects the other dissolves when the partner learns the cause of the initiator's unhappiness. Instead of competing for the support of others, the couple cooperate so that they may continue to share friends of the relationship. They collaborate to keep this secret. Whether or not they eventually disclose it, I don't know. Should the bond between the two partners weaken over time, the willingness to maintain each other's secrets may also weaken. If the gay partner decides to make this lifestyle choice public, the other partner may even collaborate in helping to break the news.

The second circumstance of going public with the same account occurs when, at separation, the partner is also ready to move on. The partner has already confided in others, secured their social support, and arrived at a stable account of the relationship's demise. As in the first circumstance, the account each has constructed places the blame elsewhere (e.g., "we just grew apart"), which allows the couple to remain cordial.

They present the same account because they have both arrived at the same point in the transition, and thus in the redefinition of relationship. Again, whether the accounts remained identical over time and to all audiences, I do not know.

20. Not only is each partner's account told in different form to numerous others, but it is also told several times to one, varying in form and content not only depending on the audience, but on the stage in the transition. McCall, in Duck, p. 225. See also LaGaipa, in Duck, p. 207. Thus, each couple presents many versions of the end of their relationship. Rubin reports (p. 51) that for many couples there are two courtships. In addition, Jessie Barnard (pp. 3–59) finds two marriages: "his" and "hers." In both these studies, however, the researcher was the audience, thus getting one version of the subject's experience. Perhaps other audiences got other versions of the courtship and marriage, thus creating the possibility of not just two but many versions of the courtship and marriage, depending on the number of audiences and their proximity to the partners. See Lillian Rubin, *Worlds of Pain: Life in The Working Class Family* (New York: Basic Books, 1976); Jessie Barnard, *The Future of Marriage* (New York: Bantam, 1972).

21. Murray S. Davis, *Intimate Relations* (New York: Free Press, 1973), p. 282.

22. Peter Marris, *Loss and Change* (London: Routledge and Kegan Paul, 1974), pp. 5–22.

23. See, for example, Maureen Baker, *Support Networks and Marriage Dissolution*, Final Report (Toronto: Connaught Foundation, University of Toronto, 1980), p. 11; Julia Brannen and Jean Collard, *Marriages in Trouble: The Process of Seeking Help* (London: Tavistock, 1982), pp. 31–46, 93–112, 113–139; Eugenia Proctor Gerdes, John D. Gehling, and Jeffrey N. Rapp, "The Effects of Sex and Sex-Role Conception on Self-Disclosure," *Sex Roles* 7(1981): 989–998.

24. Peter M. Blau, *Exchange and Power in Social Life* (New York: John Wiley & Sons, 1964), pp. 118–125.

25. Wallerstein and Kelly, pp. 49, 77–79. Kurt H. Wolff, ed. and tr., *The Sociology of Georg Simmel* (New York: The Free Press, 1950), p. 150.

26. Wallerstein and Kelly, pp. 41–45.

27. For the application of these same ideas to macro-organizational behavior, see Diane Vaughan, *Controlling Unlawful Organizational Behavior: Social Structure and Corporate Misconduct* (Chicago: University of Chicago Press, 1983), pp. 54–66.

28. See Wallerstein and Kelly, p. 30.

29. Ibid.; Austin Sarat and William L. F. Felstiner, "The Ideology of Divorce: Law in the Lawyer's Office," Paper presented at the Workshop on the Study of the Interaction Between Lawyer and Client, Rijksuniversiteit, Groningen, The Netherlands, October 1984, pp. 30–32.

30. In Chapter 3, I pointed out how initiators can be influenced by the separation of someone they know. They, in turn, at separation may become role models for someone else, triggering their own domino effect.

31. Joyce Carol Oates, *Spoils*. Performed by The American Repertory Theatre, Loeb Drama Center, Cambridge, Massachusetts, May 23, 1983.

32. Barney G. Glaser and Anselm L. Strauss, *Status Passage* (London: Routledge and Kegan Paul, 1971), p. 17; Lillian B. Rubin, *Woman of a Certain Age: The Midlife Search for Self* (New York: Harper & Row, 1979), p. 137.

33. LaGaipa, in Duck, pp. 195–196: Duck, in Duck, p. 15.

34. LaGaipa, in Duck, p. 201.

35. Weiss (pp. 130–131) notes the tendency of some husbands to leave the notification of the family to their wives. The result is an alignment between his parents and his wife. Robert S. Weiss, *Marital Separation* (New York: Basic Books, 1975).

36. David Sudnow, *Passing On: The Social Organization of Dying* (Englewood Cliffs, N.J.: Prentice-Hall, 1967), pp. 72–77; Barney Glaser and Anselm Strauss, "Awareness Contexts and Social Interaction," *American Sociological Review* 29 (October 1964): 669–678; David R. Unruh, "Death and Personal History: Strategies of Identity Preservation," *Social Problems* 30, No. 5 (February 1983): 340–351.

37. McCall, in Duck, p. 225.

38. Nicky Hart, *When Marriage Ends: A Study in Status Passage* (London: Tavistock, 1976), p. 167; Sissela Bok, *Secrets: On the Ethics of Concealment and Revelation* (New York: Pantheon, 1982), p. 91.

39. Michael P. Johnson, "Social and Cognitive Features of the Dissolution of Commitment to Relationships " in Duck, pp. 59–62. See also Eli Coleman, "Developmental Stages of the Coming Out Process," *American Behavioral Scientist* 25(1982): 469–482; and Michael P. Burk, "Coming Out: The Gay Identity Process," pp. 137–072 in Bernard I. Murstein, ed., *Exploring Intimate Lifestyles* (New York: Springer Publishers, 1978).

40. See also Weiss, p. 137.

41. McCall, in Duck, p. 222.

42. Kurt H. Wolff, ed. and tr., *The Sociology of Georg Simmel* (New York: The Free Press, 1950), p. 313.

43. McCall, in Duck, pp. 217–220; Marris, p. 195. Goffman notes that friends are ideal for helping a person adjust to an unwanted loss because their relationship is not connected to the role in which the person has failed. Friends are, therefore, free to take the responsibility for the rehabilitation process. Goffman, "On Cooling the Mark Out," p. 457. The role of friends in the consolation process is complicated in homosexual relationships, however, due to the potential for the transitional person to subsequently become a lover.

44. Wallerstein and Kelly, p. 136.

45. McCall, in Duck, pp. 217–220.

46. Willard Waller, *The Old Love and the New* (New York: Liveright, 1930), pp. 129–131; Robert K. Merton, "Socially Expected Durations: A Case Study of Concept Formation in Sociology," in Walter W. Powell and Richard Robbins, eds., *Conflict and Consensus: A Festschrift in Honor of Lewis A. Coser* (New York: Free Press, 1984), pp. 262–283.

47. Johnson, in Duck, p. 67.

48. Hart, p. 121, describes well the erosion of self-confidence that occurs in dealing with those whose negative reaction we anticipate.

49. Wallerstein and Kelly, pp. 126–129, 136. Wallerstein and Kelly also report (pp. 250–251) that the availability of alternative relationships was a part of this rejection process. Children who reject fathers who leave draw on available relationships in their environment for support: the custodial parent, stepfather, boyfriend, teacher—people whose values they could accept and who held a congenial world view.

50. Blau, p. 84; Rosabeth Moss Kanter, *Commitment and Community: Communes and Utopia in Sociological Perspective* (Cambridge: Harvard University Press, 1972), p. 83.

51. Berger and Kellner, pp. 14–15. See also Levenger's discussion of "Barrier Forces" in George Levenger, "A Social Exchange View on the Dissolution of Pair Relationships," in R. L. Burgess and T. L. Huston, eds., *Social Exchange in Developing Relationships* (New York: Academic Press, 1979).

52. Berger and Kellner, pp. 14–17. Having a larger public does not necessarily mean more support, however. Public figures who separate have to contend with greater dis-

ruption, due to the vast dissemination of information about their private lives through the media. Still, these people remain strangers, capable of objection or support only from a distance.

53. Diane Rothbard Margolis, *The Managers: Corporate Life in America* (New York: Morrow, 1979), pp. 41–66, 93–116.

54. I am speaking here only of the relative difficulty or ease of negotiating the change in the relationship in the public arena, not psychological trauma. Research verifies that regardless of legal status or living arrangement, breaking up is always emotionally disruptive and disorienting. See Eleanor D. Macklin, "Nontraditional Family Forms: A Decade of Research," *Journal of Marriage and the Family* 33 (1980): 296; K. Mika and B. L. Bloom, "Adjustment to Separation Among Former Cohabitors," *Journal of Divorce* 4 (1980): 45–66.

55. Comparisons between people who live together and those who marry indicate that cohabiters often avoid telling their families about their relationships, thus necessitating "internally generated cohesion" to compensate for the absence of the cohesion that is bestowed on those who marry by the reaction of family to the partnership. Eleanor D. Macklin, "Review of Research on Nonmarital Cohabitation in the United States," in Bernard I. Mustein, ed., *Exploring Intimate Lifestyles* (New York: Springer Publishing, 1978), p. 235; Michael D. Newcomb, "Relationship Qualities of Those Who Live Together," *Alternative Lifestyles* 6(1983): p. 86. See also discussion of resources and "fast uncouplers" in Chapter 7.

56. See, for example, Betty Frankle Kirschner and Laurel Richardson Walum, "Two-Location Families: Married Singles," *Alternative Lifestyles* 1 (November 1978): 513–525; Caroline Bird, *The Two Paycheck Marriage* (New York: Rawson, Wade Publishers, 1979). For theoretical insight into variation in relationship between units of an organization, see Alvin Gouldner, "Reciprocity and Autonomy in Functional Theory," in Llewellyn Gross, ed., *Symposium on Sociological Theory* (New York: Harper & Row, 1960), pp. 241–270, and Karl E. Weick, "Educational Organizations as Loosely Coupled Systems," *Administrative Science Quarterly* 21 (1976): 1–19.

57. Blau, pp. 118–125.

CHAPTER NINE

1. Robert S. Weiss, *Marital Separation* (New York: Basic Books, 1975), pp. 78–81; Hart, p. 111; Marris, p. 195.

2. George McCall, "Becoming Unrelated: The Management of Bond Dissolution," in Steve Duck, ed., *Personal Relationships. 4: Dissolving Personal Relationships* (London: Academic Press, 1982), pp. 217–220; Unruh, p. 342.

3. See, for example, Neil Simon, *Chapter Two* (New York: Samuel French, 1978); Simone de Beauvoir, *Adieux: A Farewell to Sartre,* Patrick O'Brian, tr. (New York: Pantheon, 1984); Nora Ephron, *Heartburn* (New York: Alfred Knopf, 1983). Nora Ephron, questioned in a PBS radio interview about the autobiographical nature of her book, replied, "If you can take one of life's tragedies and turn it into a humorous anecdote, it's yours. You own it." Wallerstein and Kelly report that a young girl whose parents were divorcing "designed and issued a magazine filled with articles, drawings and cartoons heralding the impending divorce of her parents and announcing other interesting happenings in the neighborhood. She distributed and sold the magazine in the school and the community." Judith S. Wallerstein and Joan Berlin Kelly, *Surviving the Breakup: How Children and Parents Cope with Divorce* (New York: Basic Books, 1980), p. 74.

Unruh reports this same response in people interviewed who were dying. They documented their personal history through writing memos, letters, notes, journals, and autobiographies which they planned to leave behind for others. David Unruh, "Death and Personal History: Strategies of Identity Preservation," *Social Problems* 30 (February, 1983): 342.

4. John I. Kitsuse, "Societal Reactions to Deviant Behavior: Problems of Theory and Method," *Social Problems* 9 (1962): 247–256.

5. Hart, p. 115; Kristine M. Rosenthal and Harry F. Keshet, *Fathers Without Partners: A Study of Fathers and the Family after Marital Separation* (Totowa, N. J.: Rowman and Littlefield, 1981), p. 46.

6. Marris, p. 195; Julia Brannen and Jean Collard, *Marriages in Trouble: The Process of Seeking Help* (London: Tavistock, 1982): p. 61; Steve Duck, "A Topography of Relationship Disengagement and Dissolution," in Duck, p. 17; Hart (p. 117) found the shorter the length of time since the separation, the more likely positive feelings were expressed for the spouse. As time passed and respondents grew more sure there would be no reconciliation, negative statements increased.

7. Peter L. Berger and Thomas Luckmann, *The Social Construction of Reality* (Garden City, N.Y.: Doubleday, 1966).

8. Erving Goffman, *Interaction Ritual* (New York: Anchor, 1967), p. 126.

9. Erving Goffman, *The Presentation of Self in Everyday Life* (Garden City, N.Y.: Anchor, 1959), p. 141.

10. Erving Goffman, "On Cooling the Mark Out: Some Aspects of Adaptation to Failure," *Psychiatry* 15(1962): 458.

11. George J. McCall and J. L. Simmons, *Identities and Interactions* (New York: Free Press, 1966), pp. 36, 236; Hart, p. 50; Maureen Baker, *Support Networks and Marriage Dissolution*, Final Report (Toronto: Connaught Foundation, University of Toronto, 1980), p. 56. Lenore J. Weitzman, *The Divorce Revolution: The Unexpected Social and Economic Consequences for Women and Children in America* (New York: Free Press, 1985).

12. McCall and Simmons, p. 234.

13. Weiss, *Marital Separation*, p. 52.

14. Ibid.

15. Erving Goffman, *Interaction Ritual* (New York: Anchor, 1967), pp. 39, 107.

16. Hart, p. 111; McCall and Simmons, p. 245.

17. Goffman, *Interaction Ritual*, p. 107. Barney G. Glaser and Anselm L. Strauss, *Status Passage* (London: Routledge and Kegan Paul, 1971), p. 144.

18. See, for example, Doug Harper, *Good Company* (Chicago: University of Chicago Press, 1982); Erving Goffman, "The Moral Career of a Mental Patient," *Psychiatry* 22 (1959): 123–142; Georg Simmel, "The Stranger," in Kurt H. Wolff, ed. and tr., *The Sociology of Georg Simmel* (New York: Free Press, 1950); Elijah Anderson, *A Place on the Corner* (Chicago: University of Chicago Press, 1978).

19. See, for example, Lillian B. Rubin, *Women of a Certain Age: The Midlife Search for Self* (New York: Harper & Row, 1979), p. 202; Peter M. Blau, *Exchange and Power in Social Life* (New York: Wiley, 1964), pp. 98–99.

20. Blau, p. 101.

21. McCall and Simmons, pp. 233–244; Glaser and Strauss, pp. 21–23; p. 31.

22. Wallerstein and Kelly, p. 150. Research indicates that women are more likely than men to maintain contact with their in-laws after divorce. (J. W. Spicer and G. D. Hampe, "Kinship Interaction After Divorce," *Journal of Marriage and the Family* 37

(1975): 113–119.) This tendency may be a result of maintaining their role as primary

234 / NOTES

(1975): 113–119.) This tendency may be a result of maintaining their role as primary caretaker of the children. Whatever the reason, the continued interaction has obvious consequences for identity, as noted in the text.

23. Hart, pp. 140–144.

24. Goffman, *Interaction Ritual*, p. 107.

25. See discussion in Chapter 6.

26. Sam D. Sieber, "Toward a Theory of Role Accumulation," *American Sociological Review* 39(1974): 567–578.

27. Angrist reports that women may be more prepared for uncoupling because they have been contingency-trained, or less prepared because of the salience of the coupled role and relatively fewer economic options. Shirley S. Angrist, "The Study of Sex Roles," *Journal of Social Issues* 25(1969): 215–232.

28. Michael P. Johnson, "Social and Cognitive Features of the Dissolution of Commitment to Relationships," in Duck, p. 68.

29. Johnson, in Duck, p. 68.

30. Johnson, in Duck, p. 67.

31. Hunt notes that most divorced people do not really enter the world of single people, but that of the formerly married. Morton Hunt, *The World of the Formerly Married* (Harmondsworth: Allen Lane, 1968).

32. See also Rubin, p. 137.

33. Robert K. Merton, "Contributions to the Theory of Reference Group Behavior" (with Alice Rossi) in Robert K. Merton, *Social Theory and Social Structure* (New York: Free Press, 1968), p. 324.

34. See also Hart, p. 199; John H. Harvey et al., "An Attributional Approach to Relationship Breakdown and Dissolution," in Duck, p. 125.

CHAPTER TEN

1. Murray S. Davis, *Intimate Relations* (New York: Free Press, 1973), p. 179. Simmel describes isolation as interaction between two parties, one of whom leaves, after exerting certain influences. The isolated individual is isolated only in reality, however; for in the mind of the other party, the absent person continues to live and act. Kurt H. Wolff, ed. and tr., *The Sociology of Georg Simmel* (New York: The Free Press, 1950), p. 119.

2. See also Judith S. Wallerstein and Joan B. Kelly, *Surviving the Breakup: How Children and Parents Cope with Divorce* (New York: Basic Books, 1980), pp. 26–29.

3. Paul Bohannan, ed., *Divorce and After* (New York: Doubleday, 1971), pp. 33–34. Hart, examining the length of time between separation and divorce, found that some people took months or years to rule out the possibility of reconciliation. She reports, "In some cases, it was not until the individual had finalized some other plans for the future, either in the shape of another partner, or perhaps a new occupational career, that the old life could be abandoned. Arranging for the legal dissolution of the bond was often deferred until this state of affairs had been reached." Nicky Hart, *When Marriage Ends: A Study in Status Passage* (London: Tavistock, 1976), pp. 116–117.

4. Gram (pp. 12–13), Wallerstein and Kelly (p. 149), and Hagestad and Smyer (p. 183) also note that divorce date and separation date are seldom accurate measures of the actual end of a marital relationship. In fact, in William J. Goode's classic study *After Divorce* (Glencoe, Ill.: Free Press, 1956), 22% of the couples hadn't separated when the divorce suit was filed. Seven percent hadn't separated when the decree was granted. See also William H. Gram, "Breaking Up: A Study of Fifty-Nine Case Histories of

Marital Collapse'' (Ph.D. dissertation, Northwestern University, 1982); Wallerstein and Kelly, *Surviving the Breakup;* and Gunhild O. Hagestad and Michael A. Smyer, "Dissolving Long-Term Relationships: Patterns of Divorcing in Middle Age" in Steve Duck, ed., *Personal Relationships. 4: Dissolving Personal Relationships* (London: Academic Press, 1982), pp. 155–188.

5. Marvin B. Scott and Stanford M. Lyman, "Accounts," *American Sociological Review* 33 (1968): 46–62.

6. John H. Harvey et al., "An Attributional Approach to Relationship Breakdown and Dissolution," in Duck, p. 125.

7. Hart, pp. 196–197; Willard Waller, *The Old Love and the New* (New York: Liveright, 1930), pp. 172–185.

8. See also Abigail Trafford, *Crazy Time: Predictable Stages of Divorce* (New York: Harper & Row, 1982), p. 141.

9. Wallerstein and Kelly, pp. 38–39.

10. As Berger so elegantly puts it, "Old markers may be retrieved from the debris of discarded chronologies." Peter L. Berger, *Invitation to Sociology: A Humanistic Perspective* (New York: Anchor, 1963), p. 59; Waller, p. 140.

11. Barney G. Glaser and Anselm L. Strauss, *Status Passage* (London: Routledge and Kegan Paul, 1971), pp. 90–97.

12. Scott and Lyman, pp. 46–62; George McCall, "Becoming Unrelated: The Management of Bond Dissolution," in Duck, p. 225; Wallerstein and Kelly, p. 158.

13. Waller, p. 185; Wallerstein and Kelly, pp. 154–157, 187, 193.

14. McCall describes five types of bonds: attachment, social structural bonds, commitment, benefit-dependability, and investment. George McCall, "The Management of Bond Dissolution," in Duck, pp. 212–217. See also Robert S. Weiss, "The Emotional Impact of Marital Separation," *Journal of Social Issues* 32 (1976): 138; John Bowlby, *Attachment and Loss, I: Attachment* (New York: Basic Books, 1969); John Bowlby, *Attachment and Loss, II: Separation* (New York: Basic Books, 1973); Hagestad and Smyer, pp. 161–166.

15. Jean Goldsmith, "Relationships between Former Spouses: Descriptive Findings," *Journal of Divorce* 4(1980): 1–20. In a sample of one hundred fifty separated and divorced men and women, Baker found that 23% said that they never saw their former spouses at all. Those who never saw their former spouses tended to be childless. Maureen Baker, *Support Networks and Marriage Dissolution,* Final Report (Toronto: Connaught Foundation Project, University of Toronto, 1980), p. 23.

16. Weiss notes that men seem generally to drop relationships with in-laws, even if they have custody of the children, while women tend to maintain them. Robert S. Weiss, *Marital Separation* (New York: Basic Books, 1975), p. 144.

17. Kristine M. Rosenthal and Harry F. Keshet, *Fathers Without Partners: A Study of Fathers and the Family After Marital Separation* (Totowa, N. J.: Rowman and Littlefield, 1981), pp. xiii, 157. Wallerstein and Kelly report the tendency for couples with children to maintain geographic proximity in order to continue their parenting. They also note that "the visit is an event continually available for the replay of anger, jealousy, love, mutual rejection and longing between divorced adults," p. 125. In addition one-third of both parents in their study were in active competition for the affection and loyalty of the children, p. 125. Not only for these reasons do former partners initiate interaction, but the children sometimes actively work to get their parents together. Hoping to achieve a reconciliation, some children arrange for their parents to bump into each other or create scenes and problems that will bring them together. Wallerstein and Kelly, pp. 73–74.

18. Patricia Leigh Brown, "Sharing the Pet After a Breakup," *New York Times*, November 1983.

19. Lenore J. Weitzman, *The Divorce Revolution: The Unexpected Social and Economic Consequences for Women and Children* (New York: Free Press, 1985); See also Weiss, *Marital Separation*, pp. 102–112; Wallerstein and Kelly, p. 30; Carol Smart, *The Ties That Bind: Law, Marriage, and the Reproduction of Patriarchal Relations* (Boston: Routledge and Kegan Paul, 1984). Unruh notes that documents can have a similar effect when one of the partners dies. Those who are dying use their wills to solidify their identity, affecting others' lives even after they are gone by creating or maintaining interdependencies. David R. Unruh, "Death and Personal History: Strategies of Identity Preservation," *Social Problems* 30, No. 5 (February 1983): 343. For a marvelous example, see Book 5: The Dead Hand, in George Eliot, *Middlemarch: A Study of Provincial Life* (Edinburgh and London: William Blackwood and Sons, 1871).

20. Weiss also found that expressions of hostility are attempts to maintain contact. Robert S. Weiss, "The Emotional Impact of Marital Separation," in Peter J. Stein, ed., *Single Life: Unmarried Adults in Social Context* (New York: St. Martin's, 1981), p. 76; Weiss, *Marital Separation*, p. 114. See also Wallerstein and Kelly, p. 193.

21. Davis, p. 258.

22. Rosenthal and Keshet, p. x.

23. "Dog is Ruled Couple's 'Child' in Custody Case in California," *New York Times*, 8 September 1983.

24. Edmond Rostand, *Cyrano de Bergerac: An Heroic Comedy in Five Acts*, trans. Brian Hooker (New York: Henry Holt and Company, 1924), pp. 44–46.

25. For description of some gender differences in post-separation change, see Wallerstein and Kelly, pp. 157–159. See also Rosenthal and Keshet, pp. 121–123.

26. Davis, pp. 176–177.

27. Weiss notes that "Often the spouse who took the lead in the separation will also attempt to establish a friendly post-marital relationship. This spouse, perhaps, has less to be angry at and stronger feelings of continued obligation," *Marital Separation*, p. 115. According to my interviews, initiators are more likely to try to pick up the ties because they are ahead of the partner in the transition and thus have worked through their negative feelings. Consequently, initiators are first to be able to again see the positive characteristics of the partner.

28. See also Lindsy Van Gelder, "Is Divorce Ever Final? Ten Woman Talk about Their Ex-Husbands," *MS* (February 1979): 61–70; Kathy E. Kram, "Phases of the Mentor Relationship," *Academy of Management Journal* 26, No. 4 (December 1983): 608–625; Rosenthal and Keshet, pp. 89–111, 157.

29. Weiss notes this also, stating "the farther along a couple is in their course toward divorce, the less likely reconciliation seems to be." Weiss, *Martial Separation*, p. 121.

30. George J. McCall and J. L. Simmons, *Identities and Interactions* (New York: Free Press, 1966), pp. 235–244; Barney G. Glaser and Anselm L. Strauss, *Status Passage* (London: Routledge and Kegan Paul, 1971), p. 106.

31. Waller, pp. 142, 167–168.

32. See also Wallerstein and Kelly, pp. 261–263.

33. For extensive examples, see William H. Gram, "Breaking Up: A Study of Fifty-Nine Case Histories of Marital Collapse" (Ph.D. dissertation, Northwestern University, 1982), pp. 43–50.

CHAPTER ELEVEN

1. Undoubtedly, the discovery of order was encouraged by the methodology of the study (see Postscript). The information I received was based on retrospective analysis by the interviewees. The passage of time not only allowed events to be reconstructed in an orderly way that made sense, but ordering them is also an important part of the process. Nonetheless, as I noted in the Introduction and Postscript, the interviewees were at various stages in the uncoupling process—some in the earliest beginnings, some years after separation or divorce. Despite this, the patterns I've described appeared consistently. Moreover, these patterns have been confirmed by the other methods described in the Introduction.

2. Van Gennup notes that in most societies significant transitions involving role exits and entries are marked by characteristic sequences of events. See A. Van Gennup *The Rites of Passage* (New York: Phoenix Books, 1908/1960). Also see Gunhild O. Hagestad and Michael A. Smyer, *"Dissolving Long-Term Relationships: Patterns of Divorcing in Middle Age,"* in Steve Duck, ed., *Personal Relationships. 4: Dissolving Personal Relationships* (London: Academic Press, 1982), pp. 155–187.

3. Orville G. Brim, "Socialization Through the Life Cycle," in Orville G. Brim and Stanton Wheeler, eds., *Socialization After Childhood* (New York: John Wiley, 1966), pp. 1–49; Kathy E. Kram, *Mentoring at Work: Developmental Relationships in Organizational Life* (Glenview, Ill.: Scott, Foresman, 1984).

4. Fred H. Gouldner, "Demotion in Industrial Management," *American Sociological Review* 30 (1965): 714–724; Nigel Nicolson, "A Theory of Work Role Transitions," *Administrative Science Quarterly* 29 (1984): 172–191.

5. Peter L. Berger, *Invitation to Sociology: A Humanistic Perspective* (New York: Anchor, 1963), pp. 56–65, especially p. 60.

6. Laurence A. Basirico, "Stickin' Together: The Cohesiveness of Rock Groups" (Masters thesis, Department of Sociology, State University of New York at Stony Brook, 1974).

7. John Lofland and Rodney Stark, "Becoming a World-Saver: A Theory of Conversion to a Deviant Perspective," *American Sociological Review* 30 (1965): 862–875.

8. Zick Rubin, *Children's Friendships* (Cambridge: Harvard University Press, 1980), especially pp. 80, 86.

9. David R. Unruh, "Death and Personal History: Strategies of Identity Preservation," *Social Problems* 30 (February 1983): 340–351; Helena Znaniecki Lopata, "Widowhood and Husband Sanctification," *Journal of Marriage and the Family* (1981): 439–450.

10. Elaine Cumming and William E. Henry, *Growing Old: The Process of Disengagement* (New York: Basic Books, 1961), p. 150.

11. Cumming and Henry, especially at pp. 22 and 227; E. Wilbur Bock and Irving L. Webber, "Suicide Among the Elderly: Isolating Widowhood and Mitigating Alternatives," *Journal of Marriage and the Family* 34(1972): 24–31.

12. Arlie Russell Hochschild, "Disengagement Theory: A Critique and Proposal," *American Sociological Review* 40(1975): 553–669. For other transitions exhibiting some of the patterns found in uncoupling, see D. R. Maines, "Bodies and Selves: Notes on a Fundamental Dilemma in Demography," in Norman K. Denzin, ed., *Studies in Symbolic Interaction* (Greenwich, Conn.: JAI Press, 1978), 241–265; Lee J. Cuba, "Reorientations of Self: Residential Identification in Anchorage, Alaska," in Norman K. Denzin ed., *Studies in Symbolic Interaction* (Greenwich, Conn.: JAI Press, 1984),

pp. 219–237; Marion K. Yarrow et al., "Social Psychological Characteristics of Old Age," *Human Aging: A Biological and Behavioral Study* (Washington, D.C.: Government Printing Office, 1961); Nancy Ammerman, "The Fundamentalist Worldview" (Ph.D. dissertation, Yale University, 1983); Berger, *Invitation to Sociology*, pp. 56–65, especially p. 60; Kathy E. Kram, "Phases of the Mentor Relationship," *Academy of Management Journal* 26, No. 4 (December 1983): 608–625. Kram's research is unique in its exploration of the developmental history of these relationships. See also Kathy E. Kram, *Mentoring at Work: Developmental Relations in Organizational Life* (Glenview, Ill.: Scott Foresman, Inc., 1985).

13. A theme running persistently through the work of Robert K. Merton is that choice is not simply an output of structure, but a strategic input for the system as a whole. See Arthur Stinchcombe, "Merton's Theory of Social Structure," in Lewis A. Coser, ed., *The Idea of Social Structure: Papers in Honor of Robert K. Merton* (New York: Harcourt Brace Jovanovich, 1975), pp. 23–24.

14. I do not believe that the signs of caring can be discounted on the grounds that the interviewees may have constructed accounts that would allow them to save face during the interview. First, I took as evidence of caring their behavior during the breakup and after, not sentiments expressed in the interview setting. Second, while we always distort, I believe that the degree to which those I interviewed became immersed in the telling of their account reduced the possible biasing effects of my presence. See Postscript for details.

15. Trafford describes confrontation as an opportunity to renegotiate the power relationship between two people, and argues that the continuance of the relationship depends on a successful redistribution of power. Abigail Trafford, *Crazy Times: Predictable Stages of Divorce* (New York: Harper & Row, 1982).

POSTSCRIPT

1. Lillian B. Rubin, *Women of a Certain Age: The Midlife Search for Self* (New York: Harper & Row, 1979). Rubin and her colleagues began interviewing a few people whom they knew fit the requirements of the research, asking them for referrals. Sometimes they got one referral, sometimes twenty. The next person to be interviewed was one with the most distant connection, both geographically and emotionally, from the person who referred her.

2. For a similar strategy in biographical interviewing, see Kathy E. Kram, *Mentoring at Work: Developmental Relationships in Organizational Life* (Glenview, Ill.: Scott Foresman, Inc., 1985); Julia Brannen and Jean Collard, *Marriages in Trouble: The Process of Seeking Help* (London: Tavistock, 1982).

3. The results of this pilot study first appeared in *Alternative Lifestyles* 2(1979): 414–442. See also Diane Vaughan, "Uncoupling: The Social Construction of Divorce," in Howard Robboy, Sidney L. Greenblatt, and Candace Clark, eds., *Social Interaction: Introductory Readings in Sociology* (New York: St. Martin's, 1985, 3rd ed.).

4. The three components of systematic generalization are described in Diane Vaughan, *Controlling Unlawful Organizational Behavior: Social Structure and Corporate Misconduct* (Chicago: The University of Chicago Press, 1983), pp. 132–135.

5. Marvin Scott and Stanford M. Lyman, "Accounts," *American Sociological Review* 33, No. 1 (1968), 46–62.

6. George McCall, "Becoming Unrelated: The Management of Bond Dissolution,"

in Duck, ed., *Personal Relationships. 4: Dissolving Personal Relationships* (London: Academic Press, 1982), pp. 224–231; John J. LaGaipa, "Rules and Rituals in Disengaging from Relationships," in Duck, pp. 207–209; Robert S. Weiss, *Marital Separation* (New York: Basic Books, 1975), p. 15.

7. Peter Marris, *Loss and Change* (London: Routledge and Kegan Paul, 1974).

SELECTED READINGS

Aldrich, Howard E. *Organizations and Environments.* Englewood Cliffs, N.J.: Prentice-Hall, 1979.

Ammerman, Nancy. "The Fundamentalist Worldview," Ph.D. dissertation, Yale University, 1983.

Arrow, Kenneth. *The Limits of Organization.* New York: W. W. Norton, 1974.

Baker, Maureen. *Support Networks and Marriage Dissolution.* Final Report, Connaught Foundation Project, University of Toronto, 1980.

Barnard, Jessie. *The Future of Marriage.* New York: Bantam, 1972.

Baruch, Grace, Rosalind Barnett, and Caryl Rivers. *Life Prints: New Patterns of Love and Work for Today's Women.* New York: McGraw-Hill, 1983.

Basirico, Lawrence. "Stickin' Together: The Cohesiveness of Rock Groups." Master's thesis, State University of New York at Stony Brook, 1974.

Becker, Howard S. "Becoming a Marijuana User." In Howard S. Becker, ed., *Outsiders.* New York: Free Press, 1963.

Bequaert, Lucia H. *Single Women: Alone and Together.* Boston: Beacon, 1976.

Berger, Peter, and Hansfried Kellner. "Marriage and the Construction of Reality." *Diogenes* 46 (1964): 1–25.

Berger, Peter L. *Invitation to Sociology.* New York: Anchor Books, 1963.

Berger, Peter L., and Thomas Luckmann. *The Social Construction of Reality.* New York: Doubleday, 1966.

Bird, Caroline. *The Two Paycheck Marriage: How Women at Work are Changing Life in America: An In-Depth Report on the Great Revolution of Our Times.* New York: Rawson, Wade Publishers, 1979.

Blau, Peter M. *Exchange and Power in Social Life.* New York: John Wiley, 1964.

Blau, Zena S. "Changes in Age and Status Identification." *American Sociological Review* 21 (1956): 198–203.

———. *Old Age in a Changing Society.* New York: New Viewpoints, 1973.

Bock, Wilbur, and Irving L. Webber. "Suicide Among the Elderly: Isolating Widowhood and Mitigating Alternatives." *Journal of Marriage and Family* 34 (1972): 24–31.

Bohannan, Paul, ed. *Divorce and After*. New York: Doubleday, 1971.

Bok, Sissela. *Secrets: On the Ethics of Concealment and Revelation*. New York: Pantheon, 1982.

Bower, Donald W., and Victor A. Christopherson. "University Student Cohabitation: A Regional Comparison of Selected Attitudes and Behavior." *Journal of Marriage and the Family* 39 (1977): 447–453.

Bowlby, John. "Processes of Mourning." *International Journal of Psychoanalysis* 44 (1961): 317–335.

———. *Attachment and Loss, I: Attachment*. New York: Basic Books, 1969.

———. *Attachment and Loss, II: Separation*. New York: Basic Books, 1973.

Brannen, Julia, and Jean Collard. *Marriages in Trouble: The Process of Seeking Help* London: Tavistock, 1982.

Brim, Orville G., and Stanton Wheeler, eds. *Socialization After Childhood*. New York: John Wiley, 1966.

Burk, Michael P. "Coming Out: The Gay Identity Process." In *Exploring Intimate Lifestyles*, edited by Bernard I. Murstein, pp. 257–272. New York: Springer Publishing, 1978.

Cherlin, Andrew. "Effect of Children on Marital Disruption." *Demography* 14 (1977): 265–272.

———. *Marriage, Divorce, Remarriage*. Cambridge: Harvard University Press, 1981.

Cleveland, W. P., and D. T. Giranturco. "Remarriage Probability After Widowhood: A Retrospective Method." *Journal of Gerontology* 31 (1976): 99–103.

Coleman, Eli. "Developmental Stages of the Coming Out Process." *American Behavioral Scientist* 25 (1982): 469–482.

Crosby, John F., Bruce A. Gage, and Marsha Croy Raymond. "The Grief Resolution Process in Divorce." *Journal of Divorce* 7 (1983): 3–18.

Csikszentmihalyi, Mihaly, and Eugene Rochberg-Halton. *The Meaning of Things: Domestic Symbols and the Self*. Cambridge: Cambridge University Press, 1981.

Cuba, Lee J. "Reorientations of Self: Residential Identification in Anchorage, Alaska." In *Studies in Symbolic Interaction*, Vol. 5, edited by Norman K. Denzin, pp. 219–237. Greenwich, Conn.: JAI Press, 1984.

Cumming, Elaine, and William B. Henry. *Growing Old: The Process of Disengagement*. New York: Basic Books, 1961.

Curb, Rosemary, and Nancy Manahan, eds. *Lesbian Nuns: Breaking Silence*. Tallahassee, Fla.: Naiad Press, 1985.

Dank, Barry. "Coming Out in the Gay World." *Psychiatry* 34 (1971): 180–197.

Davis, Murray S. *Intimate Relations*. New York: Free Press, 1973.

DeMontflores, Carmen, and Stephen J. Schultz. "Coming Out: Similarities and Differences for Lesbians and Gay Men." *Journal of Social Issues* 34 (1978)3: 59–72.

Devilbiss, M. C. "Gender Integration and Unit Deployment: A Study of G. I. Jo." *Armed Forces and Society: An Interdisciplinary Journal* 11 (1985): 523–552.

Duck, Steve. "The Personal Context: Intimate Relationships." In *Psychological Problems: The Social Context*, edited by P. Feldman and J. Orford, pp. 73–96. London: John Wiley, 1980.

Duck, Steve, ed. *Personal Relationships. 4: Dissolving Personal Relationships*. London: Academic Press, 1982.

Ephron, Nora. *Heartburn*. New York: Simon and Schuster, 1983.

Furstenberg, Frank F., Jr., and Graham B. Spanier. *Recycling the Family: Remarriage After Divorce*. Beverly Hills: Sage, 1984.

Garfinkel, Harold. "Conditions of Successful Degradation Ceremonies." *American Journal of Sociology* 61 (1956): 420–424.

Gerstel, Naomi, Catherine Kohler Riessman, and Sarah Rosenfield. "Explaining the Symptomatology of Separated and Divorced Women and Men: the Role of Material Conditions and Social Neworks." *Social Forces* 64 (September 1985): 84–101.

Gilligan, Carol. *In a Different Voice: Psychological Theory and Women's Development*. Cambridge: Harvard University Press, 1982.

Glaser, Barney, and Anselm Strauss. *Status Passage*. London: Routledge and Kegan Paul, 1971.

———. "Awareness Contexts and Social Interaction." *American Sociological Review* 29 (1964): 669–678.

———. *Time for Dying*. Chicago: Aldine, 1968.

Goffman, Erving. "On Cooling the Mark Out: Some Aspects of Adaptation to Failure." *Psychiatry* 15 (1952): 451–463.

———. *The Presentation of Self in Everyday Life*. Garden City, N.Y.: Anchor, 1959.

———. *Asylums*. Garden City, N.Y.: Anchor, 1961.

———. *Encounters: Two Studies in the Sociology of Interaction*. Indianapolis: Bobbs-Merrill, 1961.

———. *Stigma: Notes on the Management of Spoiled Identity*. Englewood Cliffs, N.J.: Prentice-Hall, 1963.

———. *Interaction Ritual*. Garden City, N.Y.: Anchor, 1967.

———. *Frame Analysis: An Essay on the Organization of Experience*. New York: Harper & Row, 1974.

———. "The Interaction Order." *American Sociological Review* 48 (1983): 1–17.

Goleman, Daniel. *Vital Lies, Simple Truths: The Psychology of Self-Deception*. New York: Simon and Schuster, 1985.

Goode, William J. *After Divorce*. Glencoe,, Ill.: The Free Press, 1956.

Gouldner, Alvin. "Reciprocity and Autonomy in Functional Theory." In *Symposium on Sociological Theory*, edited by Llewellyn Gross, pp. 241–270. New York: Harper & Row, 1960.

Gouldner, Fred H. "Demotion in Industrial Management," *American Sociological Review* 30 (1965): 714–724.

Gram, William H. "Breaking Up: A Study of Fifty-Nine Case Histories of Marital Collapse." Ph.D. dissertation, Northwestern University, 1982.

Harry, Joseph. *Gay Couples*. New York: Praeger, 1984.

———. "Gay Male and Lesbian Relationships." In *Contemporary Families and Alternative Lifestyles: Handbook on Research and Theory*, edited by E. Macklin and R. Rubin. Beverly Hills: Sage, 1983.

Harry, Joseph, and Robert Lovely. "Gay Marriages and Communities of Sexual Orientation." *Alternative Lifestyles* 2 (1979): 177–200.

Hart, Nicky. *When Marriage Ends: A Study in Status Passage*. London: Tavistock, 1976.

Henze, Lura F. and John W. Hudson. "Personal and Family Characteristics of Cohabiting and Noncohabiting College Students." *Journal of Marriage and the Family* 36 (1974): 722–727.

Hill, Charles T., Zick Rubin, and Letitia Anne Peplau. "Breakups Before Marriage: The End of 103 Affairs." *Journal of Social Issues*, 32 (1976): 147–168.

Hirschman, A. O. *Exit, Voice, and Loyalty*. Cambridge: Harvard University Press, 1970.

Hochschild, Arlie Russell. "Disengagement Theory: A Critique and Proposal." *American Sociological Review* 40 (1975): 553–669.

———. *The Unexpected Community*. Englewood Cliffs, N.J.: Prentice-Hall, 1973.

Holmstrom, Lynda Lytle. *The Two-Career Family*. Cambridge: Schenkman, 1973.

Hunt, Morton. *The World of the Formerly Married*. Hammondsworth: Allen Lane, 1968.

Jaffe, Dennis T., and Rosabeth Moss Kanter. "Couple Strains in Communal Households: A Four-Factor Model of the Separation Process." *Journal of Social Issues*, 32 (1976): 169–207.

Kanter, Rosabeth Moss. *Commitment and Community: Communes and Utopia in Sociological Perspective*. Cambridge: Harvard University Press, 1972.

Kirschner, Betty Frankle, and Laurel Richardson Walum. "Two-Location Families: Married Singles." *Alternative Lifestyles* 1 (1978): 513–525.

Kitt, Joseph. *Rites of Passage: Adolescence in America*. New York: Basic Books, 1977.

Kram, Kathy E. *Mentoring at Work: Developmental Relations in Organizational Life*. Glenview, Ill.: Scott Foresman, 1985.

La Rossa, Ralph and Jane H. Wolf. "On Qualitative Family Research." *Journal of Marriage and the Family* 47 (1985): 531–541.

Levenger, George. "A Social Exchange View of the Dissolution of Pair Relationships." In *Social Exchange in Developing Relationships*, edited by R. L. Burgess, and T. L. Huston. New York: Academic Press, 1979.

Levenger, George, and Oliver Moles, eds. *Divorce and Separation*. New York: Basic Books, 1979.

Lofland, John, and Rodney Stark. "Becoming a World Saver: A Theory of Conversion to a Deviant Perspective." *American Sociological Review* 30(1965): 862–875.

Lopata, Helena. "On Widowhood: Grief Work and Identity Reconstruction." *Journal of Geriatric Psychiatry* 8 (1975): 41–55.

———. "Widowhood and Husband Sanctification." *Journal of Marriage and Family* 43 (1981): 379–389.

———. "Self Identity in Marriage and Widowhood." *Sociological Quarterly* 14 (1973): 407–418.

Lynch, James J. *The Broken Heart: The Medical Consequences of Loneliness*. New York: Basic Books, 1977.

Lyness, J. F., Lipetz, M. E. and K. E. Davis. "Living Together: An Alternative to Marriage." *Journal of Marriage and the Family* 34 (1972): 305–311.

Macionis, John J. "Intimacy: Structure and Process in Interpersonal Relationships." *Alternative Lifestyles* 1 (1978): 113–130.

Macklin, Eleanor D. "Nontraditional Family Forms: A Decade of Research." *Journal of Marriage and the Family* 33 (1980): 905–922.

Maines, David R. "Bodies and Selves: Notes on a Fundamental Dilemma in Demography." In *Studies in Symbolic Interaction*, vol. 1, edited by Norman K. Denzin, pp. 241–265. Greenwich, Conn: JAI Press, 1978.

Marks, Stephen R. "Multiple Roles and Role Strain: Some Notes on Human Energy, Time, and Commitment." *American Sociological Review* 42 (1977): 921–936.

Marris, Peter. *Loss and Change*. London: Routledge and Kegan Paul, 1974.

Martin, Patricia Yarney and Marie Withers Osmond. "Gender and Exploitation: Re-

244 / SELECTED READINGS

sources, Structure, and Rewards in Cross-Sex Social Exchange." *Social Forces* 4 (1982): 412–423.

Matthew, Sarah H. *The Social World of Old Women: Management of Self-Identity.* Beverly Hills: Sage, 1979.

McCall, George J., Michal M. McCall, Norman K. Denzin, Gerald D. Suttles, and Suzanne B. Kurth. *Social Relationships.* Chicago: Aldine, 1970.

McCall, George J., and J. L. Simmons. *Identities and Interactions.* New York: Free Press, 1966.

Mechanic, David. "Sources of Power of Lower Participants in Complex Organizations." *Administrative Science Quarterly* 7(1962): 349–364.

Melson, Gail Freedman. *Family and Environment: An Ecosystem Perspective.* Minneapolis: Burgess Publishing, 1980.

Merton, Robert K. *Social Theory and Social Structure.* New York: Free Press, 1968.

———. "Socially Expected Durations: A Case Study of Concept Formation in Sociology." In *Conflict and Consensus: A Festschrift in Honor of Lewis A. Coser,* edited by Walter W. Powell and Richard Robbins, pp. 262–283. New York: Free Press, 1984.

———. "Continuities in the Theory of Reference Groups and Social Structure." In *Social Theory and Social Structure,* by Robert K. Merton, pp. 335–440. New York: Free Press, 1968.

Merton, Robert K., and Alice Rossi. "Contributions to the Theory of Reference Group Behavior." In *Social Theory and Social Structure,* by Robert K. Merton, pp. 279–334. New York: Free Press, 1968.

Mika, K., and B. L. Bloom. "Adjustment to Separation Among Former Cohabitors." *Journal of Divorce* 4 (1980): 45–66.

Milardo, P. "The Social Context of Developing Relationships." Ph. D. dissertation, Pennsylvania State University, 1980.

Miller, Brian. "Adult Sexual Resocialization." *Alternative Lifestyles* 1 (1978): 207–234.

Miller, Gerald R., and Malcolm R. Parks. "Communication in Dissolving Personal Relationships." In *Personal Relationships. 4: Dissolving Personal Relationships,* edited by Steve Duck, pp. 127–154. London: Academic Press, 1982.

Miller, Jean Baker. *Toward a New Psychology of Women.* Boston: Beacon Press, 1976.

Montgomery, J. P. "Commitment and Cohabitation Cohesion." University of Edmonton. Mimeographed, 1973.

Mortimer, Jeylan T., and Roberta G. Simmons. "Adult Socialization." *Annual Review of Sociology* 4 (1978): 421–454.

Newcomb, Michael D. "Relationship Qualities of Those Who Live Together." *Alternative Lifestyles* 6 (1983): 78–102.

Nicholson, Nigel. "A Theory of Work Role Transitions." *Administrative Science Quarterly* 29 (1984): 172–191.

Peplau, Letitia A. "Research on Homosexual Couples: An Overview." *Journal of Homosexuality* 8 (1982): 3–8.

Peplau, L. A., and S. Cochran. "Value Orientations in the Intimate Relationships of Gay Men." *Journal of Homosexuality* 6 (1981): 1–19.

Peplau, L. A., K. Rook, and C. Padesky. "Loving Women: Attachment and Autonomy in Lesbian Relationships." *Journal of Social Issues* 34 (1978): 7–27.

Richardson, Laurel Walum. *The Dynamics of Sex and Gender: A Sociological Perspective.* 2d rev. ed. Boston: Houghton Mifflin, 1981.

———. *The New Other Woman.* New York: Free Press, 1985.

Reiss, Ira L. *Family Systems in America*, 3d ed. New York: Holt, Rinehart and Winston, 1980.

Rose, Phyllis. "Catherine Hogarth and Charles Dickens." In *Parallel Lives: Five Victorian Marriages*, pp. 141–191. New York: Random House, 1983.

Rosenthal, Kristine M., and Harry F. Keshet. *Fathers Without Partners: A Study of Fathers and the Family After Marital Separation*. Totowa, N.J.: Rowan and Littlefield, 1981.

Rubin, Lillian Breslow. *Worlds of Pain: Life in the Working Class Family*. New York: Basic Books, 1976.

———. *Women of a Certain Age: The Midlife Search for Self*. New York: Harper & Row, 1979.

———. *Intimate Strangers*. New York: Harper & Row, 1983.

Rubin, Zick. *Children's Friendships*. Cambridge: Harvard University Press, 1980.

Rubin, Zick, Letitia A. Peplau, and Charles T. Hill. "Loving and Leaving: Sex Differences in Romantic Attachments." *Sex Roles* 7 (1981): 821–835.

Rueda, Enrique. *The Homosexual Network*. Old Greenwich, Conn.: The Devin Adair Company, 1982.

Safilios-Rothschild, Constantina. *Love, Sex, and Sex Roles*. Englewood Cliffs, N.J.: Prentice-Hall, 1977.

Scanzoni, John. *Sexual Bargaining: Power Politics in the American Marriage*. Englewood Cliffs, N.J.: Prentice-Hall, 1972.

Schickel, Richard. *Singled Out*. New York: Viking, 1981.

Schwartz, Barry. "Waiting, Exchange, and Power: the Distribution of Time in Social Systems." *American Journal of Sociology* 79 (1973): 841–870.

Schwartz, Pepper, and Philip Blumstein. *American Couples: Money, Work, Sex*. New York: William Morrow, 1983.

Scott, Marvin B., and Stanford M. Lyman. "Accounts." *American Sociological Review* 33 (1968): 46–62.

Shaver, Philip, Wyndol Furman, and Duane Buhrmester. "Transition to College: Network Changes, Social Skills, and Loneliness." In *Understanding Personal Relationships: An Interdisciplinary Approach*, edited by Steve Duck and Daniel Perlman, pp. 193–220. London: Sage, 1985.

Sieber, Sam D. "Toward a Theory of Role Accumulation." *American Sociological Review* 39 (1974): 567–578.

Spence, Michael. *Market Signaling*. Cambridge: Harvard University Press, 1974.

Stafford, R., Bachman, E., and P. DiBona. "The Division of Labor Among Cohabiting and Married Couples." *Journal of Marriage and the Family* 39 (1977): 43–57.

Stein, Peter J., ed. *Single Life: Unmarried Adults in Social Context*. New York: St. Martin's, 1981.

Strauss, Anselm. *Contexts of Social Mobility*. Chicago: Aldine, 1971.

Sudnow, David. *Passing On: The Social Organization of Dying*. Englewood Cliffs, N.J.: Prentice-Hall, 1967.

Sullivan, Judith. *Mama Doesn't Live Here Anymore*. New York: Pyramid, 1974.

Sykes, Gresham, and David Matza. "Techniques of Neutralization: A Theory of Delinquency." *American Sociological Review* 22 (1957): 664–669.

Trafford, Abigail. *Crazy Times: Predictable Stages of Divorce*. New York: Harper & Row, 1982.

Unruh, David R. "Death and Personal History: Strategies of Identity Preservation." *Social Problems* 30 (1983): 340–351.

Van Maanen, John, and Edgar H. Schein. "Toward a Theory of Organizational Socia ization." In *Research in Organizational Behavior, vol. 1*, edited by Barry Staw and L. L. Cummings, pp. 209–264. Greenwich, Conn.: JAI Press, 1979.

Waller, Willard. *The Old Love and the New: Divorce and Readjustment*. New York: Horace Liveright, 1930, republished with introduction by Bernard Farber. Carbondale: Southern Illinois University Press, 1967.

Waller, Willard, and Reuben Hill. *The Family: A Dynamic Interpretation*. New York: Holt, Rinehart, and Winston, 1938.

Wallerstein, Judith S., and Joan B. Kelly. *Surviving the Breakup: How Children and Parents Cope with Divorce*. New York: Basic Books, 1980.

Weick, Karl E. "Educational Organizations as Loosely Coupled Systems." *Administrative Science Quarterly* 21 (1976): 1–19.

Weinberg, Martin S. and C. S. Williams. *Male Homosexuals: Their Problems and Adaptations*. New York: Oxford University Press, 1974.

Weiss, Robert S. *Loneliness: The Experience of Emotional and Social Isolation*. Cambridge: MIT Press, 1973.

———. *Marital Separation*. New York: Basic Books, 1975.

Weitzman, Lenore J. *The Divorce Revolution: The Unexpected Social and Economic Consequences for Women and Children*. New York: Free Press, 1985.

Wheeler, Stanton. "Socialization in Correctional Communities." *American Sociological Review* 26(1961): 697–712.

White, Harrison C. *Chains of Opportunity: System Models of Mobility in Organizations*. Cambridge: Harvard University Press, 1970.

Wolff, Kurt, ed. and tr. *The Sociology of Georg Simmel*. New York: Free Press, 1950.

Zaltman, Gerald. "Knowledge Disavowal." Paper presented at the Conference on Producing Useful Knowledge for Organizations, Graduate School of Business, University of Pittsburgh, October, 1982.

Index

ABOUT THE AUTHOR

Diane Vaughan is Associate Professor of Sociology
at Boston College. She is also the author of
Controlling Unlawful Organizational Behavior.